REG KRAY

Roberta Kray ran her own media research company for ten years. She met Reg Kray in March 1996 and married him in July 1997. She is now a full-time writer and lives in Norfolk.

ROBERTA KRAY

REG KRAY

A MAN APART

PAN BOOKS

First published 2002 by Sidgwick & Jackson

This edition published 2003 by Pan Books
an imprint of Pan Macmillan Ltd
Pan Macmillan, 20 New Wharf Road, London N1 9RR
Basingstoke and Oxford
Associated companies throughout the world
www.panmacmillan.com

ISBN 0 330 49111 3

A CIP catalogue record for this book is available from
the British Library.

Typeset SX Composing DTP, Rayleigh, Essex
Printed and bound in Great Britain by
Mackays of Chatham plc, Chatham, Kent

FOR REG

Acknowledgements

With special thanks to my mother
for her unfailing love.

To my family and friends for all their support.

And last, but not least, to Robert Smith
for his help, patience and encouragement.

Contents

INTRODUCTION 1

1. INTO THE SYSTEM 9

2. A DOWNWARD SPIRAL 33

3. REACHING OUT 50

4. GETTING ON WITH BUSINESS 68

5. TROUBLE AND STRIFE 85

6. LOSING RON 104

7. CLOSE ENCOUNTERS 125

8. THE BIG QUESTION 161

9. HOPE AND HOPELESSNESS 192

10. PILING ON THE PRESSURE 227

11. FALSE HOPES, FEARS AND FAREWELLS 254

12. A ROOM WITH A VIEW 280

EPILOGUE 317

INDEX 325

INTRODUCTION

It would be fair to say I had my doubts. Hurtling down the motorway in the back of a stranger's car, the phrase 'What am I doing here?' sprang to mind on more than one occasion. It was a chilly March morning in 1996 and we were on our way to Maidstone Prison.

The phone call had come a week earlier. The caller was friendly and polite. After revealing his name he asked if I would visit; he insisted there were things we needed to talk about. I wasn't quite so sure. He persisted and eventually, if rather reluctantly, I agreed. He said he had a female friend who could give me a lift. I took her number, we said good-bye and I put the phone down. What had I done? What was I doing? It all felt rather unreal. I was not to know I had just had the first conversation with my future husband.

That's how it began. Although I suppose, in real terms, it was a little before that. Perhaps it really started several weeks earlier in a bar in North London. I was sitting with an old friend having a farewell drink. He had got a new job and was about to leave for the States. He asked if I would do him a favour; he had made someone a promise and wanted to keep it. It was an easy enough task, just some publicity for a video, a number of sheets that needed faxing to the press and to magazines. I couldn't see any problem. It sounded straightforward enough. One drink later he told me it was for Reg Kray. I laughed, thinking he was joking. Two drinks later I knew he wasn't. Three drinks later I was standing at a bus stop wondering what on earth I'd agreed to.

And so I found myself in a car heading towards Maidstone. Maureen Flanagan 'just call me Flanagan', the female friend, was sitting in the passenger seat and her boyfriend Derek was driving. They chatted as the road slipped by and our destination approached. A part of me was still uncertain about what I was doing. It would be untrue to say I didn't have *any* preconceptions about the Krays but I didn't have many. My information was limited to vague memories, a few newspaper articles and the media coverage following Ron's death. The only fact I was sure of was the immense amount of time they had spent in prison. Was I worried at the prospect of meeting Reg Kray? I did feel a sense of trepidation. It wasn't just to do with who he was or his reputation. It was something more. I felt uneasy. I put it down to a combination of curiosity and nerves.

The prison was surrounded by an imposing grey stone wall. From the outside it looked like a fortressed city. That is probably not a bad description for (as I was to learn) a community existed inside, a microcosm of society, with its own hierarchical structure, rules, conventions, beliefs and principles. It was a place of friendship and betrayal, loyalty and deception, hope, desperation and hypocrisy. It was a community exiled from society but in many ways not so very different from our own.

Inside, after Derek had left, we met up with another visitor there to see Reg. The bare magnolia waiting room was crowded. It was filled primarily with women and children although there were a few men too – fathers, brothers and friends. Many of the women were young. Despite the cold they were minimally dressed, bare legged and high-heeled, some with a generous abundance of cleavage on view. I found myself wondering if that was better or worse for the men inside – knowing they could look but not touch. Attired in a grey woollen jumper and matching grey trousers, I felt like a house sparrow in an aviary of exotic birds. The children shouted and slammed the doors of the unused lockers. The babies screamed. Who could blame them? An empathic headache spread throughout the visitors. There was a low hum of conversation. Every now and again the door opened and a number was announced. A few more people were swallowed. The crowd shuffled forward.

Eventually our number was called. We went through the door and into a small room. There were three prison guards waiting inside. We laid our coats and jackets on a table and then passed through the metal detector. One officer checked through all my pockets. Another female officer frisked me. I found myself mentally switching off. I didn't feel violated, that would be too strong a word, but I certainly felt something, perhaps simply an invasion of privacy. I knew the process was necessary but I recoiled from it. Being under suspicion is an uncomfortable feeling. It took me back to those long-gone school assemblies where one elderly and bespectacled headmistress, her face white with rage, surveyed her girls and apportioned blame. *You know who you are.*

From here we passed through another door into an open courtyard. Accompanied by an officer we walked across to the visitors' building. Once inside we had to wait again. The room was stark. With its long rows of formica tables and chairs it had the appearance of a works canteen. From a hatch on the left-hand side, tea and chocolate bars were being sold. We chose a place and sat down. By the entrance there was a raised platform; four or five prison officers presided over us. There were barred windows to the left and right. There was plenty of light but neon strips ensured additional illumination. A few tiny windows, close to the ceiling, were open for air. There were pigeon droppings on the ledges, inside and out. Gradually the tables filled. We sat and made small talk. We glanced around.

It was at least ten minutes before a door at the back opened and the inmates started to filter out. Reg was one of the first to appear. As if unwilling to waste even a second he moved rapidly into the room, scanning the tables while he walked until he saw us and waved. He came quickly over. Introductions were made and handshakes exchanged. He was wearing jeans and the regulation blue and white striped shirt. His hair was cropped short and grey. Around his neck was a gold cross and chain. I probably had the same initial impressions as many people – that he was older, smaller, fitter and less intimidating than expected.

We all sat down, Flanagan to his left, myself to his right, the other gentleman directly opposite. The visit commenced. I don't remember much of the conversation we had. I know we talked about the video and made the necessary arrangements. I know we set dates and times. I know he was cordial and humorous. He thanked me for my help. The video was Reg's tribute to Ron; he had recorded his thoughts and feelings on tape and these had been incorporated into a documentary. He was not entirely satisfied with the final product but the anniversary of Ron's death was approaching and there was no more time to work on it. He was pleased, he said, that he'd been able to do it at all – it was not the easiest of tasks from inside prison. After many months, through phone calls and visits and with the help of some good friends, he had managed to complete the project. He spoke quickly and quietly, sometimes so softly it was hard to hear him at all. He leaned in to the table and gathered us closely around, our heads almost touching as if in some grand anarchical conspiracy. At one point he turned to me and said, 'I talk a lot don't I?' I couldn't disagree. Reg laughed. He explained how he always looked forward to visits and spent time beforehand musing about what he wanted to say or do. His thoughts and ideas, he said, built up and then just all tumbled out. There were only two hours and he didn't want to waste a minute of them. While we were talking he produced numerous notes on small pieces of paper and once the subject had been covered he tore them into pieces and threw them away. His writing, an indecipherable scrawl, lay like confetti across the table.

I was surprised by his spirit and determination, perhaps even more by his obvious sharpness. He was far from the rather puerile TV parodies that had been prevalent through the eighties. I was not sure, though, how much I actually liked him. The jury was still out on that one.

What remain in my memory aren't words so much as impressions. When he turned to speak to the others I was able to watch more closely. Despite his bluff exterior there was something frustrated and distressed about him. Even when he laughed his hands remained bunched in two tight fists on the table. He was like a rolled-up ball of anxiety. I watched his face, the right-hand side that was exposed to me, and noticed the way a pink flush spread periodically across his cheek, rose and subsided and disappeared. It was less than a year since Ron had died and I appreciated that his sense of loss was still immense. It was clear, however, that he was suffering in other ways too.

I won't say that I pitied him for I had gleaned already that Reg Kray was not of a character to welcome such an emotion. He would have found it, in the same way he found self-pity, to be at best worthless and at worst demeaning. Perhaps it is fairer to say that I felt pity for his situation. His crimes although deplorable had been far exceeded by recent and more vicious criminals, men who had committed the most terrible atrocities but whose sentences would run for only twelve or fifteen years. Reg, when we first met that day, was in his twenty-eighth year of imprisonment. It was hard to comprehend.

Towards the end of the visit I started to look forward to the time I could leave. The room and the presence of the prison officers were oppressive. Reg Kray was disconcerting. I found him, if I am honest, uncomfortable to be with. There was so much suppressed emotion. He appeared outwardly determined and confident, inwardly frustrated and vulnerable. It was a disturbing combination. I had done what I had promised. I sat and waited for the visit to end. I thought to myself, 'I will never come back here again.' I was sure of it.

↗ ↗ ↗

Four and a half years later, standing in winter sun at Chingford Cemetery, that fateful meeting seemed a lifetime ago. Together we had travelled an unlikely road. It had been a journey of great hope and terrible disappointment, of friendship, understanding and love. Reg died of cancer on Sunday, 1 October 2000. Having endured over thirty-two years of incarceration, his life had ended after only five weeks of freedom.

Looking around I saw a sea of faces, some familiar, others not. Over a thousand people had gathered in the cemetery. Many more had lined the streets to watch as the cortège passed by. Amongst them were men and women who had known him – but most had only ever known *of* him. Some were gathered to pay final respects, others to witness the finale to what had been an incredible, and in many ways tragic, story. Some had grown up with Reg Kray, others had not even been born when he was sent to prison. Some genuinely loved him, others hated and despised him. Some felt admiration, others only contempt. Whatever their emotions, whatever their beliefs, few if any were indifferent. The name of Kray was guaranteed to provoke strong opinions.

Time is a great healer. That's what everyone said. Time blunts the edges, makes loss gradually more bearable. But over the following year as I was trying to come to terms, to make sense of what had happened, I was faced not just with

the terrible reality of Reg's death but with a seemingly endless flow of new 'revelations' about him. The floodgates
opened to a stream of vilification. From strangers it was to
some degree predictable, from former friends and associates
it was truly shocking.

The Krays. How many books have been written about
them and around them? You have only to walk into any
bookshop and scan the shelves to witness the enduring fascination. It has become almost an industry in its own right
annually spawning new myths and legends with all the reality of a bad soap opera. Once Reg was no longer able to
respond the details of his life became a free-for-all. Like dogs
fighting over a bone, his 'biographers' battled to claim the
juiciest rewards.

But who was the real Reg Kray? Who was the man lost
beneath the layers of attitude and opinion, exaggeration and
distortion? Why was he destined to spend so much of his life
behind bars? What did he feel? What did he want? These
are the questions that have never been answered. I knew
Reg only in his final years. They were intense, tumultuous
and sometimes despairing times. We lived through them
together. It would be an arrogance to claim I knew him
absolutely. I didn't. It is never possible to completely understand another person. We supported, respected, trusted and
most importantly loved each other. I was moved when Reg
wrote in *A Way of Life*, 'Rob's loyalty to me has never faltered
and, as a result, she has got to know me better than anybody
else.'

Through writing this book I wanted to try to reveal more
of the real man, to untangle the web of misrepresentation, to
separate the human being from the associated myth and
legend. Reg seemed destined to be trapped forever in the
image that was created for him. He was a 1960s David Bailey
photograph, a black-and-white symbol, a smart-suited irre-
deemable gangster – the epitome not only of violence and

menace but also of a perverse 'glamour' that became entrenched and then embellished through the years. It was an image that appealed both to his admirers and his detractors, an image that was mutually satisfying for opposing reasons.

It is beyond doubt that the mythology surrounding the twins contributed to their long and unforgiving incarceration. Theirs was a myth perpetuated by the Establishment, the media, fellow criminals, the public and, most dramatically, themselves. Originating in childhood, flowing through an active life of law-breaking and violence, it gathered credence as it grew. When they each received a thirty-year sentence for murder in 1969, the myth of the 'eternal gangster' was sealed. Reg and Ron Kray became the perfect symbols of unrelenting and absolute criminality. For the rest of their lives they would be despised, feared, glamorized or glorified – depending on the advantage to be gained from those who wished to take it.

This book is partly about the years we spent together; the personal and public struggles, our marriage, our hopes and dreams, the campaign for Reg's freedom, and his final determined fight against cancer. It is also about his past, his relationships and experiences and the deleterious effects of prison. It is not a dissection of his criminal career about which so much has already been written. I cannot be Reg's voice but through the use of letters, documents and conversations, I can at least try to redress the balance and reveal a little more about the real Reg Kray.

The following words are not intended as a eulogy or a rose-tinted portrait. Reg would not have wanted that. He was what he was, no more and no less. He was not an angel but he was not a devil either. He was a human being and his failings, like his virtues, were human ones. If he is to be judged then it cannot be by fiction or conjecture. It can only be by the truth.

1. INTO THE SYSTEM

Reg's past was always a distant country to me, the geography only partially mapped by his memories, letters and books. It was a place heavily populated with newspaper reports, articles, biographies, documentaries and films, sources of varying accuracy and interest. His own attitude was often ambiguous. Reminiscence could evoke pain or pleasure, most usually a mixture of both. Although he would sometimes talk about the past, he would later claim it was a mistake to look back. He had too many regrets. He had made too many bad decisions. Nothing could be changed. Even the comfort of nostalgia, the remembrance of happier times, was only ever temporary; with it came the knowledge of everything he had lost.

Reg wrote at length about his prison experiences. It was only after his death when I was passed a number of old official papers – officers' reports, reviews and medical records – that I realized how much more was revealed in their pages. His daily battles, on both a practical and psychological level, were well documented. His separation from Ron, the loss of his parents and his struggle to retain some kind of sanity were starkly highlighted against the regimental demands of the system. The first fifteen years of his imprisonment had a profound effect. It was a time spent almost exclusively in segregation or hospital units. They left a terrible legacy of paranoia and depression. He later found ways to cope with the psychological as well as the physical realities of prison. Faced with the possibility of never being released, he strove to find a purpose to his life. It was rarely easy. He could have slipped, as so many do, into the destructive emotions of self-pity and bitterness. In the end he chose hope over despair.

To even begin to understand the man Reg Kray became, the man I met in Maidstone Prison in 1996, it is necessary to look back. It seemed the brothers were singled out from birth. As identical twins they were always the centre of attention. It was not just Violet, their mother, who showered them with attention and affection, but also relatives, friends and neighbours. They were instilled with the knowledge that they were special. It was a status they would not readily relinquish.

From an early age success in the boxing ring, and violent scuffles out of it, brought them to the attention of the news-papers. This media recognition became a driving force in their lives. To be acknowledged, for any reason, symbolized success. It gave them kudos and added to their growing reputations. For most aspiring or established criminals, anonymity is everything but for the twins accomplishment without recognition was meaningless. They craved publicity. Raised on stories of East End heroes, boxers, fighters and successful thieves, Reg and Ron were imbued in childhood with a respect for violence and villainy. Encouraged to admire the men glorified by their father and grandfather, it is not surprising they later sought also to emulate them. To be 'someone' was everything. To be recognized was to have respect.

There were, of course, stories of people who fought their way out of East End deprivation through determination, hard work and a modicum of luck. Their success was admirable but also the exception to the rule. Many of Ron and Reg's peers took the same road, with varying success, as the twins. With little education but plenty of aspiration, the rewards of villainy were appealing. But the small-time occupation of petty theft was not for the Kray brothers. They wanted something more. They had no desire to escape the East End, only its likely inheritance – a lifetime of anonymity and impoverishment. Although their father Charlie was wily and smart, he was also frequently missing, on the run from the army or 'on the knock' buying jewellery and other saleable goods from households all over the country. In his absence their mother Violet often struggled, pawning her wedding-ring on occasions to pay for food. The memories of these times provided additional fuel for their growing ambitions.

The environment in which they were raised provides no excuse for their future criminal careers. It simply offers part of the reason. The more essential motivation lay within their own characters and their relentless appetite for fame and success. Their effectiveness sprang not just from their ambition but their confidence in achieving it. An additional advantage came with their status as twins. There is something extraordinary and incomprehensible about identical twins. The mystery added to their power. Although they fought ferociously with each other they also had an incredible understanding. Their mutual loyalty was absolute. Separately they were daunting but together they became formidable.

Both Reg and Ron were promising young boxers. Trained by their older brother Charlie, the sport provided an outlet for their energy and aggression. At seventeen they both turned professional. Of the two, Reg had the greater skill and went on to win all seven of his bouts. Ron, although powerful, lacked his twin's discipline and out of six fights lost two. By the end his interest was waning. There were faster and easier ways to make money. The lure of a different and more lucrative career had taken hold.

It was inevitable that Reg, although he had a promising

future in boxing, would follow his brother's lead. His more equable nature was no match for Ron's single-minded determination. Anyway, they were twins and whatever they did, they would do together. The decision was made. Their rise through the echelons of the criminal world has already been recorded in detail and there is little point in repeating it here. Both the twins were violent but Ron's vicious unpredictability provided an edge. No amount of logical thinking could anticipate the next move of a man who rarely knew it himself. Their ruthlessness propelled them quickly up the criminal ladder; fear and reputation compounded their power. As their notoriety spread, others gathered round, eager for a share in the spoils. It was a time of plenty. By 1968, however, the party was over.

On 8 March 1969, after almost a year on remand and one of the longest criminal trials in British history, Reg and Ron Kray were each awarded a minimum of thirty years in prison. Judge Melford Stevenson did not disguise his pleasure at the sentence. If it was a victory for justice, it was an even greater one for the Establishment. The Kray twins, friends to so many Lords, MPs and figures of social influence, had finally been brought down. Revenge was sweet. It would also be long. There was to be no forgiveness.

They had been convicted of the murder of two fellow villains, George Cornell and Jack 'The Hat' McVitie. Reg had not been present, and had not known about Ron's intention to kill Cornell, but was still held to be responsible. Although also tried for helping Frank Mitchell to escape from Dartmoor, they were cleared of his subsequent killing due to lack of evidence. Their criminal empire comprising fraud, protection, gambling and extortion had been crushed. If it was to some degree an end, it was also a new start. The real mythology of the Krays was just beginning – along with their life sentences.

After the trial Reg and Ron were kept in Brixton Prison

for a further month until their future location was decided. Although not completely unprepared, they were still disheartened to learn they would be separated – Reg to be despatched to Parkhurst and Ron to Durham. It was not the first time they had been apart, both had served short sentences whilst the other was at liberty, but this was something different. Already facing a lifetime of incarceration they were now confronted with the equally fearsome prospect of never seeing each other again. It was a major blow.

Their parents were stunned. They didn't believe the twins could survive and lobbied the Home Office for them to be reunited. They also asked for help from Dr Clein, a psychiatrist who had treated both the brothers on the outside. On 4 July he wrote to the Home Office and to the Senior Medical Officer at Brixton Prison expressing his concerns. He claimed that Ron was 'a well-maintained schizophrenic' whose worst symptoms, such as hallucinations or delusions, were controlled by medication. Although Reg had been the more stable of the twins it was Clein's opinion that the death of Frances had caused a great deterioration in his mental state. He believed that separation for such a lengthy period would have serious effects and that Ron, or perhaps both, could have a major breakdown in the near future.

Four days later, Charles and Violet, accompanied by a family friend called Thomas Cowley, attended a meeting with the Home Office representatives Mr Weekes and Mrs Becks. It was a fruitless interview. Mr Weekes said that medical opinion would obviously be taken into account but there were few special security wings and great care was taken in deciding where individual prisoners should be placed. It was, he insisted, normal policy to split up the leaders of gangs so as to avoid any control problem. He explained that the decision to send the twins to different prisons had been taken after a great deal of thought and assured his visitors, perhaps not altogether convincingly, that this was in no way

a punitive measure. On their departure he promised that
their views, and those of Dr Clein, would be carefully considered. It was cold comfort to Charles and Violet Kray.

While the argument raged, Reg settled into the Special
Security Block which was to be his home for most of the
next six years. It was filled with high-security Category 'A'
prisoners. There were some familiar faces, including a few of
the Great Train Robbers and Eddie Richardson, a contempo-
rary and well-known South London villain. There were also
a number of very disturbed inmates like John Straffen, the
child killer. They were all, regardless of their crimes or
mental state, mixed together. The Block consisted of a series
of cells over three floors with primitive showers and bath. Its
only redeeming factor was a gym with some weightlifting
equipment.

Living in such close proximity, with little hope for the
future, it was inevitable that tensions would surface. It
wasn't long before Reg had a serious row with a con called
Mick Copeland. They had taken an instant dislike to each
other. After some minor disagreements they met face-to-face
and fought until they were separated. Reg was fined and
Copeland shipped out to a different prison. It was to be the
first of a series of violent episodes. Cooped up month after
month, relationships between inmates became strained. Attitudes differed. Trivial matters took on a disproportionate
importance. Grievances fermented. Patience was strained
and tempers flared on an almost daily basis. Another fight
followed with John Richard Jones over a derogatory comment he had made regarding a photograph of Reg's late wife
Frances. The pressure was relentless. With all the men facing
long prison sentences, their lives reduced to the scant
resources of the Security Block, anger and frustration were
never far from the surface. In *Our Story*, Reg says: 'Life in
Parkhurst was a living hell. It was like living in a jungle – a
constant battle for sanity and survival.'

They were not the only ones feeling the pressure. In a different part of the building, in October 1969, the Parkhurst riots took place. The jail was overcrowded and a number of conflicts had already arisen between the officers and inmates. These culminated in a bloody confrontation. Frank Fraser – who had worked with the Richardson brothers in South London – received a further five years, on top of the fifteen he was already serving, for his part in the proceedings.

During this time Reg was found to be suffering from a condition called otitis externa, an uncomfortable and chronic ear infection, requiring regular treatment. It persisted for the rest of his life and resulted in partial deafness. He was also still taking Valium, prescribed for depression after the death of his wife. Reg rarely talked about Frances but he often thought of her. On visits and through letters he occasionally shared his feelings with me. He had gone to pieces after her death, experiencing all the guilt and remorse that suicide inevitably brings. Could he have done something else? Could he have stopped her? Did she kill herself because of him? Their relationship was never easy, strewn with problems created both by their own personalities and by the actions of others.

In the late fifties and early sixties Reg always considered his emotional life, apart from his family, to be secondary to the 'business' interests he pursued. Although he had a few short-lived affairs, they were not important. He lived for the intrigue and challenge of the criminal life he was now involved in. Making deals and building a reputation were more important than a date with a girl. He often stayed out half the night, doing the rounds of the pubs and the clubs, making new contacts and reinforcing established ones, looking for opportunities whilst picking up ideas and information.

One of Reg's girlfriends became pregnant by him while

he was in his early twenties. Together they went and talked to the local priest. They were young, unsure of themselves, and less than ready for a life-long commitment. Eventually she decided an abortion would be best. Reg didn't argue. Although relieved at the time, he later had huge regrets. He often thought about the child he might have had and felt guilty about what they had done.

Ron's sexual preference was always for young men. A number of books published since Reg's death have claimed that his tastes were identical and that he married both Frances and myself to cover up his homosexuality. Reg, however, told me that although he had experimented (as many young men do) he had never perceived himself as even bisexual until he was almost fifty. His years of celibacy after imprisonment would seem to reinforce this. Further evidence came in the form of some interesting Government files released in October 2001. Dating from 1966, when the murder of George Cornell was being investigated, they included a statement to the police from a man called Charles Clark. Clark was a close confidant of Ron Kray's and he described his friend's inner turmoil over his sexuality: 'He once told me the tragedy of his life was that he was the twin who was born the wrong way round sexually. He said he cried inside himself every day. Indeed he cried in my presence a few times.' It's a testimony that sheds light not just on Ron but also Reg. As Ron was undoubtedly the person who knew his twin brother best, his confessions to Charles Clark suggest that Reg was far from sharing his own sexual leanings.

Reg was simply not interested in long-term relationships of any kind. They were a distraction from his driving ambition. His was a man's world and women were, on the whole, of secondary importance. Reg did enjoy their company however. Handsome, charming, and with his pockets full of cash, he was rarely short of offers. (Even on the night of their arrest, while Ron slept with a boyfriend in the room next door, Reg was in bed with his current girlfriend Carol.) Sometimes he slept with them, occasionally he met them again, but he was never drawn towards anything permanent. That is, until he met the young and beautiful sister of a friend. Her name was Frances Shea.

His attraction was instant and enduring. She was extremely pretty and at only sixteen years of age still had an appealing innocence. To Frances he must have seemed the epitome of sophistication. She was flattered by the attentions of an older man and beguiled by his apparently glamorous lifestyle. It was not an easy courtship. Although her father worked at one of the clubs owned by the twins, Frances's parents were against the relationship. The reputation of the brothers was growing and they didn't like what they were hearing. It wasn't the future they wanted for their daughter. They tried to push them apart, to intervene, but Reg and Frances continued to meet. Their first date had been at the Double R Club, a fashionable venue in the Bow Road, East End. Owned by Reg, and managed by Reg and Charlie, the idea was conceived in the absence of Ron who was then serving a three-year sentence in HMP Wandsworth. Reg had always dreamed of founding a club equivalent to any West End venue and through the Double R he achieved that ambition. It rapidly gained popularity and soon became a regular haunt of many East End families and their friends, as well as gaining favour with celebrities, musicians and writers.

Reg, recalling his early days with Frances claimed, 'I was totally oblivious to anyone else.' He took her to restaurants, clubs and parties. He introduced her to a different world and a different lifestyle. In 1963, when she was nineteen they went on holiday together to Milan. It was a happy time. They enjoyed the sights of the city and saw *Madame Butterfly* at La Scala. The relationship continued and they later travelled together to Barcelona. Her family remained united against

the partnership but when the couple returned from Spain
Reg went to see Frances's parents and asked for her hand in
marriage. It was refused.

Shortly after, Reg was sent to prison for six months,
accused of 'demanding money with menaces'. His brief
imprisonment in Wandsworth proved a telling time. He was
tormented by the thought that Frances might leave him. He
wrote to her frequently and she wrote back with the assur-
ances he craved. On his release, Reg began a determined
campaign to make Frances his wife. Her parents were
determined to thwart his plans but in the end they could
not prevent the inevitable.

After five years, on 19 April 1965, Reg and Frances got
married. She was twenty-one and Reg was thirty-one. It was
a huge society event. Ron was best man. Celebrity guests
abounded. David Bailey took the photographs. Looking at
Frances, it is hard to believe she was anything but happy.
The only downside to the day was the obvious disapproval
of her parents. To make a point her mother wore black to the
wedding. Reg saw the gesture as an act of spite and never
forgave her for it.

They went to Athens for their honeymoon. It was the
first time they had spent an extended period alone. Other
trips had been made with friends. Problems began almost
immediately. They had fought so hard and for so long to be
together, the reality was perhaps bound to be less than
idyllic. During the day they went sightseeing but in the
evenings, without the usual distraction of entertaining company, they were thrown back on their own resources. One
morning, over breakfast in a street café, Frances told Reg that
he seemed 'out of place' there, 'like a different person'. He
took it as an insult and was stung. She had hit him where it
hurt most. Away from his usual London crowd, he was less
confident and less sure of his place in the world. Nobody
knew or recognized him. Nobody paid him attention. There

was no special treatment. They were just a couple of tourists in a strange city.

Things did not improve on their return. Reg decided they should move to the West End, in part for the nightlife but mainly to escape the influence on Frances of her parents and of Ron on himself. He hoped it could be a fresh start for them both. It was not to be. Reg took his new wife to view the West End flat shortly before they moved in. She seemed happy on the journey across the city and in good spirits. When Reg unlocked the front door he found the carpets had not yet been laid and the boards were bare. Frances followed him inside. Suddenly, for no apparent reason, she began to scream. Reg was stunned. He held her in his arms and tried to calm her down, she was crying uncontrollably. Even when the tears subsided she could not explain what was wrong or why she felt the way she did. Before the end of the year she was to suffer her first breakdown.

Frances was lonely in the West End. She missed the company of her friends and family. Reg was often out until the early hours. Despite his frequent absences he remained wildly possessive, refusing to let her go out to work or even learn to drive. He told me he later regretted his attitudes but in those days a married woman working suggested that her husband couldn't afford to keep her. For him, it was a matter of pride. He understood, in retrospect, that she would have been much happier in an occupation. Bored and lost, her life at the early age of twenty-one seemed cast in stone.

Neither of them was happy in the new flat and a decision was made to move back to the East End. At this point Reg made another mistake. Without consulting Frances he chose to take an apartment in Cedra Court, in the same block as his twin brother. Ron was overjoyed. He didn't attempt to hide his resentment of Frances. He often taunted and insulted her, sometimes in the presence of Reg, who found himself torn by conflicting loyalties. If he objected Ron would say he was

only joking, only teasing. What was the matter with him?
Had he lost his sense of humour since he got married? Was
he going to let a woman come between them? Ron tormented
Frances out of jealousy, fear and insecurity – she was a real
threat to his relationship with Reg. If the marriage worked,
if it was successful, if they had children – then what would
become of him? She would take him away. He needed Reg
and he needed *all* of him. It was only Reg who could see him
through the darkest times. It was only Reg that truly understood.

Ron did everything he could to tear them apart. He held
parties and invited his young male friends. The music was
loud and the alcohol flowed. He encouraged Reg to join him
and he often agreed, relieved to get away from the bad
atmosphere in his own flat, relieved to escape the constant
rows and arguments. Frances was afraid. She knew what
Ron was trying to do. Reg would have none of it. He said she
was imagining things. He refused to face the truth. Frances
turned more and more to the comfort of her parents. Sensing
her weakness and unhappiness they encouraged her to leave.

They had married and separated within a year. It was a
disaster. Reg truly loved her but couldn't make the compromises she needed. Their lives were complicated by other
people and other issues, by the animosity of Ron, the interference of her family and by Reg's lifestyle. In addition they
both had deep emotional problems. Frances had suffered
severe depressive episodes since childhood and Reg was
trapped in a complex and destructive relationship with his
twin brother.

Even after she left, Reg could not accept that he had truly
lost her. Each night he went around to her house. Mr and Mrs
Shea would not allow him in and Frances talked to him
through an open window. He began courting her all over
again, taking flowers and gifts. Despite a period in hospital
and then a suicide attempt, Frances could not break away.

She moved to live with her brother but Reg would not give up. Occasionally they went out. Away from Ron, they spent some better times together. Gradually she came to trust him again. In June 1967 when Reg suggested a holiday abroad, a second honeymoon, she agreed. He bought the tickets. The night before they were due to leave Reg went round to see her. She seemed uneasy and distant, fussing with her hair and reluctant to talk. He stayed for a couple of hours and then left. Tomorrow they were going on holiday. Tomorrow everything would be different. Tomorrow everything would be fine. Just like the good old days.

What went through Frances's mind that night? It's impossible to know. She would have heard about the killing of Cornell. In early 1966 Ron had walked into the Blind Beggar pub and very publicly, and at point-blank range, shot George Cornell dead. The reason was unclear. It has been claimed that Cornell had slighted or insulted him but a greater motivation probably lay in Ron's increasing desire for power and control. Delusional, believing himself untouchable, he had committed the ultimate act of destruction. Now his reputation was sealed. Reg, who was not present and who'd had no idea of his twin's intention, was astounded. He was also left to pick up the pieces. While Ron was replaying his moment of glory, Reg found them a safe house, disposed of the evidence and tried to ensure that any possible witnesses stayed silent. Ron was out of control and Reg was in the middle of it all. Frances must have known that he could never escape from his twin. Would anything be different in the future? Could Reg protect her from Ron? Would Reg ever change? Could they ever make each other happy? To go on holiday, to reconcile, might mean the beginning of a whole new nightmare. No one can know for certain what made Frances take the decision to end her life. No amount of speculation can ever reveal the truth. It was a final, personal and desperate act.

There has been endless rumour and conjecture about Frances's death. Many people have blamed Reg for her suicide, not least of all Reg himself. He always felt responsible. He knew that he had let her down. Their complicated relationship undoubtedly provided some of her motivation but perhaps not the whole of it. Ron's contribution was not insubstantial. The pressure from her family also added to her distress. When Reg and Frances were together she often said that she believed she would die young – it became, eventually, a self-fulfilling prophecy.

Reg had grown up with a strong woman at the helm of the family. Violet Kray was kind, determined and generous. She supported her boys without question, accepting them as they were, giving stability and security to their precarious lives. His two aunts, Rose and May, were also strong characters. Frances was a different species altogether. If it was her innocence that attracted him, it was also that innocence and lack of knowledge that stood in the way of any kind of understanding. Tormented by her death he began to drink excessively. On cocktails of booze and tranquillizers he stayed up all night, roaming the pubs and clubs. His moods swung between rage and grief. He embarked on the bitter road to self-destruction, a road that culminated in the killing of another villain, Jack McVitie, and his eventual imprisonment. Her memory and how she had died was like a weight that he always carried. He understood what he had done and what he hadn't; both in their own ways were equally terrible.

In March 1970, after the Parkhurst riots, there was a general shake-up and Reg was suddenly moved to Leicester Prison. At the same time Ron was transferred from Durham down to Parkhurst. It is possible that the two vehicles, travelling in opposite directions, passed each other somewhere on the road. The twins were to remain separated.

If Reg had thought Parkhurst confined it bore no comparison to Leicester, which had an even smaller Security

Block. There were fewer cells and fewer inmates but it contained an equal if not greater amount of bad feeling. Eddie Richardson was moved at the same time. He had been to Leicester before and warned Reg about its shortcomings. In the Block a small cell had been converted into a shared kitchen area and there was one tiny shower room. A concrete yard was provided for exercise. Unable to escape each other's company, conflict predictably arose. One dispute between Reg and Pete Hurley, an armed robber, was over a doughnut. It resulted in a violent fight. Another incident followed with John Duddy, who was serving time for his part in the killing of three policemen. Duddy made some sneering anti-gay remarks and Reg, believing he was referring to Ron, attacked him. He also witnessed a number of violent disagreements between other inmates. The atmosphere was volatile and while vicious quarrels flared and died their legacies remained.

It was a relief to Reg when the news came through in February 1971 that he was to be transferred back to Parkhurst. He had spent almost a year at Leicester and described his time there as 'mercifully short'. Even better news came with the confirmation that Ron would still be at Parkhurst when he returned. It had finally been decided that the twins could be together again. This was not the result of any humanitarian decision on the part of the Home Office but of a purely practical one – Ron was out of control. Reg, it was hoped, could restore the peace.

If Reg was hoping for a happy reunion his expectations were soon dashed. He arrived back to a tense situation. Ron had been removed from the Special Security Block (SSB) to the hospital after attacking another inmate, Bernie Beattie. He had hit him over the head with a bottle. It was the second attack in a matter of days, the first on a different inmate, and both had come completely out of the blue.

Reg was taken twice weekly to the prison hospital to see

his brother. In addition they had a joint visit with their parents, an uncle and Christine Boyce, Reg's former girlfriend. Ron gradually became calmer but the authorities were not happy about returning him to the SSB. Both the staff and inmates expressed their concern. It was not simply Ron's violence that worried them but the possibility that Reg, far from being a restraining influence, might actually join with him in any future attack. This possible outcome had not, apparently, occurred to the senior decision-makers. What had seemed a good idea at the time was rapidly assuming the semblance of a major mistake.

Despite their misgivings, Reg was actually accepted by the other cons without difficulty. A prison officer wrote: 'He has, of course, always been more popular with his fellow prisoners than has his brother. His own conduct and manner have been unexceptionable and he has obviously been at pains to allay the fears felt by other prisoners about his brother's possible return which he, naturally, is very keen should happen when his treatment is finished.'

Ron responded well and in a matter of weeks was deemed fit enough to leave the hospital. Behind the scenes the debate continued as to whether he should be returned to the SSB with some officers claiming he not only remained a control problem but would also adversely affect both morale and the atmosphere on the block. The only alternatives were to keep him in hospital, consider him for C Wing or confine him in what was referred to as a 'segregation situation'.

In the end, either in the hope that Reg might eventually have a stabilizing influence or more likely the result of a reluctance to admit a mistake had actually been made, Ron was allowed back into the Special Security Block. For most of the next eight years the twins remained together. They were far from peaceful times. On top of the usual daily disputes, Ron had an argument over his medication with an officer and hit him in the face. He received fifty-six days' soli-

tary confinement as punishment. A number of other incidents followed. Reg's frustration was reflected in a letter he
wrote to a friend: 'I haven't seen Ron for three days as he is
over the hospital. The other night he smashed up his cell and
shouted at an officer the following morning. He goes up for
punishment on Monday. Will you write him a letter *direct* to
the hospital and try to tell him what a fool he is being, tell
him to try and settle down. Don't pull any punches in your
letter, be firm with him. It's about time we thought of my
mother more as she worries.' If the friend's letter was ever
written it certainly didn't change anything. The rows and
arguments persisted. There was one particularly bad altercation with an inmate called Roy Grantham ending in a
vicious fight and a charge on the twins of malicious wound-
ing. It began to look as if the worst fears of the authorities
were coming true. There was talk by the Home Office of
splitting them up again.

By August 1973 Reg was being prescribed Librium and
Stelazine. The former is often used to treat anxiety, the latter
is an antipsychotic drug for the treatment of mental disorders such as schizophrenia or manic-depressive illness.
Although Reg was never diagnosed as schizophrenic he suffered periodic bouts of paranoia and depression, afflictions
undoubtedly exacerbated by the highly stressful conditions
of his imprisonment.

There is always a burden, especially on a high-profile
inmate, to keep his 'position' in the hierarchy of prison.
In order to maintain respect he has to respond to every
challenge, threat or public slight. Failure to do so leads to
vulnerability and loss of face. This in turn leads to further
danger. In addition to real intimidation there is also the
imagined. Every perceived insult, slander or reproach is
another episode on which to brood. To secure his place he
therefore embarks on a perpetual and exhausting cycle of
confrontation and retaliation, attack and counterattack,

collision and resistance, leading to a state of almost constant
fear and anxiety. It is not impossible to imagine the psychological effect of such prolonged pressure.

In October 1974, five years after Reg was sentenced, Dr
Cooper, one of the Medical Officers at Parkhurst, wrote the
following statement about him:

> Over the past months he has shown increasing tension
> which has manifested itself in headaches and paranoid
> ideas towards staff and others. These symptoms have
> been controlled with tranquillisers. Physically he is in
> reasonably good health with the exception of his ears
> which are subject to recurrent bouts of severe dermati-
> tis and secondary infection. In my opinion he is a
> highly neurotic individual with strong paranoid traits
> which under stress can become borderline psychotic.
> There was an episode two or three months ago in
> which he thought people were talking about him
> and one prisoner in particular. Fortunately I have a
> reasonably good rapport with him and when these
> symptoms do occur he invariably comes over to the
> hospital. I would recommend that he still be regarded
> as dangerous and left on the Category 'A' list but that
> serious consideration be given to his removal from the
> confines of the special security wing. He has been there
> many years now and he is showing signs of deteriora-
> tion. A move out of the special security wing in the
> near future may go a long way to prevent further
> deterioration and potential violent situations extend-
> ing from his and his brother's attitudes towards the
> claustrophobic conditions of the SSB. I would not rec-
> ommend that he be moved from Parkhurst but either
> into the C Wing situation or the hospital which offer
> unique and probably *the* best means of testing his reac-
> tion to the general prison situation. If the experiment

in integration did fail we could always place him back
in the SSB for a further period.

Reg and Ron moved shortly afterwards on to the newly
opened psychiatric wing. It housed some of the worst psy-
chopaths in the country, many of them under heavy medication. Among their number were a high percentage of sex
offenders. There was the usual level of bullying and intimidation. Within the first couple of months they witnessed a
prison officer taken hostage by three inmates. There were
other violent incidents to follow. It was a strained and brutal
environment; attacks and beatings were commonplace. The
first of several murders came less than a year later. An
inmate called Doug Wakefield strangled another lifer, Terry
Peake, whom he had befriended. Further killings took place
in the main wing of Parkhurst. The prison was steaming,
a hot-bed of uncontrollable viciousness both between the
inmates themselves, and the prison officers and the inmates.
Parkhurst in the 1970s was a place not just of unregulated
punishment and retribution but also of constant threat and
menace. With so many dangerous and frustrated inmates
thrown together, and so little hope on offer, the consequences
were often fatally predictable.

The Medical Log through the next couple of years
describes Reg as 'well-behaved' and having a 'good influence on his brother'. However, on 23 December 1975, it is
reported that Reg 'cannot stand people around him'. This
may have been due to the reduction in Stelazine and the
resurfacing of some paranoid tendencies. By early 1976,
however, the medical staff are claiming there is 'no evidence
of paranoid ideas' and reiterating that he is a good influence on Ron. In 1977, eight years after sentencing, there
is a notable change. In January the Medical Log notes
that he 'seems to be depressed – it is noticeable that Ron is
becoming the dominant party again'. Around this time Reg

is also recorded as suffering considerable pain due to an ear infection. By the end of the year the Hospital is reporting: 'This man has been in C Wing for three years. Over the past three or four months he has become increasingly depressed and anxious. He is obviously under some stress from his brother who has become infatuated with another prisoner and behaving in a very demanding manner and making intolerable demands upon his brother. Admitted to hospital for observation. Librium 10 mg tds [three times a day]. He was anxious to come into hospital and since his arrival I have noticed a remarkable change in his attitude. He seems relaxed and less depressed.'

There is no doubt that the most important person in Reg's entire life, and the greatest influence, was his twin brother Ron. It was a complex relationship. Fraught with emotional difficulties, conflict and frustration, their mutual love was never uncomplicated. Although fiercely loyal they had many bitter fights and arguments, some incredibly ferocious. It is impossible to be sure where the roots of their hostility lay. Perhaps all the normal elements of sibling rivalry were exacerbated by their status as identical twins and the need to establish an individual identity. Ron's prolonged stay in hospital as a child might also have made a difference. At the age of four the twins had caught diphtheria, a dangerous illness that killed many children in the East End. The two boys were separated and sent to different isolation hospitals. Although Reg recovered quickly, after three months Ron was still in a critical condition. Removed from the closeness of his family, deprived of his mother's love, he must have felt fearful, resentful and abandoned. In the end, Violet made the brave decision to remove him from the hospital and tend to him herself.

From the moment he returned home to Bethnal Green Ron fought to gain Violet's attention and to re-establish his place in the family. His subsequent convalescence provided him with the attention he craved. He became fiercely protective of his position. Reg was always more placid and easy-going. He would often, for the sake of peace, bow to his brother's demands. It was a habit that was to continue into their adult life.

The deterioration of Ron's mental state added a further complication. Little was known about paranoid schizophrenia and it was to be years before he was correctly diagnosed. It was only when he was committed to Broadmoor that he got the continual treatment and medication that he needed. Throughout their lives Reg felt a tremendous responsibility. Most of his emotions, to the detriment of his own relationships, were permanently focused on his twin. Ron's illness made him unpredictable, violent and depressed. Reg was constantly on the lookout, alert for the signs that might indicate an imminent explosion of temper or a dangerous withdrawal into himself. Reg knew he had to take care of Ron, to always be there for him. Sometimes he resented it. He craved a life of his own, not apart from his twin, but independent of him. It has been claimed that Ron was dominant and that Reg simply followed where he led, but that is not entirely true. Reg had a good business brain. He also had his own ideas and ambitions and proved, with the establishment of the Double R Club, he was more than capable of carrying them out. He often had to be the stronger of the two, taking care not just of business but also of his brother. If Ron created a situation, Reg could not walk away from it. For everything Ron did, Reg always shared the consequences. He might have found an escape if his marriage to Frances had been successful. His life could have taken a different direction. It was not to be. His destiny was inextricably entwined with Ron's and their fate, like that of many of their victims, was a terrible one.

By 1978 the twins were living on the hospital wing of Parkhurst. It was to be their final year together. They were placed on F2, the observation landing, and were locked up for most of the day. Reg seemed to feel some respite despite, or perhaps because of, the restrictions. Ron's unpredictability, infatuations, and frequently violent outbursts were creating an intolerable strain. Reg was described as settling well on F2 but also identified as being 'the more vulnerable of the twins'. It was considered that a move might be useful for him in the near future. By October, a couple of weeks before his forty-fifth birthday, his mental health had taken an upward turn. A doctor wrote: 'Over the past weeks he has shown great improvement. He is no longer so depressed or anxious as before. Seems to have settled very well in hospital. His relationship with his brother is back on an even keel again. It is interesting to note that over the years I have known him he appears to have phases of anxiety and depression which is cyclical but depression has never reached the intensity of a true indigenous state.'

Reg's improved state of mind was short-lived. By the end of November he was finding it increasingly hard to deal with Ron and by the following spring he was slipping again into depression. One of their co-defendants at the trial arrived at Parkhurst. This man had been told he would not be reviewed for release for a further five to six years. The message for Reg was loud and clear – he had a long long wait ahead of him.

Ron could not settle. He found it impossible to simultaneously deal with prison life and the problems of his own illness. Although capable of long periods of rational thought, he was aware of the damage and strain he put on Reg during his unpredictable and uncontrollable relapses. Reg wrote in *A Way of Life*, 'One day the alarm bell rang on three different occasions when Ron had fights with other cons in the hospital. To put it mildly this was a bit of a strain on my nerves. I used to watch Ron like a hawk wherever he moved.'

In 1979 Ron was told he was being committed and transferred to Broadmoor. He was not unhappy about the decision. His ties to Reg were intense but the situation at Parkhurst was intolerable. Haunted by paranoia, anxiety and fear, his life was a nightmare. At Broadmoor he could at least get the treatment he needed. He knew he had to leave.

For Reg, as for Ron, the move evoked mixed emotions. He found it hard to envisage another separation; it was a terrible prospect. At the same time there was an element of relief. Reg continued to be drawn again and again into Ron's conflicts and emotional difficulties. Bound through love and loyalty to support him it added to the not inconsiderable strain of his own personal problems. Reg understood that Ron couldn't deal with ordinary prison conditions and knew he would continue to suffer for as long as he remained in them.

It was a traumatic time. They were twins and had shared the burden of Ron's illness throughout their lives. It was hard to let go. When Ron left for Broadmoor neither brother could have envisaged its permanency. They could not have imagined they would never spend, at any one time, more than a few hours together for the rest of their lives.

Reg continued his now slightly quieter existence on the hospital wing. He had been imprisoned for over ten years. Librium and Stelazine were still being prescribed. Life in the hospital was occasionally surreal. There were numerous inmates who had not yet been assessed and were waiting for their allocation. Some would go on to Broadmoor or Rampton but in the meantime they were Reg's constant, and often strange, companions. Many had major psychiatric problems. Reg admits to not feeling completely sane himself at this time but remained more or less aware of what was going on around him.

There was one particular ritual that Reg kept each year. Every Christmas, when it was dark, he would go to the toilets, stand on the pipes and peer out through the high window overlooking the Isle of Wight. In the distance he

could see the Christmas lights. They reminded him of everything he had lost . . . and some of the things he hoped one
day to recapture.

By the end of July Reg was once again fighting off
depression. Although freed from the pressure of Ron's
unpredictable behaviour, the separation produced its own
anxieties. With Ron settled at Broadmoor, Reg would have
to face the future alone. The hospital surroundings were not
exactly conducive to a balanced mind but he felt he couldn't
cope on the main wings. The authorities decided otherwise.
A decision was made to force Reg back into the mainstream
of prison life. Eighteen months after Ron's transfer, changes
were instigated. They would have a permanent and irrevocable effect.

2. A DOWNWARD SPIRAL

Reg's transfer in January 1981 into what was known as the 'dispersal system' proved an almost disastrous experience. The system had been introduced in 1969 and its purpose was to prevent a concentration of high-security inmates in any one place. By scattering them among other prisons, and frequently moving them around, the official aim was to lessen their ability to cause disruption and make any kind of mass breakout less serious. For the prisoners it meant they could be shifted at any time, usually in the early hours of the morning, and always without notice. Psychologically, the effect was profound. Knowing what was likely to happen made it difficult to settle or adjust. For those who had already spent long periods in highly regulated and highly secure conditions their entrance into the dispersal system could be especially traumatic.

The restrictive regime of Parkhurst had not prepared Reg for the very different environment of Long Lartin in Worcestershire. On arrival he appeared, according to staff reports, as 'a man completely disoriented and unable to cope with life in the wing situation'. The periods of open association, where most of the prisoners mixed freely together, were particularly threatening. He had difficulty relating to other inmates and initially could not deal with even a one-to-one conversation. In the presence of larger groups he withdrew to his cell. The Medical Officer described him as 'an odd little man whose management should present no real problems'.

Reg continued to have infrequent visits with Ron but these too were a source of anxiety. He believed he had a responsibility to help and support his twin but usually returned from their meetings in a state of frustration, his high hopes and expectations consistently dashed. At this time it was probably Reg who was more vulnerable. Ron's withdrawal had not just been physical; his emotional reliance had also lessened. Although they would always retain a fundamental need for each other, Ron was starting to deal with his problems on his own.

Gradually, over a period of three or four months, Reg began to gain a little confidence. Although primarily a loner he picked his few friends from former acquaintances, people he had known on the outside. One of these was Patsy Manning. They had met back in 1958 when Patsy had stopped him in the street and asked for directions to a barber. Reg had sent him down the road to 'Chris the Greek' and told him to drop by the snooker hall if he wanted a drink afterwards. That chance encounter had been the start of an enduring friendship. It was Patsy who came up with a solution when a girl Reg wished to see was refused permission to visit by the prison authorities. Under a different name it was arranged that she would visit Patsy instead, her visits coinciding with those of Reg with his mother. In this way they were able to sit near each other and have some brief conversations. For a while this arrangement worked well but eventually the staff realized what was going on. The visits were stopped and both Reg and Patsy were reprimanded.

Upset by what had happened, Reg was further distressed by the news he was to remain a high-security prisoner. The Governor of Long Lartin, in a report to the Category 'A' Committee at the Home Office, acknowledged that he no

longer warranted this status but accepted that 'the degree of
notoriety attached to him will make any downgrading of his
security category unlikely at this stage of his sentence'. The
Assistant Governor on Reg's wing was of a similar opinion:

> For institutional control reasons alone, I consider that
> Kray no longer needs the security restrictions of the Cat
> 'A' list. With regard to escape potential he has shown no
> indication of being involved in any escape attempt and
> it is possible after thirteen years inside he no longer has
> the support from anyone outside to mount an escape
> attempt for him. However the name Kray continues to
> attract considerable publicity and this is likely to con-
> tinue through reported plans to publish a book about his
> mother and through his brother Charlie's reported
> attempts to promote a film about the 'Life and times of
> the Kray Brothers'. This notoriety will make it difficult
> for the Cat 'A' Committee to approve a downgrading of
> Kray's security category, although this is recommended
> by most of the attached reports.

After a visit one afternoon Reg stood up to leave the hall
and found himself unsteady on his legs. Feeling dizzy and
light-headed he embarked on the long walk back to the wing
but had to stop halfway along the corridor. Another inmate
helped him back to his cell. Later an old friend, a magistrate
called Dora Hamilton, suggested he might be suffering
from agoraphobia. It is described in the dictionary as a fear
of public and open spaces but its roots lie in much deeper
places, in feelings of exposure, anxiety and extreme self-
consciousness. It was a reasonable diagnosis. Reg's twelve
years on the Isle of Wight had left him ill-equipped to face
the new challenges of Long Lartin. At Parkhurst social inter-
action had been minimal and determined more by necessity
than any genuine expression of friendship: confrontation

was commonplace; violence was routine; suspicion, fear, and stress were constant companions. Thrown from comparative isolation into open association, his subsequent difficulties were perhaps inevitable.

By this time it was September. The small improvements Reg had been making came to an abrupt halt. It was as if the reality of his situation suddenly hit home. Despite his attempts to integrate and adapt, the position of the authorities remained clear – he was to remain a high-security prisoner for the foreseeable future. Symptoms of his earlier paranoia re-emerged. Unable to trust even the closest of friends, he began to attribute betrayals. At night, in the darkness, he thought he could hear a persistent series of clicks. Was his cell being bugged? Were all his conversations being monitored? Was something being planned? His mind became filled with imaginary threats.

On 23 October 1981, the night before his forty-eighth birthday, a senior officer was alerted by Wing Patrol. It had been reported that 'Reginald Kray was distressed'. Officer Ramsay attended. He said:

> I went to see him and found him to be worrying about a letter, card and a book he had received during the day. It was from a Miss Beverley Derbyshire. Because of comments such as 'All my love forever' and 'This book is to remind you of me', 058111 [Reg's prison number] was convinced she was going to commit suicide. To reassure Kray I informed the Night Orderly Officer and then telephoned Kray's mother as Miss Derbyshire is not on the phone. The mother's number was unobtainable despite repeated tries. I went to see Kray and again found him in an upset condition. He stated his wife had committed suicide and he was getting bad feelings after reading his correspondence from Miss Derbyshire. I read them and went over them

with him and could not find anything in them to warrant Kray's concern. To placate Kray I made a telephone call to his brother, a Mr Charles Kray. His reply was that Miss Derbyshire had been in the best of spirits when he had seen her less than 24 hours previously and obviously after she had posted letters etc. In fact she was coming to visit Kray's mother the following day. His message was tell Reggie everything is fine, not to worry, and he would phone tomorrow. I went to see Kray again but he still would not accept that his fears were unfounded. He kept repeating that there was a 'message to him in what she had written'. He wanted the police contacted, to go to Miss Derbyshire's home and if necessary force an entry.

Reg was haunted by the suicide of Frances. Her death left wounds that would never heal and for the rest of his life he remained terrified the same thing might happen again. Unbalanced by his move to Long Lartin, Beverley's simple birthday inscriptions assumed more sinister implications. That night he didn't sleep. He paced his cell asking the same questions over and over as the staff came regularly to check on him. It was early morning before his mind was finally put at rest. Officer Ramsay's report was sent to the Medical Department. The doctor responded with a brusque and unsympathetic note: 'If the woman wants to commit suicide so be it. I am not concerned.'

Beverley was not the only person for whom Reg was afraid. He imagined all his loved ones were at risk, alone and friendless because of what he had done. Pursued by demons he withdrew ever further inside himself. His deteriorating condition, although blatantly obvious to his family, was either overlooked or ignored by prison officials. At the end of November Ron wrote a letter directly to the Medical Officer at Long Lartin:

Dear Sir,

I ask you to help my brother Reg Kray as Mother told me on a visit that he seems verry [sic] ill mentally. He told my mother that he thought his radio was bugged and that his food was being poisoned. He dose [sic] not write to me very often and has lost a lot of weight. I, as you no doubt know, have had mental illness all my life. I can tell by my brother's letters that he is now mentally ill.

Thank you sir.

From Ron Kray

Dr Green sent a response to the Medical Superintendent of Broadmoor Hospital: 'Enclosed is a letter from your patient Ronald Kray whose brother Reginald is an inmate of this establishment. Would you kindly explain to Kray that his brother is in excellent health and that he does write regularly even though not as often as he, Ronald, would wish, i.e. every single day.'

Violet tried to help her son. To her, as to Ron, it seemed quite clear what was happening. She enlisted the help of Dr Clein, the psychiatrist who had treated Reg on the outside, but his repeated attempts at a discussion with a prison doctor proved unsuccessful. After one of his phone calls the following was recorded by an officer in the Hospital Case Papers: 'The substance of the conversation was that an hysterical Mrs Kray had asked him to telephone the prison hospital. He went on to tell me more about Reggie Kray's past history than to enquire about his present state. He requested that I informed the Medical Officer that he had called. *Security informed*.' Although Dr Clein was on record as having previously treated Reg, his input was clearly neither wanted nor appreciated.

In December 1981 events took a turn for the worse. Despite their long friendship, Reg had a series of quarrels with Patsy Manning. The rows, although initially trivial, slowly took on a more serious aspect. Reg mistakenly became convinced that Patsy was plotting to kill him – Patsy was trying to poison him, Patsy was collaborating with other inmates, Patsy was working with the authorities. *Everyone*, he was sure, wanted him dead. The time had come for a confrontation. Reg left his cell, found Patsy and attacked. The fight was broken up by officers and both men were sent to the Segregation Unit. They were placed in solitary confinement. The Assistant Wing Governor later wrote, 'From this point in time Kray started to act very strangely, seemed dazed, confused, needed most conversations repeating several times and generally appeared to be not with it.'

The next morning Reg was found at 9 a.m. bleeding from both wrists. Convinced his death was inevitable and perhaps even necessary, he had smashed his spectacles on the floor and used the broken glass to inflict the injuries. The cuts to his right wrist were reported as 'superficial' but there was a much deeper cut to his left wrist and a divided tendon was clearly visible. In *A Way of Life*, Reg says: 'I was in a terrible state. I had reached the climax of despair.'

He was stitched up and returned to the Segregation Unit. A couple of days later, on Christmas Eve, he was visited by his older brother. Charlie was understandably concerned about both his physical and mental state. He talked to the doctor, describing the 'bizarre conversation' he'd had with Reg, but was reassured that there was nothing to worry about. On the same day the Hospital Case Papers (HCP) reported: 'After considerable effort and verbal persuasion he allowed staff to clean out his room, remake his bed and change his pyjama jacket but not trousers. Conversation continues vague, repetitive and generally negativistic.' Reg was prescribed Largactil, a brand name for chlorpromazine, used primarily in the treatment of schizophrenia, mania and other disorders in which confused or abnormal behaviour may occur.

Over the next few days Reg showed increasing signs of the breakdown he was undoubtedly going through. He was forty-eight years old and less than halfway through his sentence. On 27 December the HCP revealed that he was 'still acting in a strange manner, moving bed everywhere in his cell. Doesn't have much to say to anyone. Needs careful watching.' The next day showed no improvement: 'Remains negativistic, smokes endlessly, asks for "proper" tea to be made for him. Several efforts at making "proper" tea have been made to no avail. Asked a.m. if he could dress in his day clothes, these being issued shortly afterwards he threw his shirt and trousers out of the door flap. Asked if he did not require these articles he feigned deafness and merely asked for a light.'

As 1982 dawned, the start of a new year, Reg claimed he didn't wish to return to the wing. His paranoia had not subsided. He was convinced that, one way or another, his life would end at Long Lartin. The doctor dismissed his fears and premonitions as 'nonsense'. On 16 January he was returned to the wing. Believing it was only a matter of time before Patsy tried to murder him Reg promptly attacked again. Once again he was confined to the Segregation Unit. Once again he was found next morning with wounds to his wrist and arm. This time he had used a razor blade. The Assistant Governor wrote:

> At 11.14 a.m. on Sunday 17 January 1982 Kray was found in his cell in the Segregation Unit covered in blood, with some cuts showing on his left wrist and arm. A considerable amount of blood was spread around the cell. A stretcher was called for by Segregation Staff and Kray was taken to the Prison Hospital Wing. The Duty Doctor was called, and Dr Green, Medical Officer also came in to attend on Kray. Some stitches were inserted in Kray's injuries, which were then dressed and he was placed in

a strip cell. Within minutes he had attempted to remove
these dressings and did this again during the afternoon.
Whilst receiving medical treatment Kray was seen by
myself and the Chaplain but he was not able to say very
much.

Reg would not, or perhaps could not, discuss what he
had done. When asked for a reason he simply answered, 'I
was fed up.' The medical staff reported, somewhat incredibly, that they believed his actions were 'manipulative in
nature and not indicative of mental ill health'. His fellow
inmates were of a different opinion. They made representations to the Wing Governor claiming that Reg's mind 'had
gone' and that he shouldn't be punished. They asked if he
could be sent somewhere to get proper treatment.

Reg Kray was a highly unusual prisoner, a mandatory
lifer only halfway through a thirty-year sentence. He had
no indication or even any hope of a possible release date. It
is impossible to lock anyone up for a prolonged period of
time, especially in high-security conditions, without consequences for their mental health. Whilst at Long Lartin Reg
was described on various occasions, and by various officers, as being 'rational', 'vague', 'subdued', 'aggressive',
'normal', 'erratic', 'alert', 'dazed', 'confused', 'bemused' and
'depressed' – an incredible litany of adjectives and surely
indicative of a person with serious problems.

Unable to settle on the wing, finding himself constantly
overwhelmed, Reg turned again and again to the emotional
security of the Segregation Unit and the Hospital. There was
little evidence of sympathy from either the medical staff
or the officers. That Reg could not find a way to cope was
apparently a failure of his own making. He received no help
towards addressing any of his fears or anxieties. His desperation was almost contemptuously ignored.

Reg tried to explain to the doctor that he was unable to

deal with life on the wing. They had a long conversation
where Reg reiterated a need to be on his own. His paranoia
was such that he could trust neither others nor himself. The
doctor wrote in his report: 'He seemed surprised when I told
him Doctor Cooper would not have him in Parkhurst Hospital. I feel he is hankering after Parkhurst or Broadmoor.'
He prescribed Imipramine, an antidepressant drug. Shortly
after Reg set fire to some toilet paper on his bed. The doctor
warned him that should he persist with his behaviour he
would arrange for his admission to Rampton: 'I am sure his
behaviour is entirely manipulative. Advised Seg staff to put
him in the strong box and dress him in Terylene suit.'

On 5 February Reg was forced back on the wing. It was
not a successful reintroduction. At 6.20 p.m. an officer
reported that 'Kray is cracking up'. Reg returned temporarily to the Segregation Unit but the next day tried again. He
spent the afternoon moving between the wing and the Unit,
deciding he wanted to be in one place and the next minute
changing his mind and transferring to the other. A senior
officer wrote:

> From the outset his whole behaviour pattern was of
> bemused non-comprehension. The wing staff and
> myself tried hard to persuade him that it was in his
> best interest to remain on the wing but all our counsel
> and advice was met with a wall of indecision. The gen-
> eral consensus of opinion amongst the other inmates
> appeared to blame the authorities for 'sending a man
> to normal location in that state'. The majority of
> inmates acknowledged Kray's presence but that was
> all. They did not seem to want to get involved when
> they saw the way he was behaving. Kray spent most of
> the afternoon pacing up and down in between frequent
> visits to the wing office for advice, which he did not
> heed anyway.

Reg remained in the Segregation Unit. It was stressed that he shouldn't be allowed either matches or any cutting instruments in his cell. It was also recommended that he should not only continue to take the antidepressant drug but that the dose should be increased. His whole family were by now extremely anxious. Ron, aware that his twin was suffering, asked his solicitors to try to intervene. They sent a letter. On 10 February Long Lartin responded with the information that 'Kray' was under mental observation and that there was no evidence of psychosis. They claimed, inaccurately, that Reg was not receiving any medication. They also wrote: 'One of his problems is that he is a fallen idol and is at present endeavouring to find a way of coping with this situation.'

The following morning Reg set fire to his bedding again. He had persuaded a visiting priest to leave him some matches to light his cigarettes. Reg was removed to a protected room. He was now beginning to worry about something else – that he would be sectioned and sent to a mental hospital. Dr Green recommended that he be kept in the strip room with the flap sealed. Less than a week later an entry in the Hospital Case Papers claims: 'Kray today has been at great pains to convince us that he is "quite normal, I'm not mad". He is obviously very frightened since the topic of Rampton was raised. Has been picking at the old wrist wounds.'

Over the next few days his conversation with staff was described as repetitive. Although always receiving an identical answer he asked the same question sometimes five or six times. He remained convinced that other inmates were antagonistic and developed a new belief that there had been some publicity – of which he knew nothing but they knew everything – about him. His medical report stated there were 'a few signs of paranoia'. Despite his obvious confusion he was declared fit to travel and to visit Ron. Reg refused to go.

Convinced there was something wrong, some element of trickery, he withdrew to his cell. He became preoccupied, once again, by bad premonitions. A doctor declared: 'This reinforces my opinion that Kray is suffering from *paranoia* without depression or schizophrenia.'

On 25 February a prison officer submitted the following report about Reg:

> Last evening I decided that Kray ought to have a bath. The whole procedure took precisely an hour. After much indecision when he appeared to be conversing with some unseen adviser, he said 'all right then, just to please Charlie'. As he believed he was not being observed he very quickly disrobed and placed a foot in the bath, took it out and went through the motions of drying his whole body. When I said you have not bathed properly he denied this. After much persuasion he again disrobed and sat in the bath, for some three seconds, he threw some water on his chest, jumped out and dried himself then dressed. When dressed he told me, 'In confidence, when I know someone is talking about me I get a burning sensation going up and down my back'. On examination of back no rash or irritant evident.

At the beginning of March Reg was described as rational but evasive. He was full of worries – about Ron, his mother, his father's health and his rows with Patsy Manning. In trying to explain what he'd done he could only say, 'A lot of things got me down. I suppose I had some sort of breakdown.' The doctor, in his subsequent report, claimed Reg was 'afraid of certification and transfer to Rampton or Broadmoor'. That was certainly true.

It is a sad indictment of the prison system that staff could perceive of only two alternatives: either Reg was sane and behaving badly, in which case he had to be punished, or he was insane and certifiable. There was no middle ground. Despite clearly stated convictions that he was not mentally ill a request was still made for a Rampton psychiatrist to make an assessment. The motives in instigating such a report seem questionable. The prospect was in itself implicitly menacing. As he waited for the interview Reg's fears grew. A part of him knew that he was ill, knew that he was paranoid, knew that he was behaving irrationally. What he needed and wanted was some basic help. What he was offered was the probability of being sectioned.

On 6 March, four days before the meeting, an officer wrote in the Hospital Case Papers: 'Allowed out of cell to slop and take breakfast. Making comments as "Something's going to happen today" and "What's happening, I'm all mixed up." Kray was told that staff didn't have the time to spend with him at this hour of the day and to return to his cell.' He claimed that Reg had 'come very close to offering violence' and should be treated with 'extreme caution'. The doctor added that he was 'accepting his treatment with difficulty'.

On 10 March Dr Pickering arrived from Rampton. He was informed, oddly, that Reg had no history of psychiatric problems. This was untrue; his difficulties at Parkhurst were on record as well as his earlier history of extreme depression after the death of Frances. The psychiatrist's report, after a long interview, read:

I examined this patient in the Hospital at HM Prison, Long Lartin, at your request, yesterday. We had some discussion about the case and I was kindly enabled to read your current hospital case papers about Reginald Kray. Although the voluminous Parkhurst HCP [Hospital Case Papers] were available I did not see them, partly because of the time factor, but also because it seemed more worth while to concentrate upon Mr Kray's present state of mind. However, I learned from you that, unlike his twin brother, he has not had any past psychiatric history.

Mr Kray was, of course, already known to me by repute but I had not met him previously. I was a member of the Prison Department when he and his brother were received in prison and I recall the deliberations that took place – largely about the security implications. We were advised that his brother, who had an in-patient history of schizophrenia, would be better managed if Reginald was around. So both brothers were then placed in Parkhurst and Reginald was transferred from there about 15 months ago.

He has been in Hospital, off and on, since last December. He is, I understand, inclined to be moody and only yesterday morning had thrown a bowl of water over two officers. Because of his security category (Category 'A') he has to have two additional guards when he is moved about.

I learned from the hospital staff that he has lost face with the other inmates and that they no longer regard him with the same awe as in former times.

At interview Mr Kray proved co-operative and quite eager to talk about himself and his problems, about his life and his family. There seemed to be nothing wrong with his more distant memory. He told me he was now in the fifteenth year of his life sentence and said he was . . . 'a bit depressed'. He does not believe he will ever be released. His sentence was fixed as a minimum of thirty years by the trial judge – Mr Justice Melford Stevenson.

He has premonitions of death. When he arrived at Long Lartin he felt he would never leave it. So he may have suicidal ideas.

He was a little deaf. I had to remember to keep my voice up. You explained to me in discussion afterwards that he had suffered otitis externa and had become resistant to every antibiotic. Apart from a little greying of his hair, Mr Kray looked remarkably well and still like his well-known photographs. He told me he took pride in keeping physically fit. He apologized for his costume . . . his feet were bare. (Was this a security device or his own decision?)

Long Lartin he said, is the first 'Dispersal Prison' in which he had served and he would like to go to a smaller, ordinary prison. I noticed in his HCP that last December he made a request to be transferred to Dartmoor at a time when his conduct was described as being 'erratic'.

He gave me a strong hand-clasp on our meeting and again when he left. Otherwise there was nothing to infer he was a former 'boss' of the criminal fraternity.

He wished to reassert that he did not need to be treated as a VIP or Category A. Could I arrange for his Category A status now to be withdrawn. I pointed out that I could only make recommendations and it would be the responsibility of others to make the decisions.
Conclusions

He impressed me as being an uneducated man of not particularly bright intelligence but who must once upon a time have been a strong personality. Now he is just rather pathetic.

Reg, recollecting his own memories of the interview wrote: 'I was anxious about the meeting. I was worried that he might decide I should be detained indefinitely at Rampton. I didn't fancy going there at all . . . I was terribly scruffy and dirty, wearing an old blue prison singlet. I hadn't shaved or bathed properly for some time . . . At the end of the interview Dr Pickering told me to relax as he had no intention of certifying me. He told me I was quite sane.'

Four days later, despite the psychiatrist's reassurances, Reg was still in a state of fear and confusion. In the evening he was temporarily released from his cell. He was given a cigarette to smoke and allowed to sit in the TV room. For a few minutes everything was calm. Then, after he had smoked the cigarette, he suddenly picked up a table and threw it at the television. Restrained by a couple of prison officers, he made no attempt to resist. He showed no violence towards the officers. He was taken away and put into isolation.

The next day Reg was seen by a doctor. He was described in the report as 'perfectly rational'. Reg told him, 'I had a premonition when I came into this prison I wouldn't get out alive.' The doctor wrote that he was afraid of retribution. Reg said, 'I'd be happy to stay in my cell, have my radio and do my writing . . . I just don't fit in here and I never have. I wish I could.' The doctor reported that he had taken his injection of Seranace (an antipsychotic drug) quite willingly. At 3 p.m., five hours later, it was recorded that the drug had 'not had a noticeable effect'. At 8 p.m. he was given a further 200 mg of Largactil. Shortly after Reg apologized for the trouble he had made. He was told he could remain in the Hospital until arrangements were made to transfer him back to HMP Parkhurst.

To Parkhurst? Having been informed that he could not and would not return it came as a shock. It was a backward step but one that he welcomed. Or thought he did. Although initially relieved, his feelings soon turned to guilt. Both Ron and his mother had hoped he would eventually settle at Long Lartin. Once again he felt he had failed the people he loved. He asked if he could go back on the wing, if he could try again, but the decision had been made. It was final. He became frightened and aggressive. During his last few days in the prison he was described as 'agitated'. He was warned that if he continued with his behaviour he would 'end up permanently in Rampton or Broadmoor'.

Eighteen years later, Reg wrote in *A Way of Life*: 'I had many disturbing experiences at Long Lartin . . . I had partly lost my identity . . . This is the worst thing that can happen during a prison sentence, but the risk is always there – on a long sentence it is almost unavoidable. It has to do with anxiety, followed by a loss of confidence. Perhaps the main factor is just being in a strange and abnormal environment.'

On 26 March 1982 Reg was transferred back to Parkhurst.

3. REACHING OUT

It was with some relief that Reg returned to Parkhurst in March 1982. His troubles, however, were far from over. Damaged by the ill-managed attempt to reintegrate him into 'normal' prison conditions, he was haunted by paranoia. He was placed on the F2 observation landing and returned to the care of Dr Cooper. The presence of the doctor was reassuring but Reg still struggled; he could not shake the idea from his head that his continuing existence threatened the future of his entire family. He found it impossible to sleep and was filled with guilt at having refused to visit Ron.

Despite being cheered by letters from both Ron and his mother he remained in a state of mental distress. On 1 April, less than a week after being transferred, he used a piece of glass to once again slash his left forearm. The officers, who discovered him on unlocking, described the wound as deep with considerable bleeding. He was taken to the hospital but when the doctor attempted to apply a dressing Reg began to struggle. He was given Valium and the antipsychotic drug chlorpromazine. Although superficial veins had been cut there was not any tendon or nerve injuries. His arm was bandaged and he was taken back to his cell where he was put on Special Watch.

By the end of the month Reg's depression was starting to lift. He expressed a desire to stay in the hospital and the medical staff agreed that this was probably the best location for

the immediate future. Over the next few weeks he made
slow but steady progress. Reg believed his real turning point
came with a visit from an old friend, Fred Bone. Fred left a
book for him, an autobiography of the Mafia boss Meyer
Lansky. It was a book with a simple but penetrating message
– one should never give up even in the face of terrible odds.
It is impossible to know if it was the influence of the book,
or simply a gradual reassertion of his natural spirit, that led
Reg back to some kind of equilibrium. It was not the end of
his problems but provided at least a temporary reprieve. He
began to take more interest both in himself and others.
He washed and shaved. After sorting through his mail he
started to write again, a correspondence with friends and the
public that was to continue for the rest of his life.

Alarmed by what had happened at Long Lartin, he tried
to analyse his ongoing mental difficulties. He wanted to
understand what had happened to him – and why. His
inability to integrate into mainstream prison life was a major
problem. Always suspicious of the motives of others, unable
now to trust or even socialize, he looked towards his past for
answers. Reg recognized the perpetual cycle of violence in
which he had been involved not just within prison walls but
also outside. In *A Way of Life*, he explains: 'I had grown up
in the tough environment of the East End and had learnt
to be aggressive. I slighted easily and often responded, as
others did, with violence. It continued in prison. I felt I was
in a position where I had to stand up for myself or I'd be
trodden underfoot. I met aggression with more aggression.
I needed to express myself verbally, to talk, rather than
holding my tongue and letting all the pressure build up
inside me.'

The familiarity of Parkhurst helped Reg cope with what
felt like a perpetual struggle against his irrational fears.
Dr Cooper was helpful and supportive. Support came too,
as always, from his mother. After the frightening events of

Long Lartin she was glad he was back on the Isle of Wight; it might be a backward step as regards his freedom but at least he was safe. These better days were short-lived. Reg's father was still ill. Violet, worried by his condition and exhausted by the long journeys she frequently made to see both her imprisoned sons, told Reg she might not be able to visit for a while. He understood. He also knew how much he'd miss her and expressed the heartfelt hope that they would see each other soon. Sadly, it was not to be. Violet was seriously unwell herself. A few months later she was admitted to hospital with terminal cancer. On 4 August Reg received the devastating news that his mother was dead.

A brief entry in the Parkhurst Medical Log marks the occasion: 'His mother died in her sleep last night – Brother rang to inform him, took it rather badly – tearful etc. Was very close to his mother. Governor informed – requests to visit funeral.'

Both Reg and Ron were given permission to attend the service but it was not the dignified occasion they would have liked. The authorities, determined to turn the day to some advantage, ensured that both brothers were handcuffed to extremely tall prison officers. The manoeuvre, somewhat trite in its intention, was designed to show the 'smallness' of the twins in every respect. The media were also out in force indulging in an unseemly scrum for quotes and photographs. It was the first time the twins had been seen in public for many years.

Reg travelled from Parkhurst to Chingford in the back of a van, squashed between two prison officers and handcuffed to both. There was a heavy police escort with screaming sirens. It was not a journey conducive to reflective thoughts. Looking down he noticed the brightly coloured socks of one of the officers. It was only a small thing but it stayed in his mind; they somehow symbolized a more general indifference.

Although both Ron and Reg arrived before the service began they were kept apart and not allowed to talk to each other. Reg recalled in *A Way of Life*: 'We were shown separately to the front of the church where we sat down with our escorts. Our father was sitting behind and there were other close people all around but, handcuffed to the screws, I felt no warmth. All through the service, through the hymns and the prayers, I couldn't get it out of my mind that I was handcuffed to strangers and separated from those I loved.'

There was no respite outside. Crowds had gathered to catch a glimpse of the 'infamous' twins. Amidst the security, noise and curiosity, the solemnity of the occasion was lost. It was turned into a spectacle. The authorities, whilst determined to appear humane, effectively turned the day into a reminder of their own superior force. It was an opportunity they must have relished.

This was the first time, since his conviction, that Reg had lost anyone he truly loved. He found it hard to grieve properly. Without the closeness of family, surrounded by strangers, he experienced only emptiness. He felt both grief and guilt but was unable to express either. He was sure that some responsibility for her illness lay at the feet of her sons; their imprisonment had made her life a misery. In losing Violet, Reg lost his greatest source of strength and comfort. She had provided not just the unfailing and constant support of all good mothers but that most precious of gifts – unconditional love. When she died an irreplaceable sense of security was removed forever.

Shortly after the funeral Dr Cooper received a letter from David Tidmarsh, the consultant psychiatrist at Broadmoor. He explained that Ron had requested to see him regarding his great concern over his twin. On their last visit Reg had apparently been upset and confused and was talking about their mother being tortured. He had also claimed that a girl who was visiting him was Jack McVities daughter – although

she wasn't. Ron said that at their mother's funeral Reg had
been tense and extremely silent and at some stage later
had talked about 'pulling out one of the veins in his arm to
kill himself'. After sharing his worries Ron had asked for the
information to be relayed to Parkhurst in case they were not
aware of Reg's state of mind.

In addition to Reg's emotional difficulties he was also
facing physical ones. The problem with his ears and hearing
had not improved. This made it even more difficult for him
to communicate. A week after the letter, on 24 August 1982,
there is an entry from a doctor in the Medical Log: 'Predic-
tion: If the deafness increases, the resultant social isolation
may precipitate the schizophrenic psychosis that, luckily for
him, has been floating on the surface. If that happens the
twins would be united in Broadmoor? The relatively stress-
free conditions in prison seem to have kept the emergence of
a psychosis at bay.'

That conditions in a high-security prison should be
described as 'relatively stress-free' is perhaps more indicative of an attitude within the prison service than any accurate reflection of reality. After the death of his mother, it was
inevitable that Reg would be distraught and disoriented.
He had not even been able to see or talk to her before she
died. His loss, beyond the original peremptory note, was
never mentioned again in reports. It ceased to be relevant.
The doctor's query as to whether he might eventually join
Ron in Broadmoor was not pursued either. To have been
able to pronounce both brothers 'insane' might have been a
welcome result for the Home Office – but the evidence was
simply not there.

Three months later, on 24 November, Reg wrote to the
Broadmoor authorities. He was missing Violet badly and
craved the comfort of his twin. Only part of the letter sur-
vives: 'Sir, I hope you will consider letting my brother Ron
back here with me. He seems more like himself after the

treatment at Broadmoor and I feel he can settle down well here as he knows the staff here and some of the inmates. I know my mother would be pleased if he were back here with me.' At around the same time Ron wrote a similar letter to Parkhurst: 'Dr Cooper, I would like to come back to Parkhurst if you will have me back with my brother Reg. I feel we should be together. Now even more so. Would you please write back and let me know if possible.' The twins had an instinctive knowledge and understanding of each other's state of mind. Happiness and pain were shared emotions. Although Ron suffered immensely as a result of his illness he was the stronger at this time and aware of Reg's intense need for him. Despite being settled at Broadmoor, and knowing that a move back to Parkhurst could be personally disastrous, he was still prepared to make the transfer.

It was inevitable that such a reunion would not be permitted but even the prospect of it helped ease some of Reg's worst symptoms. At the end of the year, in December 1982, he requested a move to the main prison and it was agreed that he could join C Wing after Christmas. By January he was looking forward to the relocation. He was described in medical reports as having 'no evidence of psychosis'. He wanted to make a fresh start, to deal with things, but his improved frame of mind didn't last. Within a couple of months he was involved once again in some minor altercation and claimed he could not cope with the new environment. Although appreciative of the other cons and their kindness to him, he was bemused by the activity and speed of the wing. He felt he was too old or perhaps simply too tired for it all. His paranoia, that old familiar enemy, had returned. He was re-admitted to F2 and prescribed a further dose of Stelazine.

Reg remained in a state of agitation. He talked repeatedly about his mother, father and Ron. Was Ron coming back from Broadmoor? He was unable to sleep or to think clearly. He became convinced that someone was 'talking about him' but could not identify the person or the words they had spoken. He sat alone for long periods in his cell. The hospital staff could make no connection with him. Their assessment, firmly underlined in the log, reads bluntly and coldly: 'He is *psychotic*.'

Victim to anxiety, paranoia and depression, Reg found it hard to establish any kind of settled life. Before he had even begun to recover from the shock of Violet's death he was given the terrible news, barely seven months later, that his father had also died. Although they had not been as close, he still felt the loss keenly. He drew even further inside himself. With Ron he made the decision not to attend the funeral. Neither of them wanted the publicity that had marred their mother's burial.

Within a few days Reg began asking about the possibility of going to Broadmoor. It was a desperate request. Aware that Ron had recently tried to join him, he was willing to make an equal sacrifice. Although he valued what he referred to as the 'freedom of my thoughts', a freedom which he always feared would be lost within the confines of a mental institution, he wanted and needed – whatever the cost – to be with his twin.

There was a negative response. Reg might be ill but he was not, as the Rampton psychiatrist had confirmed, certifiable. Over the next few weeks he made a sustained effort to return and adapt to the main wing. Perhaps he had finally acknowledged the prospect of a permanent separation from Ron for, although no one could ever take his place, he began to search for a surrogate. He yearned for someone who could provide at least a little of what was missing from his life. Reg had by now been incarcerated for almost half of his allocated sentence. He was forty-nine years of age and had lost, through death or separation, almost everyone who meant anything to him.

It was at this stage that Reg's life underwent a dramatic

change. After years of celibacy he embarked on what would become a series of intense emotional and sometimes sexual relationships with younger inmates. There has been a lot of conjecture, rumour and gossip about these partnerships. Much of it is ill-informed or simply salacious. It doesn't begin to address the real reasons why he so desperately needed to be involved.

Reg had grown up not just with his twin but as a part of him. They had relied on each other for unquestionable love and loyalty. It was not always a peaceful alliance but it was certainly a committed one. He had taken an early responsibility for his brother, looking after him during the worst periods of his paranoid schizophrenia. These episodes had become more pronounced as the twins entered their twenties. On occasions Ron was completely incapable of dealing with the outside world. Confused and suspicious, he withdrew to his room unable to recognize members of his family and convinced that even his twin was an impostor. Reg stayed with him providing comfort and support and ensuring he received the medication he required. Even when the worst was over Ron's unpredictability and volatile emotions continued to be a danger both to others and themselves. Reliant on Reg to stand by him and see him through his dark depressions, Ron feared and resented his attachment to anyone else. Reg's relationships, especially his marriage to Frances, suffered as a result. It could only ever end, as indeed it had, in disaster.

After Ron was committed to Broadmoor, Reg felt utterly alone. He was also bequeathed a terrible legacy – the knowledge that his twin could survive without him. Ron not only coped with the separation but positively thrived. He had a small but loyal group of friends on the outside and rapidly acquired new partners on the inside. Within the confines of Broadmoor and with the drugs he needed, Ron was relatively content.

Reg was the opposite. He had lost Frances and he had lost his daily contact with Ron. The final blow was the loss of his mother. With the death of Violet his external support system was swept away. Although he had friendships, they were not deep enough to fill the void. Facing a lifetime's incarceration there was little left to fight for. This was the point when Reg began to form relationships with other inmates. By transferring all his energy and attention to another person he created a reason to carry on. Within the dull monotony of prison routine, an emotional attachment provided some essential spark of interest and purpose. He needed not just someone to care for but someone who would also care deeply for him. He wanted a partner who could embody everyone and everything he had lost – Ron, Frances, his mother, his hopes and his dreams – the perfect 'other half'. It was an impossible ideal but one he clung to through the next twenty years.

There are always opportunities for sexual encounters in prison. As in most communities sex can be bought or bartered for. What is more important, and certainly more interesting, is that many inmates – especially during prolonged incarceration – develop relationships that are as much to do with emotional as with physical need. In the prison environment where deceit and deception are rife and violence and betrayal commonplace, a trusted friend provides a sense of safety and security. such a friend also provides an essential outlet. In order to maintain status and not to betray any sign of weakness, it is often impossible for a man to express basic human emotions – tenderness, anxiety and fear must all be suppressed. A confidant provides a haven from that constant pressure: worries can be shared and comfort given and received without jeopardy to reputation.

Suspicion and loneliness were Reg's two greatest enemies. For as long as he had confidence in close friends they helped allay many of his fears and prevent the escalation of a lurking paranoia. By looking out for another person he regained a sense of self-worth and responsibility. He also received, if only temporarily, the reassurance of feeling loved and needed. There was, however, a corresponding down side. Reg's emotional vulnerability left him open to both personal and pecuniary exploitation, which was to cause significant problems for the rest of his time in prison.

Although some of Reg's relationships with other inmates were sexual, the majority were not. It was trust and loyalty that he sought most. At Parkhurst he found them in a young inmate called Steve Tully. They embarked on a project collecting cockney, criminal and American slang words to make into a book. During the following months Reg dredged through his memory trying to recall all the common phrases of his childhood; he also wrote to everyone he knew. Between them, and in collaboration with his now-released old friend Patsy Manning, he and Steve Tully produced a manuscript. It was named simply *Reg Kray's Book of Slang*. On its completion Reg felt a tremendous sense of achievement.

His friendship with Steve contributed to a general feeling of well-being during this period. If Steve had any problems Reg would try to sort them out, a process that meant taking responsibility and getting involved. This gave him a purpose. While he was thinking about someone else he was less inclined to succumb to his own, often self-destructive, anxieties. For most of the next three years, until Tully was released, they spent much of their time in each other's company.

It wasn't until October 1983 that any signs of Reg's former depression re-emerged. He began to sleep badly and to suffer occasional panic attacks. The knowledge that he would probably have to serve the full thirty years of his sentence preyed on his mind. The approach of his fiftieth birthday served as a distinct reminder, if he needed one, of both the passing of time and his slow progress through the prison system. He was in his sixteenth year of imprisonment.

Most had been spent in the high-security conditions of Parkhurst where he was still designated an 'A' category prisoner.

Despite his worries, Reg's birthday proved to be a memorable event. A large party was organized and over eighty inmates attended bringing food, gifts, cards and an adequate supply of illicitly brewed alcohol – commonly known as 'hooch'. It was a special evening for Reg and one that would always remain with him. The prison officers, perhaps unwilling to provoke unnecessary strife, stayed away. As Reg moved between the cells, listening to the music and chatting to his guests, he was reminded of the past. For a couple of hours he was transported back to his days of freedom.

1985 marked the beginning of another Category 'A' Review that would debate his suitability for a security downgrade. His future, once again, was in the balance.

12th September 1985 – Report from J. Rumball,
HMP Parkhurst Governor, to P2 Division
(Lifer Section, Home Office)
You will be aware of the background to this prisoner so I will not repeat the details. He asked for a personal interview with me and I saw him on Tuesday 10th September 1985.

He is aware that he has a review next year (1986) and has an expectation that a target will be set for consideration of his release. Understandably he is anxious about the outcome of this review – this was apparent by how and what he said and by his general manner.

He is anxious to remain here for his review, and this I would support, adding that I advised KRAY he would not normally be considered for a transfer in the time leading up to a review.

We then discussed the future. KRAY states that he

would prefer to remain here rather than go to another dispersal prison. He feels settled here and says he is able to find peace of mind here. It is of note that he constantly referred to his 'peace of mind'. If he is to be moved, he would wish it to be out of the dispersal system to a Category 'B' prison. He specifically mentioned Nottingham and Kingston. We discussed these suggestions at length, and I hope that I persuaded him that because of the nature of Kingston he could not expect to go there from here; equally I did not rule it out totally in the future, as I advised him that his future location(s) were a matter of very careful consideration.

KRAY appears to be thinking sensibly and positively about a release date and does not have unrealistic views. He is aware of his thirty-year recommendation, and he sees that period as a time for him to serve.

He is quietly spoken and appears to have some difficulty in hearing. Further, each point has to be clearly and concisely explained to him, with repetition being required on each occasion. He appears to have a further difficulty in absorbing and understanding new information easily. This may be a mannerism or a genuine situation. I do not comment as I believe this is a matter for the Principal Medical Officer (to whom this is copied).

Summing up, KRAY would benefit from the review setting a plan for him. It would give him targets at which to aim and a purpose to his sentence. However, this makes the assumption that it is planned that KRAY will be released eventually as in our discussion we did agree that the life sentence could mean exactly that – life.

He was quiet and respectful on the interview, yet made his points quite strongly. I enjoyed the discussion.

Forwarded for information and any action deemed necessary.

This was an interesting report. It stated, for the first time, that Reg would benefit from a sentence plan – *if* the authorities were ever intending to release him. It was, and is, normal procedure for most prisoners to receive such instruction and provides them with at least some idea of how long imprisonment may last and what is expected from them. The failure to provide Reg with any such information in 1985, so many years after conviction, suggests either an unfortunate oversight or a quiet acknowledgement that there was no intention to ever free him. It is discouraging to note that as late as 1995, ten years later, Reg's then-solicitor remarked on the surprising brevity of reports and information on a man who had spent so long in prison.

For Reg there was little incentive or encouragement. Aware of his abysmally slow progress through the system, he began to lose faith in any prospect of release and relied increasingly on the world 'inside'. By late 1985, Steve Tully had left Parkhurst and Reg was alone again. He continued to see Steve on visits and worked with him on a few projects but things were not the same. Faced with old problems, Reg struggled to find a reason to carry on. This changed in December when a new con arrived on the wing from HMP Coldingley. His name was Pete Gillett. The two struck up a friendship and were soon inseparable. Gillett was young and ambitious.

Reg recognized Gillett's ambition and Gillett recognized Reg's usefulness. Inside prison they made plans that could bring 'success' to them both. A show-business career for Pete, based perhaps more on wishful thinking than any real evidence of talent, was devised and lingered over. For Reg it provided the opportunity not just of closeness within prison but also of a future, if vicarious, external life; for Gillett it offered hope of a better future.

In January 1986 Dr Cooper wrote a report to the Lifer Division at the Home Office. He claimed there was 'no evidence of mental illness at present' and that Reg had adapted well to the routine of the wing. 'In the past Kray has been subject to several relatively severe depressive episodes which have responded to treatment . . . He has a curious relationship with his brother – almost 'love/hate' in nature – and I am told by officials at Broadmoor that sometimes on visits hardly a word is exchanged between them.' He also registered his concern that the complexity of Reg's relationships with other inmates was creating a drain on his emotional resources.

It was Dr Cooper's opinion that Reg no longer represented a physical threat but that if he was transferred from Parkhurst he would need to go to a prison with a full-time Medical Officer.

In early 1986 Reg was sent on a 'lay-down' to Wandsworth Prison. This is usually the penalty for what is termed 'an act against the prison system' but no specific reason was either given to Reg or declared in his reports. He was due to stay for a month. It was cold and icy. Exercise was taken in a caged concrete yard. He walked alone for an hour each day and for the rest of the time he was locked up. Wandsworth brought back many memories. He had served a short sentence there when he was courting Frances, fretting that she might leave him, determined to make a better life for them both when he got out.

When the month was over, Reg looked forward to returning. Instead he was sent to Wormwood Scrubs for a further four weeks. Again, no reason was provided. It may have been connected to a strike that was taking place at Parkhurst. Also, in his absence, another murder had been committed. The prison was in a state of unrest.

Eleven years later, when he was at Maidstone Reg, recalling the lay-down, wrote in a letter to me: 'I used to lie on the bed for 23 hours and switch off like a corpse. Eventually I went back to Parkhurst . . . Before I did so I went to the church service . . . all the faces had changed but it was the same story, all waiting to go wherever, all praying for freedom. Like they were all waiting for a bus in a queue. I'm still waiting for that bus!'

When Reg arrived back he renewed his friendship with Pete Gillett and the two continued making plans. Unable to foresee any freedom of his own, Reg concentrated instead on his friend's. He had high hopes for his success. Reg's association with Gillett was later to create a minor scandal in the newspapers.

By this time *Slang* had been published but, due to various problems, it met with little success. Distributed through Patsy Manning, major bookshops seemed reluctant to take the title, probably due in equal parts to its infamous author and its publishing origins – an unknown company called Wheel and Deal. In 1985 it was rare for a convicted criminal to write any kind of book. It wasn't until 1988 when *Our Story*, compiled in conjunction with Fred Dinenage, was published that the floodgates opened and the public's fascination with the world of crime revealed an entirely new career option for a number of ex-cons in search of a more comfortable retirement.

The book *Slang* was slight but interesting enough. It had a quirky originality. Copies were certainly sold in London and through various outlets including pubs, clubs and friends but it wasn't until 1989 that Sidgwick & Jackson published the more widely distributed and hardback version. It is now out of print.

It was during his last years at Parkhurst that Reg discovered there could be more to life than a routine existence in prison. Many ideas occurred to him. Although sometimes unrealistic they occupied his mind and provided the impetus he needed to keep going. By far the most fascinating prospect was one suggested by Roger Daltrey; he had expressed an interest in making a film. It was still in its early

stages but was something to look forward to. Reg also made
big plans with Pete Gillett. Interviews with journalists record
a number of projects in which they were interested – cloth-
ing, security, pubs, restaurants and clubs.

It is impossible to know how much Reg was earning from
his various extra-curricular activities but it was not vast.
Most of the ventures came to nothing. The mythology that
had already grown around the twins drew certain people
towards him. Prospective investors, believing in the huge
hidden fortunes of the Krays, were more than happy to
advance a few hundred in the prospect of a much greater
return. They had, as Reg soon learned, no intention of sharing any future profits.

He proceeded to give money away as quickly as it was
received. Reg had a compelling need to provide for his
friends. This was down to a combination of factors. It was
part generosity, part responsibility, but mainly the result of a
deep-seated insecurity. He felt, sadly, that money might bind
them in a way emotion never could.

His attachments to young inmates did not go unnoticed.
It seems his relationship with Pete Gillett was especially significant. In February 1986 Reg spoke to a local BBC crew
who were visiting Parkhurst. In a brief interview he said: 'I
would just like to mention a friend of mine. He is a kid of
twenty-five, Peter Gillett, and he is the best entertainer I
have ever seen. I knew Sammy Davis Jnr when I was on the
outside and Peter is even better than him.' Reg's faith in
Gillett's abilities was to be sorely tested – but that was all in
the future.

Later that month a scandal erupted when a tabloid newspaper claimed that Gillett was Reg's lover. There was talk of
writs and legal action. Gillet wrote a letter from Parkhurst to
the editor, demanding an apology.

No apology was forthcoming.

In October of 1986 Gillett had four days' home leave from

Parkhurst. Reg made sure it was spent in style. He arranged
for a white Rolls Royce to be waiting as his friend stepped
off the ferry. Gillett was then whisked off for an interview
with the BBC news programme Coast to Coast where he
talked about his hopes and plans for a show-business career.
Reg also arranged for him to start negotiations for a recording contract and to sing at a nightclub. A publicity sheet, produced around this time, claimed: 'Pete's singing style is
unique and as individual as the man himself . . . Pete Gillett
is very ambitious to be a top star and a millionaire, and has
the talent to make his ambitions come true . . . Pete derives
a lot of pleasure by making others happy and will go a long
way.' Whilst on home leave Gillett gave an interview to a
national newspaper. In it he talked about his friendship with
Reg, denying that he was having a gay affair: 'It's an intimate
relationship, but we're not bent . . . it's like a homosexual
relationship without the sex. But I'm closer to him than I've
been to anyone – even my wife.'

He also gave interviews to a number of regional papers.
The *Portsmouth News* recorded that: 'Parkhurst prisoner Pete
Gillett has revealed that he wants to set up home in the country with gangland killer Reg Kray when he leaves jail.'
Gillett is quoted as saying that his taste of freedom had been
'quite confusing' and not quite up to what he had expected.
He added, 'Everywhere I went people were saying that I was
gay, which I am not, and some people were throwing themselves at me just because I am Reg's best friend. When I come
out I want to settle down with a woman but she will have to
realize that Reg will always be part of my life.'

The rumours about Reg's sexuality would not be easily
dismissed. Gillett's comments only added fuel to the fire.
There was no shortage of ex-cons, 'friends', and journalists
willing to add to the debate.

As the year progressed talk began again about the possibility of moving Reg. It was getting more difficult to justify

his continuing status as Category 'A'. There are four main categories of prisoners. Category 'A', the most secure, is described as 'prisoners whose escape would be highly dangerous to the public or to police or the security of the state'. Category 'B' includes prisoners for whom the very highest conditions of security are not necessary but for whom escape must be made very difficult. Category 'C' is for those who cannot be trusted in open conditions but are not perceived to have the ability or resources to make a determined escape attempt. Category 'D', with the lowest security, is for prisoners who can be trusted in open conditions. There has been some controversy over the methods used to assess an inmate's categorization. Often prisoners who are perceived as a control problem or have difficulties adjusting to prison life – but are still highly unlikely to attempt to escape – find themselves in a higher category than their risk factor actually warrants.

In January 1987, eighteen years after his trial at the Old Bailey, Reg finally received his de-categorization to a 'B' status and his transfer out of HMP Parkhurst.

4. GETTING ON WITH BUSINESS

By 8.15 a.m. on 22 January 1987 Reg's life on the Isle of Wight was over. As the gates closed behind him he could not have envisaged his temporary return thirteen years later or the terrible circumstances.

The officers, probably under instruction, refused to divulge their destination. It was a wise decision; Reg's response would not have been convivial. He was expecting a shift into an ordinary 'B' category and not a dispersal prison. He had no wish to repeat his experiences at Long Lartin. Various discussions with officers and governors had been reassuring; they had agreed it would be better not to send him back to any prison in the Midlands. Reg was hoping for a placement in the south but as the journey continued and the hours passed, it became increasingly obvious that the hope was an empty one.

They arrived in Leicester, at HMP Gartree, around lunchtime. He was shocked to find himself, despite his decategorization, not only back in the Midlands but also back in the dispersal system. Although officially divested of his high-security status he was still being treated as a high-security prisoner. He was to remain in Gartree for the next two years. Reg was told that he was there for the purpose of 'assessment'.

Within a couple of weeks it became apparent that Reg's assessment consisted of a certain amount of provocation. The practice of 'testing', which is still in place to some extent, involves the creation of situations where the inmate might snap and prove himself unsuitable for further progress through the prison system. It is especially prevalent in 'C'-category institutions where prisoners may be close to release. Reg's 'testing' involved, amongst other things, a couple of officers arriving every Saturday morning and asking Reg to recite a list of everything he had in his cell . . . week after week after week. Reg complained to the Governor, claiming he was 'too old to be part of their rituals' and the Saturday visits eventually stopped.

Reg's medical notes from Gartree describe his mental state as that of 'chronic anxiety'. He was prescribed Tranxene, an anti-anxiety drug, as well as Stelazine to help control his paranoia. It has to be said that there is something bizarre about creating stressful circumstances for inmates and then giving them drugs to counteract the effects. The pharmaceutical companies must be grateful for the business.

There were a few familiar faces at Gartree including Harry Roberts, who had been involved in the killing of three policemen, and Paddy Hill of the Birmingham Six. Reg also met an inmate called Raphael Rowe for the first time. He was one of three men jailed for life for a murder and a series of robberies around the M25. Four of the six victims had claimed that at least one of the offenders was white but all the convicted men were black. Raphael, after a long battle, was eventually freed on appeal in July 2000. Their initial meeting was significant. When their paths crossed again at HMP Maidstone in 1996, Raphael encouraged Reg to see his own solicitor Trevor Linn. The introduction was a turning point. Trevor agreed to take on Reg's case and worked tirelessly on his behalf for the next four years.

Gartree was not a peaceful prison. Reg described it as 'a

human cargo warehouse', a place of violence and retribution, anger and frustration. Prisoners were simply being taken out of circulation, held for a while, and then passed on. There were no notions of rehabilitation. Reg's hopes for a different environment were quickly shattered. He had seen it all before. It was not all doom and gloom however. Small things, like being able to switch his own light on and off in the cell, meant a lot. He was grateful too for the absence of cockroaches! Having lived side-by-side for so many years, it was a relief to be free of them. One of the few high points came one afternoon. Descending from the skies, a helicopter landed in the exercise field and two cons quickly clambered on board. A minute later they were gone. It was a fast and audacious escape. The prison authorities were in turmoil; security had been well and truly breached. The remaining inmates made the most of the situation. Unofficial posters quickly appeared on the notice board offering helicopter trips, referrals to the Chief Security Officer for tickets, and advice on checking luggage before flights. For a few weeks the atmosphere was considerably lighter than normal.

Things were also looking up on the business front. Reg had a visit from Roger Daltrey and discussions began in earnest about the film. A script had already been commissioned after an agreement made in 1982. The proposal was serious; Daltrey wanted to produce a film that explored the real issues of the Kray twins' lives. He was not looking for a Hollywood 'gore and violence' movie. His interest lay in the psychological rather than the sensational. Had such a film ever been made it might have provided some interesting insights. Reg and Ron, however, were more concerned with cash than character. Although they approved of Daltrey's intentions, and were seduced by the prospect of celluloid fame, their primary motivation was always financial.

Around this time Reg had another visitor, a woman who would have a greater impact on Ron's life than his own but

whom Reg met for the first time at Gartree. Her name was
Kate Howard. She had written to him and he had written
back and phoned her. They became friends and after a few
months Reg suggested that she visit Ron in Broadmoor. He
was later to regret that he had ever made the introduction.

In addition to his move to Gartree, Reg had other problems on his mind. His twice-yearly visits with Ron were
becoming a major bone of contention. Whilst Ron could see
any other visitors in the Main Hall, all his visits with Reg
were conducted in a small room and in the presence of
prison officers. It made for self-conscious and limited conversation. Now that Reg was no longer high-security, the
arrangements seemed unduly severe. He asked the Gartree
Medical Officer to intervene on his behalf explaining that the
circumstances of the visits made them both anxious. If they
were not to be allowed to meet in the Main Hall perhaps the
officers could sit just outside the open door, a proximity that
would keep them within sight but not sound? Dr De Silva
wrote to the consultant psychiatrist at Broadmoor relaying
Reg's concerns. Dr Tidmarsh replied that the visits had been
taking place long before he started looking after Ron Kray
and that he had, until now, seen no reason to prevent them.
Over the past year, however, they had become 'a constant
headache' with Reg and Ron always making complaints. He
appreciated that the presence of the prison officers annoyed
both brothers but claimed that close supervision was necessary. He referred to a recent occasion where the twins had
become heated in their criticism and Ron had threatened one
of the nursing staff. 'As it happened he calmed down quickly
and was apologetic . . . but I very nearly decided to terminate the visit then and there and refuse to allow any more.'
Dr Tidmarsh stressed that his enthusiasm for the visits had
never been high and that other patients saw them as 'an
unearned privilege for an undeserving case'.

The argument persisted and both Reg and Ron continued

to lobby Broadmoor for a change in arrangements. The twins' relationship tended to be stormy at the best of times and their visits only added to the tension that always lay between them. They were more frustrated than normal due to difficulties over the film – there seemed to be endless complications. Unable to openly discuss the matter, issues festered between them.

Although Daltrey had been working hard little progress had been made. A company called Bejubop was now trying to forge a workable script. Fugitive Films, in the form of Ray Burdis and Dominic Anciano, was getting ready to actually put the movie together but there were problems with finance. Rumours were beginning to circulate that Daltrey might sell his rights and let someone else pursue the project. Both Reg and Ron were disgruntled by the constant setbacks.

Another on-going interest was a book they had agreed to write with the TV broadcaster and former journalist Fred Dinenage. It was not the first time they had embarked on such a project. Back in 1967, less than a year before their arrest, the author John Pearson had been approached with a view to compiling a work about the Krays. He had recently finished a biography of Ian Fleming and the James Bond connection provided a certain cachet that appealed to the twins. He was flown over from Rome and introduced to all three brothers. Over lunch, in the baronial splendour of a country house, the idea was discussed and an agreement reached. At a time when most criminals preferred to keep a low profile it was an extraordinary proposal but perhaps not such a surprising one. The twins had always craved not only success but, more importantly, *public* success. The idea appealed on two levels – one purely financial, the other of a more egotistical nature. It is interesting to note that Reg's great underworld hero Billy Hill had published an autobiography in 1955. Emulation was perhaps the sincerest form of flattery.

For the following months Pearson was given access to

friends, associates and family, all of who knew exactly what they could and couldn't say. Despite these limitations there was still plenty to record. Both Reg and Ron were happy to share their memories and spent many hours reminiscing about the past. Family members made their contributions and a host of local characters added their own unique perspective.

Pearson had only been working for a few months before a change in the East End became apparent. Rumours started to circulate. There was a subtle alteration in atmosphere, a nervous caution permeating the most innocent of conversations. The activities of the police were developing more sinister undertones. Local whispers were of secrets and treachery. The authorities, kept at bay for so long, were gradually closing in. Suspicion grew alongside rumour. The mighty edifice of the Kray 'empire' began to tremble. Fear, once the mortar that bound, gradually became the substance of betrayal. The balance between advantage and self-interest tilted and for the first time people began to talk. If the Krays were going down, they were not going down with them. Reg's hopes of an early retirement began to assume a less than voluntary aspect.

Pearson's position became precarious. His own information-gathering, despite being sanctioned by the twins, laid him open to suspicion. They no longer trusted anyone. In April of 1968 he visited them for the last time at their mother's flat. Shortly after, they were arrested and the rest, as they say, is history. Freed from their restrictive parameters, Pearson continued with his research. The facts were beginning to surface. With Reg and Ron behind bars, and with the general opinion they would remain there for a not inconsiderable time, tongues became loose. Everyone had a story to tell. Details of the Krays' power and influence were gradually revealed. Along with their numerous and widespread criminal activities another interesting, and for the authorities far more embarrassing, truth emerged – the extent of the Krays' contact with members of the Establishment. Most were perhaps only minimally scandalous and easily covered up. Others, especially Ron's friendship with Lord Boothby, were potentially dangerous and damaging. Two mysterious break-ins, one at Pearson's home and one at the office of his agent, resulted in the theft of letters from Boothby to Ron. They were never recovered.

It is interesting to think how much the twins might have revealed in the witness box had they desired some instant retribution of their own. But that was not their style. The code of loyalty, once their great strength, now prevented them from speaking out. They would not expose their Establishment 'friends'. It was not simply to do with protecting others but, even at this late stage, a matter of reputation.

John Pearson's book called *The Profession of Violence* was published for the first time in 1972. It is still in print today. Initially fractious about some of the inaccuracies, both Reg and Ron eventually came to terms with it. By the time of its publication they had embarked on a lifetime of incarceration. If nothing else it stood as a symbol of everything they had 'achieved', a record of perceived past glories and a permanent reminder of their place in criminal history.

Many years were to pass before John Pearson and Reg met again. In the meantime another author arrived bringing the opportunity of a completely different kind of book. This time Reg and Ron would have the chance to say exactly what they wanted. Fred Dinenage met and talked with both the twins. He began to put together a manuscript based around themes. Using the alternate narratives of Reg and Ron, he explored a number of subjects including their memories of childhood in the East End, the issue of crime and punishment, Reg's life in Gartree and Ron's life in Broadmoor. After almost twenty years in prison, the twins could at last tell their own story. It might not be an entirely truthful account but that was a detail of a minor nature.

The finished manuscript was published in 1988. It met with mixed reviews. Some found it compelling but others objected to the lack of moral tone and its 'attempt to defend the indefensible'. Sales, of course, were good. What *The Profession of Violence* had started *Our Story* continued. It marked the beginning of a flood of books about the Krays, some by Reg and Ron but the majority by other authors. Former members of 'the firm' had recently been released from prison. A lucrative and completely legal market was there to be exploited. Who could resist? The twins had opened a can of worms . . . and the lid was never going back on.

In the spring of 1987 Pete Gillett was released from prison. The plans they had lingered over could now be put into action. For Reg it provided the prospect of mental escape from his own continuing imprisonment. There was only one fly in the ointment – when he requested a visit from Gillett the authorities refused. Reg took the news badly. A report from the prison, dated 19 March 1987, states: 'According to information Kray is very upset and has said that he does not know now what he will do. He has said that it is not worth carrying on if he is not allowed to see this inmate (Gillett).' A further report from the doctor advised staff to keep Reg under observation because of his past history and suicidal tendencies. Despite his bitter disappointment he remained calm. Eventually the Governor reconsidered the request and granted the necessary permission.

For the next few months, while Gillett adjusted to life outside, Reg worked hard. He wrote letters, made telephone calls and had visits with those who might help catapult his protégé to stardom. Reg believed he had found in Gillett his perfect 'other half', that all-important person who would fill the emotional void in his life. In an interview with the *People* newspaper on 15 November, Gillett talked at length about his friendship with Reg. He claimed 'All his life he has been searching for someone to share his life with and now he has found it . . . He is obsessed with me and says he lives in the outside world through me.'

A few days later Gillett made his first public appearance at a nightclub called Raquel's in Basildon. (Many years later the club became infamous through its connection to the Leah Betts tragedy.) The signing of a contract with International Record Syndicate (IRS) soon followed. His first record 'Homeless Child' was to be released in January. Reg was pleased. Gillett's career was taking off and he had no reason to suspect that anything could go wrong. As his manager he would be able to share in the future glory of his success. Tabloid interest had not waned and regular reports were still appearing about Pete's progress.

It was fortunate that Reg had something to lift his spirits for early the following year he got the news he was dreading; he had been turned down yet again for a transfer out of the dispersal system. For the immediate future he would have to remain at Gartree. After almost twenty years there was still no progress. Reg's application for a move coincided, somewhat ironically, with the death of Judge Melford Stevenson on Boxing Day 1987.

Reg turned his attention back towards his other major problem, the visits with Ron, and this time enlisted the help of his solicitor Stephen Gold. He wrote to him: 'In all institutions they have the option to curtail a visit if patients or inmates misbehave. This option should be open to Ron and I. We know how to behave. The only reason we swore was because staff were present, too many of them on top of us. I don't suppose the Ripper [Peter Sutcliffe] has lost his urge to kill women since his short stay at Broadmoor but he has use of the main hall in the presence of women. If the option is open to him and other patients who are certified then it should be open to us too.' Ron also requested better visiting conditions but on 1 February received a definitive rebuttal from Sir David Brown, the Chairman of Broadmoor.

He claimed he could see no reason for the arrangements to be changed and that proper supervision could not be provided in the main hall. The visiting room in Glastonbury ward was the only suitable place available. Responding to the complaint that the escort were able to overhear all their conversations, he said that this was not due to the size of the room but because 'you and your brother are somewhat deaf and tend to talk loudly to each other . . .' He finished his letter with the comment, 'I must remind you that these visits are a privilege and if you do not want them to continue there is no reason why they should.'

Broadmoor was adamant but the persistence of the twins, and their solicitor, eventually paid off. They were later allowed a few valued visits together in the relative privacy of the Main Hall before the old restrictions were reimposed.

Despite his knockback, Reg continued to contemplate future freedom. There was talk in the newspapers that his incarceration might not last much longer. The *Sunday Sport* in a front-page article pronounced: 'Former gangland boss Reggie Kray is to have the rest of his cruel life sentence dramatically HALVED. Instead of serving out the rest of his 30-year term – due to run out in 1999 – we can exclusively reveal that Reggie, 54, has been told he'll be FREE in six years time.' Although Reg had been told no such thing, and all the direct evidence pointed to an outcome distinctly to the contrary, such 'revelations' must have led him to wonder if the future might be less bleak than anticipated. Despite the lack of any official encouragement Reg began to make enquiries in regard to Ron. The issue of whether his twin would have to return to ordinary prison conditions before consideration of release weighed heavily on Reg's mind. He was worried that Ron would be unable to cope after the comparatively relaxed regime of Broadmoor. Reg wrote to Stephen Gold: 'The

answer will be the foundation to any future plans for Ron.'
Enquiries were made but responses remained ambiguous.
The newspapers could claim what they wished – the author-
ities knew better.

Reg had a good relationship with Stephen Gold and
wrote him a vast number of letters. Gold answered the correspondence and also provided Reg with regular copies of a
law journal. In response to one article Reg commented:

> I found the article on hanging in the journal enlightening,
> if not stimulating, there but for the grace of God go I!
> Pierrepoint once wrote how he would have personally
> liked to have hung the Krays – one of my biggest fans!
>
> I go to see Ron on the 2nd of June and look forward
> to a convivial chat and hope we are promoted to the
> main room at a later date – it's a long time since I last
> saw the Ripper! When I was at Parkhurst he was a
> neighbour of mine – since then the yuppies have moved
> in.
>
> As I get older I get more mystified what life is all
> about because I seem to cause a great deal of consterna-
> tion here with those in charge because I voice disap-
> proval at rapists and other such scum and I begin to
> wonder why they are locked away if seen in such a good
> light by the custodians.
>
> Just a thought to start the day!! There is hope even
> yet!

In May, despite continuing problems, publicity about the
film began in earnest. The Spandau Ballet brothers Martin
and Gary Kemp were confirmed as the main protagonists.
Photographs were splattered over the tabloid press; suited
and booted, the brothers posed, tight-lipped and severe, in
mock-reminiscence of the infamous twins. It was not an
image that went down well with everyone. The hot potato of

'notoriety' raised its head again. There was debate in the papers and criticism not just of the concept but also of the actors involved. The Kemps, idols to a generation of teenagers, were accused by some of contributing to the glorification of crime. Undoubtedly there was even greater debate behind the scenes. The roller coaster of the Kray mythology was gathering pace and the authorities were powerless to stop it. The collaboration of Reg and Ron was known; their participation would not be forgotten and it would certainly never be forgiven.

In the meantime contractual complexities, demands and confusions still hindered any real progress with the movie. The twins did not trust Charlie and were wary of the deal he was trying to put together. Reliance on others, even those closest to them, was anathema. They had more time than most to dwell on past iniquities; experience had left a bitter taste. Relationships with Charlie were especially strained. They both knew their older brother harboured resentment and would never forgive them for the prison sentence he received. His bitterness, in some respects justified, eroded what remained of any mutual trust or loyalty.

Charlie had often been involved in criminal activities but they were not of a major nature. As a young man, after leaving the navy, he had made a reasonable living as a 'fence', a purveyor of stolen goods. His younger siblings, however, had far more ambitious ideas. Whilst he may not have approved of all his brothers' actions, he could not resist the temptation of a share in the proceeds. He rapidly learned to turn a blind eye to their more unsavoury tactics. For a number of years he reaped the rewards of their violent and profitable career. He helped to run many of their businesses. He enjoyed the life and the lifestyle. He spent the money and made the most of the advantages it brought. There was, inevitably, a price to pay. It came with the murder of Jack McVitie in 1967. The following year, as everything spiralled out of control, Charlie found himself in court. Although he had not been present at the killing he received a ten-year sentence for helping to dispose of the body.

On his release in 1975 Charlie was determined to go his own way. He needed money and decided to authorize a biography about 'The Krays' from his own unique perspective. It was not successful. Over twelve years later he decided to republish. A row with the twins quickly followed. His revised book was due to be released at the same time as *Our Story*.

Reg barely had time to argue. He was facing other major difficulties. He wrote to his solicitor: 'I'm not too happy today because things seem out of my control at the moment. I am in the dark as something tells me I have a personal problem. I have not heard from Pete for four days and I take it as not a good sign, also Ron and I are not seeing eye to eye on many points lately. I tell you these things as I do consider you a friend and I am not all robot or just business and material things in life.' Perhaps in an attempt to regain some control Reg then created a crisis by insisting that Pete Gillett, who had no acting experience, took a leading role in the film. He asked Stephen Gold to write to Roger Daltrey. Ron, when he heard, was incensed. In a letter to their solicitor on 23 May 1988, he wrote: 'I don't want you to send *no more letters* saying that unless Pete Gillett gets a star part there will be no film, like the one you sent to Roger Daltrey. I strongly object to it.' Reg in turn wrote to Mr Gold: 'Ron is driving me crackers. Maybe he wants me to join him at Broadmoor!! He is of the opinion I'm rocking the boat in all directions and that I am too cocky in trying to be clever to get part etc. Please get him off my back by sending him calming letter that *we* have all under control!!!, and to leave to us while he relaxes with an occasional cigarette!!'

Reg's demands of the film-makers did not produce the desired response. Burdis and Anciano had recently returned from a productive visit to Cannes. Their promotion for the movie was going well. They were less than happy, therefore, to find a pile of disgruntled letters from Reg. Burdis replied and said his partner now wanted Fugitive to pull out of the film due to Reg's constant objections. He declared: 'Reggie, I feel this project is falling apart.'

A lot of time had passed since the original idea was mooted and it soon became clear that Roger Daltrey was going to sell his rights. His control over the content of the film would be simultaneously removed. A company called Parkfield was to take over financial responsibility. Daltrey wrote to Ron saying a settlement was near and if the deal went through he would expect them to start shooting the film in August. The script rapidly assumed a more commercial aspect; the borders between truth and fiction were about to be irretrievably merged.

In order to placate Reg and to promote better feeling, the producers eventually offered Gillett a minor part. Ron and Charlie, who rarely agreed on anything, raised a collective eyebrow. They both disliked Gillett and were concerned about his increasing influence over their brother. Reg was not only giving him large amounts of money but also, through his attempts to promote Gillett's career, jeopardizing negotiations. Feelings ran particularly high while filming was taking place. Rumour has it that during his short scene, where he was punched by an irate 'Reg Kray' whilst admiring his car and its passenger (Frances), Charlie asked for Gillett to be despatched with a little more realism than might normally be called for.

The year of 1988 ended with the emergence of old squabbles. The publication of Charlie's book resulted in a row of huge proportions. The twins were not just irked at its publication so close to *Our Story* but also enraged by its content. Such was their anger that Reg made a public declaration claiming they had 'disowned him'. He alleged that Charlie had not visited in two years, had forgotten to send them even a birthday card, had snubbed their countless pleas to see him and had made large amounts of money by trading off their name. In the book there were passages of what Reg described as pure 'self-pity' with Charlie complaining how hard it was to be associated with the twins and how he was labelled a gangster just because he was their brother. There were references as well to Ron's sexuality. Charlie's response to this public outburst by his siblings was more or less predictable. He was quoted in a paper as saying: 'I don't care – they've been getting on my nerves anyway . . . it's true I haven't visited them for nine months but that's because they don't appreciate all the things I have done for them in the past. All I get from them is aggravation.' Later, when another edition of the book was published in 1997, Charlie wrote in the foreword: 'Not surprisingly, *Me and My Brothers*, first time round, failed to make any ripples in the publishing pond. Mostly everyone – Ronnie and Reggie included – hated it. And so did I. Like many things done for the wrong reasons, the book lacked emotion, conviction and, I have to admit, honesty.'

The bad feeling between Charlie and his younger brothers raged, on and off, for the rest of their lives. Although they knew he exploited their name – and reaped the profits – through numerous private deals including T-shirts, records and merchandize, it was hard to prove. In return they were equally evasive, trying to cut him out of any business that came their way. This was especially true of the film where they objected to Charlie's payment of £85,000, one-third of the total sum of £255,000. Reg had lobbied hard for a contract that included a share of the royalties but it is rumoured that Charlie, who was in financial difficulties, deliberately opted for a one-off up-front payment.

Whilst fraternal arguments took their usual, if erratic, course Reg received his final medical report from Gartree. It was written by Dr C. P. Smith who claimed to 'know him well' and had been the first Medical Officer to examine him at Brixton Prison twenty years earlier. Dr Smith wrote:

> I have treated him on several occasions during the last two years at Gartree Prison, both for bodily and nervous complaints . . . He remains subject to chronic nervous tension for which he receives continuous medication. He is now approaching his 55th birthday, and already his appearance shows some signs of ageing. I understand however that his bodily health is at present satisfactory, apart from a recurrent inflammation of the outer ears. In my opinion, Reginald KRAY is a man of about average intelligence, with a severely emotionally unstable personality, including depressive and paranoid tendencies, with moreover a record of violence, homicide and suicidal attempts. I have always found him a cooperative and grateful patient, and my reading of his medical records suggests that other Medical Officers have regarded him likewise. I have to state however that his personality disorder is so severe that I find it difficult to see him surviving long outside institutional care.

Reg was told in early 1989 that the move he so badly wanted had finally come through – he was to be shifted out of the dispersal system and into an ordinary 'B' category prison. His destination was HMP Lewes in Sussex. In anticipation he quickly packed his property and placed it in reception; he was at last one step closer to freedom. However nothing, as usual, was straightforward. Although the transfer had been confirmed no exact date was forthcoming and the days passed into weeks and then the weeks into months. Reg's frustration was expressed in a letter to Stephen Gold:

> With my supposed move it has become a case of mental cruelty because *no* one knows when I am going to Lewes

(1) *No* one this end (2) No one at Lewes (3) And no one at the Home Office. All keep passing the buck.

I was first told I was going in February, then it was put back to March and now I am told it could reach into mid-April . . . that's how it stands at the moment. So in reply to your question when you should visit me and where I cannot truthfully answer the question. I just don't know what I am doing from one day to the next. So I suggest you just make arrangements to see me as normal and if you waste your time then hold someone responsible or of course you can get on to Lifers Division at the Home Office to see if I have got to do another 21 years in a dispersal prison.

Reg's long wait came to an end on 19 April 1989. He was not just leaving the high-security conditions of the dispersal system but also heading south, back into more familiar territory. It was almost like going home.

5. TROUBLE AND STRIFE

Reg settled quickly into the more relaxed routine at Lewes. The pace was slow and the atmosphere calm, a welcome relief after almost twenty-one years. There were green fields around the prison and views of the distant Downs. Even the air smelled fresher. He felt the environment was good for him, reducing his tendency to slip into depression. He used the gym regularly, went on daily walks in the small compound, played football and kept up his correspondence with the outside world. Being closer to London also made it easier for friends to visit.

Such was his optimism at this time that he once again put in a request for Ron to be allowed to join him. He was convinced his twin would be able to cope in the quieter surroundings. It was a constant worry that Ron would never be released while he remained at Broadmoor. The request, unsurprisingly, met with a stern rebuttal. A medical report from 25 May reads:

> I strongly oppose this proposal on the grounds that:
> 1. Ronald Kray has schizophrenia.
> 2. Reginald Kray has a disturbed personality and paranoid ideation.
> 3. Their criminal history shows a tendency to reinforce the other's criminality. If together, I would expect their paranoid cognitions to be mutually reinforced

and I would predict an increase in disturbed behaviour which would be in the interests of neither themselves nor the establishment containing them.

If it is felt that the two twins should be reunited, the appropriate setting would be a top security special hospital.

It is unlikely that Ron had any desire to leave Broadmoor at this stage. His life was settled there. He presented few problems to staff and received the medication he needed on a regular basis. Reg was disappointed but took the decision philosophically. He had at least tried. Where once the response would have hurtled him into chronic anxiety, now he simply accepted it.

Over the following months everything went well. Reg made new friends, gained confidence and was generally more optimistic. He felt he had turned a corner. His life was back on track. Although Lewes was still a prison it was at least a restful one. For once the future looked a little brighter. In early November Reg was surprised to hear that Ron intended to marry again. He had recently been divorced from mother of two Elaine Mildener. This time his partner was to be none other than Reg's old visitor Kate Howard.

Many inmates form attachments, through letters and visits, to women on the outside. For some it is just a temporary distraction, for others – who may rarely, if at all, have contact with family and friends – it fills a greater emotional need. For long-serving prisoners especially, the knowledge that somebody cares can provide an essential lifeline. A proportion of these relationships inevitably ends in marriage. It is impossible to make sweeping generalizations as to why women choose to marry lifers. For some there may be an element of emotional or physical safety attached to their partner's incarceration – the day-to-day realities (and possible dangers) of living together are removed.

Although his sexual preference was always for men, Ron certainly enjoyed the company of women. He missed the love and support of Violet. By marrying Elaine, who was aware he would never be released, he could once again be the recipient of a woman's affections without any physical obligations. Her two children added to the sense of 'family'. They stayed together for a few years but gradually drifted apart. The marriage generated a great deal of publicity and most of the pressure, and lack of privacy, was borne by Elaine. It generated something else as well – the opportunity of financial benefit. Ron had been quick to capitalize on it, arranging for numerous stories, including an interview about his divorce, to be sold to the press.

To the more cynical his next marriage was viewed as a purely exploitative exercise, a second bite, so to speak, of the cherry. Kate was both more worldly and more extrovert than Elaine. She enjoyed the attentions of the press and was happy, like Ron, to make the most of them. It would be untrue, however, to claim that it was simply a marriage of convenience. On the contrary, they seem to have had a great deal of affection for each other.

For Reg, the forthcoming wedding created a dilemma. He naturally wanted to attend – it was a chance, if nothing else, to see his brother – but Pete Gillett asked him not to. After his release it was rumoured that Gillett had indulged in a short-lived affair with Kate; she, in return, vehemently denied it. He insisted that Reg should stay away, that to go to the wedding would be a betrayal of their friendship and a signal to Kate that Reg was taking her side. Reg was torn between conflicting loyalties. Over the next few weeks he decided not to go, then changed his mind, then changed it back again, and finally after much soul-searching declared he *would* like to go. By this time it was all too late. The prison

authorities had had enough. Arrangements needed to be
made in advance and Reg had lost his opportunity.

In his absence, the wedding went ahead and photographs of the happy occasion adorned the pages of the
tabloid press. Reg regretted his indecision. His feelings
towards Kate continued to be coloured by her alleged relationship with Gillett and suspicion about her motives in
marrying Ron. He found it hard to accept that she had
passed from being his friend to becoming the wife of his twin
brother.

After the success of *Our Story*, Reg developed a taste both
for the written word and its financial rewards. He decided to
embark on a more comprehensive account of his life. To this
end he began to make notes and dictate to other inmates
his many memories of the past. He had recently become
friendly with a reporter called Carol Clerk and she agreed to
help with the manuscript, typing out the pages and doing
the editing work. An agreement was reached with a publishing company. The autobiography was to be called *Born
Fighter*. Reg saw Carol on visits and he was also able to send
sections of the book through the post. The work kept his
mind occupied and gave him something to aim for. He was
pleased with the final result. He felt it was an accurate reflection of his thoughts and feelings, as well as his experiences,
through the years.

There was during this time a gradual deterioration in
his relationship with Pete Gillett. Reg wrote to his solicitor
claiming that Gillett was no longer looking after his affairs
and that he should take no instructions, especially as regards
Born Fighter from him. Reg had offered him a generous third
of the proceeds from the book but he complained that it was
not enough. In a further letter to Stephen Gold Reg wrote:
'Pete says he is entitled to a larger cut but I do not see this.
It is the life story of Ron and I. Also I wrote the book so shares
will be as I state. I consider I have been more than reason-

able.' A couple of weeks later Reg adds: 'I had another row
with Pete. Even now he is not satisfied. He should drop that
writ. He is headed for big trouble.' Gillett had taken out a
libel action against the *Sun* newspaper after they claimed
that he and Reg were having a gay relationship. Reg, more
pragmatic in his attitude, knew that Gillett's action would
probably create more trouble and even more publicity. By the
middle of the next month his rows with Gillett were increasing, as was his distrust. He offered Gillett the opportunity to
try to sell some overseas rights for the book but was again
writing to Stephen Gold shortly after to explain: 'Last
Monday I told Pete Gillett I wished to help him by letting
him negotiate in foreign countries but now I learn from him
he has sought out legal advice to see if he is in the deal so
that means to me that he did not accept my hand in good
intent and in friendship, so now I will be all legalities too and
he will *only* be entitled to what he is due legally. Also please
tell me how I can make Pete's Power of Attorney which I
gave him some time ago null and void?!'

Although Reg no longer trusted him, he continued to see
Gillett. Despite their differences, and perhaps in the hope
that things would improve, he was unwilling to terminate
the friendship. Reg had given Gillett a large proportion of
what he'd earned from the film – but his investment in his
protégé had been more than financial. He knew, rationally,
that their friendship was ending but emotionally he still
struggled to hold on. It was not just a case of separation but
of letting go of all his trust, hopes and aspirations. He was
still worried about the legal action against the *Sun* and
events took an unexpected twist when Ron, in a fit of rage,
talked to a reporter and called Gillett 'a liar, gay and a ponce'.
It was just what the paper needed and the comment was
published. Reg was infuriated. Ron, although he privately
stood by the sentiments he had expressed, regretted the
public outburst and tried to build some bridges with his

brother. Letters went back and forth. Ron despised Gillett, and Reg objected to Ron's interference. Old conflicts raised their head again. It was not the first time such a scenario had been played out; the subject might change but the song remained the same. The twins' relationship resembled an eternal battleground – if they were not fighting their enemies they were fighting their friends, the system or, with equal alacrity, each other. It was part of the familiar pattern of their lives. Altercations came and went. The months were littered with minor skirmishes. In between came periods of reconciliation, closeness and harmony.

Despite these difficulties, Reg remained content at HMP Lewes. A report from the Visiting Psychiatrist, J. D. A. Whitelaw, reinforces the view that he was doing well and making steady progress: 'I have interviewed this man and read his records. I also reported on him last year and he seems much more alert and settled this time. Last year I felt that he was showing signs of mental deterioration in relation to memory and in coherent thought but there is no evidence of this now. He exhibits humour in discussing his situation and a realistic approach to the subject of transfer which has arisen. He refuses to become over optimistic or make plans until the future is clear.'

As 1990 drew to a close, only twenty months after his arrival at HMP Lewes, Reg's brave new world was split apart. With no warning at all he was suddenly shipped out. A message from a friend to Stephen Gold said: 'In the early hours of Saturday morning Reg was removed from Lewes to Nottingham – he doesn't know why. He hasn't even got socks and he is going up the wall. Can you please find out when he will get his belongings.'

This was followed a few days later by a letter from Reg himself: 'Would you visit me as soon as possible. I have been told that an enquiry is going on at Lewes Prison and that if and when I am exonerated I will be reconsidered for a Cat

'B' prison. All I know is that allegations seem to have been made against me which are the reason why I am in this prison.'

It later transpired that Reg had been transferred due to a 'gun scare'. It was claimed that a firearm had been smuggled into the prison and that Reg was planning an escape. After twenty-two years, and with Ron in Broadmoor, the idea was preposterous. If Reg escaped he would never see his twin again. Within a week he was moved on, this time back to Gartree and back into the dispersal system. Although he tried to make the best of the situation, it was not easy to accept. Having recently taken one step forward he had now taken two steps back.

As if this was not bad enough the tax-man was also at his heels. An inspector called Michael Allcock had noted the publication of *Our Story* and, with all the dedication of a true Inland Revenue employee, decided that some monies must be due to Her Majesty's Government. Contact was made with Stephen Gold and he arranged a meeting. Reg wrote: 'Please take tax man to nearest river! Only joking! Take him to a nice inn.' Eventually, Mr Allcock and Reg met personally. Reg found him affable and the visit passed without any bad feeling. A legal agreement was made and everything was settled. An interesting postscript to this story occurred in 1996. Allcock found himself in the Old Bailey accused, and at the end of the trial convicted, of taking bribes including expensive holidays and thousands of pounds in cash payments from businessmen he was investigating. The judge ruled that the names of some people 'prominent in public life' who might be mentioned during evidence must remain anonymous. There was something faintly familiar about such instructions. Reg was amused – the judicial system, obviously, had not changed one iota. The other perhaps less flattering but still entertaining aspect was that Allcock had not even bothered to ask *him* for a bribe!

Several months later, officials arrived from HMP Lewes with the information that Reg had been cleared of all charges. It was good news. He would not, however, be returning to Sussex. After his brief reacquaintance with Gartree, he was to be sent back to Nottingham Prison. It was not what he wanted but his impressions of the place from his short visit were relatively positive. One encounter in particular stayed with him. He had met a young man from the area called Paul Marcus (also known as Paul Henry), who had asked him for a number of autographs and engaged him in conversation. It was to be the start of another enduring but self-destructive friendship.

On his arrival Reg was given a large ground-floor cell. As a lifer he was allowed a single cell on his own but on this occasion was allocated a rather generous double. It wasn't long before Paul bumped into him again and, over a glass of hooch, began to grouse about his current circumstances and the inadequacies of his accommodation. Reg, in the process of a confusing break with Gillett, offered to share his own cell and Paul eagerly agreed. He put in an application for a move and it was accepted.

There are some prison officers who take the view that inmates can be more easily controlled if they are emotionally involved with another con – it makes for a generally less volatile and more peaceful life. To this effect staff will often go out of their way to ensure that willing inmates are able to be together and will help them move from one wing or cell to another. These pairings provide an element of stability and prevent frustrations, which can quickly turn to violence, from spilling over into day-to-day routines. The overall result is usually advantageous to everyone. Although such arrangements are unofficially endorsed, officially they are still frowned upon. This double standard creates a situation where what is actively encouraged on a day-to-day basis is subsequently condemned when it comes to parole reports. It is one of the many hypocrisies within the prison system.

Paul Marcus was in his early twenties, a habitual criminal since his teens and rarely out of institutions. He had already served sentences for theft and burglary. He and Reg shared a love of music and Reg was soon encouraging him in his hopes of becoming a DJ. They were rarely out of each other's company and Reg became heavily involved not just with Paul but with his family. Paul's sister, Maria, had a young son also called Paul – Paul Stapleton. Sadly he was suffering from muscular dystrophy. Reg met the four-year-old on a visit and never forgot his brightness or courage; he quietly and consistently gave financial help for the next ten years. He died just after Charlie in April 2000.

In 1990 *The Krays* premiered in the West End without the presence of its protagonists but with all the usual publicity associated with them. A few months passed before Reg had the opportunity to watch it for himself on video. Although the concept may have been seductive, the reality was something else. Dramatic licence had not only reduced Ron and Reg to a pair of cartoon gangsters but also drastically misrepresented their mother. They especially disliked the scenes where she was portrayed swearing at hospital staff. As an accurate portrayal of the twins it had all the credibility of a cardboard box, and about as much charm.

The finger of blame was quickly pointed . . . and Charlie was in the firing-line. Why hadn't he checked the script? Why had he allowed so many falsehoods to go unchecked? Why had he allowed the false depiction of their mother? Charlie had signed away their rights in a contract that provided instant cash but no royalties and it soon emerged that he had also accrued additional and not unsubstantial amounts for acting as a consultant on the set. The twins were unhappy.

Charlie put his head down. He had better things to do than argue. The film had provided a windfall and for the first

time in years he was free to enjoy himself. He had recently
met a young woman called Judy Stanley and was eager to
share his good fortune with her. The money, after his debts
were paid, was gradually frittered away on expensive
restaurants and nightclubs. He regretted his excesses several
years later when penury led him down the road of no return.
Desperate for cash he became embroiled with a couple of
shady businessmen from Birmingham and found himself,
far too late in life, back in the dock and facing serious
charges.

In the meantime, back in Nottingham, Reg was once
again sharing and trying to promote someone else's ambitions. Unfortunately Paul had neither direction nor focus
and his social skills were limited. Having spent so many of
his formative years in prison, and with on-going drug problems, it was always going to be an uphill battle. In the
summer months Reg became so involved that he wrote to his
solicitor saying: 'Would you ask to see my new friend Paul
Marcus Henry. He is here with me. I intend to leave him in
my will.' Reg's desire to fill the emotional space left by Ron,
and later Gillett, was desperate and intense. He needed someone to believe in. This new friendship was the only hope he
had left. It was, however, far from sunshine and roses. Paul's
bad habits created complications with other inmates; Reg
frequently had to intervene to prevent his young friend
being beaten and was drawn into unnecessary and unwelcome conflicts. Paul was unconcerned. Confident of Reg's
affection, and assured of his protection, he continued to abuse
his trust. It didn't stop with other inmates. One evening, after
lock-up, Paul hurled a honey jar at Reg and hit him in the
face. The injury was bloody and needed treatment but Reg
covered up for him claiming it was an accident. Neither the
medical staff nor the other cons were convinced.

In September 1991 Reg received another four-year knockback on his parole. When he wrote to inform his solicitor he

said, good-humouredly, 'My stars predicted it would be a memorable day!' Despite the disappointment Reg remained in a good frame of mind. In October, he wrote to Stephen Gold again, this time about a prospective visit to see Ron at Broadmoor: 'I suggest you write to the Governor of Nottingham Prison Mr Lavender, who I am sure will concede that he is happy for his staff to sit in the main visiting room when I have visits knowing that I am in their sight while they are plied with coffee and buns. I leave you to do the barrister work in return for your drastic fees! Please do not send me the bill till early next year due to recession etc!'

Shortly after, perhaps because of his friendship with Paul, the decision was made to shift Reg yet again. He was sent temporarily to HMP Leicester where he waited to hear about his next location. Upset by the separation, he started writing letters to his old cell-mate. It was a correspondence that would come back to haunt him. There were plenty of journalists more than eager to snap up the innermost feelings of Reginald Kray.

In February Reg was moved to HMP Blundeston in Suffolk. He had only been in Nottingham for ten months and, before that, Lewes for twenty. It was disorientating to be moved around so much. In *A Way of Life* Reg explained: 'Unless one has been separated the way I have from close friends during my time in jail it may be difficult to comprehend the terrible feeling of loneliness that comes about from having to leave without any forewarning. There is hardly time to say farewell. And then one is taken to a new but similar environment, to a cold bare cell, and left alone with thoughts of those you have departed from. It brings about a sense of loss.'

Convinced that he would probably be moved on again, Reg did little to make his cell comfortable and kept most of his property in storage. In fact he was to spend the next two years at Blundeston. It was not an especially bad prison. The worst aspect was the disturbing tendency of some of his neighbours to set fire to their cells. Being locked up with smoke sliding under the door was not an ideal start to any evening.

Reg, more capable now of controlling his own temper, kept out of trouble. He had learned how to diffuse rather than aggravate difficult situations. For the time being he made the best of a bad job, renewed old friendships and generally got on with his sentence. There was some element of social life and a steady supply of hooch for anyone who wanted it. Cons would meet in a bustling passageway, known because of its length and activity, as Bond Street. Information and gossip was exchanged, deals and arrangements made. There was a steady trade in drink and drugs. Reg would usually have a drink if any were available; it relieved the boredom and provided a temporary escape. He never became aggressively drunk and in all his thirty-two years in prison was not charged once with any alcohol-related offence. Despite unorthodox methods of distillation and an often profoundly unpleasant smell and taste the resultant product served its purpose. I read various reports in newspapers after Reg became ill, echoed in more recent books, that his liver was severely damaged by his prison drinking. This was not the case. Although I would not advocate the imbibing of large amounts of prison hooch, Reg suffered no obvious ill-effects. His liver, as the doctors can testify, was not affected.

Reg remained on Stelazine and anti-anxiety drugs. His health was generally good but his hearing was growing progressively worse. His deafness increased with each passing year. According to a consultant surgeon his eardrums were scarred. This made it difficult for Reg to engage in conversation with too many people and he tended to shy away from large groups.

One of the sadder moments at Blundeston came with the

news that his old pal, Harry 'Hate-'em-All' Johnson, had died during a heart operation. He was only forty-six and had spent too much of his life in prison. It was a reminder to Reg of his own mortality. He wondered, not for the first time, if he too would die in jail.

More bad news arrived in the shape of Pete Gillett. Despite some initial success, his show business career had failed to take off and he had quickly slipped back into crime. In February he was on remand for drugs charges at HMP Belmarsh. Reg wrote to Stephen Gold: 'Gillett and I are no longer friends as you rightly foresaw would be the case.' It would be a few years before they met again in Maidstone Prison.

In July 1992 Paul Marcus was released from HMP Nottingham and began visiting Reg regularly. Reg tried to make sure he had money and, as with Gillett, began introducing him to people he felt might be useful. One in particular was not impressed. Wilf Pine, a close friend of Ron, arrived one day to relay some messages. Finding Paul already at the table, and unwilling to share his confidences in his presence, he gave Reg an ultimatum, 'Either he goes or I do.' Reg prevaricated and Wilf shook his head, got up and walked out. It was a good few months before they talked again.

The friendships Reg made in prison had begun to affect some of his older ones outside. Even Ron expressed concern. If Reg liked someone he believed all his old mates should automatically trust and like them too. It was an unrealistic expectation. Reg thought they were unreasonable and churlish. They feared he was laying himself open to being badly used.

News soon got back to Reg that Paul was keeping bad company in Nottingham. He began to worry about the letters he had written; there were rumours that Paul was trying to sell them to the press. In October, in an interview with the *Sunday Mirror*, Paul claimed that Reg had been asked to take an Aids test by the prison authorities and refused. It was not true but made for a good headline. The paper commented that Reg had been moved to another jail following concern over his relationship with the twenty-three-year-old. Paul was quoted as saying: 'He's sent me hundreds of letters. Some of the things in them are very personal.' He added: 'I have had a jailer say, in front of 250 men, that we were lovers. After that, when they moved Reg, I had to defend myself against the whole jail. But the rumours were not true. It's just jealousy because Reg is good to me – we're like father and son.' They were familiar words and it was not the last time they would make their way into a newspaper.

Paul, unable to stay out of trouble, was shortly up on another charge. Reg helped arrange legal representation. A good barrister kept him out of prison on this occasion but it was not long before Paul reoffended and was back inside. Despite his behaviour, including further attempts to sell the letters, Reg never turned his back on him. It was a matter of loyalty. Although frequently hurt and frustrated by his behaviour, he could not and would not forget the friendship they had shared. For all the bad times there had been plenty of good ones too.

A report from Blundeston in mid-1993 claimed Reg had initially found it hard to settle but that the situation had improved. His energy and good humour were noted – as was his propensity to be occasionally volatile. He was described as having a negative reaction to attempts by staff to discuss his feelings. It was also stated that although he made efforts to distance himself he was held in awe by some fellow prisoners and that his case continued to attract media attention and public notoriety.

While Reg had been writing *Born Fighter* Ron had decided to make his own contribution to the ever-growing Kray genre. Once again he enlisted the help of Fred Dinenage and together they started work on a book to be named

My Story. Although the idea appealed in theory, in practice
Ron was not that forthcoming. Dinenage struggled to get the
angles he needed to create a new manuscript. He visited and
talked to Ron but progress was slow. Back before their arrest
Ron had freely, and often humorously, reminisced about the
past but all these years later that essential spark was gone.
He had contributed as much as he could to their earlier collaboration, *Our Story*, and now had nothing much left to say.
Fred Dinenage was left with scant resources.

As Ron was worrying over the past with Fred, his wife
Kate suggested a new and different book with an alternative
perspective. She wanted to write about the *present*. The idea
appealed to him. He was tired, like Reg, of all the farcical
stories in the press. What appealed even more was that he
wouldn't have to make any contribution – Kate would do it
all. He didn't have any worries; his relationship with Kate
was good and she could write about the person he was today
without any of the media hype. She could tell the truth. He
knew he could trust her; she would never write anything
he would disapprove of.

In the summer of 1993, Ron suddenly developed serious
problems. Charlie Kray claimed the doctors at Broadmoor
had reduced his medication level, 'another experiment presumably,' and out of the blue, and after many years of calm,
Ron attacked another patient called Lee Kiernender. It made
headline news in the *Daily Star*. They claimed:

> The 60-year-old East End twin was said to have flipped
> after being continually pestered by Kiernender, who has
> a reputation for hassling patients . . . The attack took
> place in the ward they share with other killers, includ-
> ing Yorkshire Ripper Peter Sutcliffe. Kray has been on a
> reduced drug treatment and was feeling 'irritable' when
> [Kiernender] picked on him. A worker at the top-secu-
> rity hospital in Berkshire said: 'Kray suddenly snapped.

The other guy had been winding him up. Kray might easily have killed him. It took quite a few nurses to get Ronnie off.'

What was going on? Nobody really understood. For Ron, everything was falling apart. He regretted the incident and although he calmed down quickly after the attack nothing was ever quite the same again. The situation grew worse when he received the published copy of *My Story*. Angry and frustrated, he claimed unfairly that Dinenage had misinterpreted many of the things he had said.

Only a week later Ron received another major shock. Kate's book *Murder, Madness and Marriage* was published. Ron was horrified. He had not bothered to read through any of the manuscript and had not realized how much would be revealed. Kate had discussed her recent two-year relationship with a married car dealer called 'Pa'.

Although Ron had been aware of the affair he had never objected to it. He knew he was unlikely to leave Broadmoor and, understanding the reality of their position, never demanded fidelity. He enjoyed the time they spent together on visits; her sense of humour and extrovert personality appealed to him. He trusted and to some degree confided in her. The relationship, although unorthodox, was mutually advantageous. In return for her loyalty, support and friendship he offered the same, as well as a share in any financial profits that might come his way. She was free to do as she wished. It is doubtful, however, that he expected to have to read about her affair in the book.

Ron felt that her revelations made a public mockery of their marriage – and of him. He felt simultaneously angry and bewildered. It was not just a matter of hurt dignity; he believed she had betrayed his trust. He realized, despite their years together, that he really didn't know her at all.

Ron's mental state, still delicate after his attack on Kiernender, rapidly deteriorated. Despite their differences in the past, he turned to his older brother for help. It was a time of crisis. In September 1993 Charlie visited him in Broadmoor. Ron was bitter and wretched. He claimed he wanted a divorce but was worried about what Kate might do next. Charlie was also concerned about the situation. To complicate matters even further Kate had formed close friendships with many of Ron's associates. What would happen if he divorced her? What would happen if he didn't? The whole situation was a mess.

Over the next week Ron's mental and physical condition worsened. Under strain, he struggled to make a decision. The pressure was building. He couldn't cope. At the end of the month he collapsed and was admitted to Wexham Park Hospital in Ascot suffering from what was thought to be a mild heart attack. Even in hospital he continued to dwell on his problems. He wrote to Reg expressing his worries. Reg, believing he was partly responsible for the marriage, felt guilty. What had he done? His reason for the original introduction had not been without ulterior motive. Gillett's alleged affair with Kate, and its subsequent fallout, had compromised his friendship with both. To prevent any ill-feeling he had encouraged Kate to meet Ron in the hope she would transfer her interest from one twin to another and thus resolve an embarrassing dilemma. He had no idea that Ron would actually decide to marry her. It was a disaster. Even worse, it was a disaster of Reg's creation.

Several days later Ron was returned to Broadmoor. He was told, despite having all the symptoms, that he had not actually suffered a heart attack. Ron was not convinced. He was not convinced of anything any more. He felt ill and betrayed. He continued to share his fears with Reg. He also sent numerous letters to his solicitor. On 20 October 1993, he wrote: 'Dear Stephen, I would like to start divorce proceedings with Kate and I would like to put in the press that I am getting a divorce over her book. God Bless, Ron Kray. Your friend.'

In a letter to Stephen Gold, written the next day, Reg wrote:

Stephen, Ron wants to see you urgent. He hopes to see you next Friday if not sooner. Last night I spoke to him over the phone. He seems to think he did have a heart attack but Ron says they are covering it up because it is political! He could be right but I don't know how much of this statement is due to paranoia or not. Trouble is that if he has too much bad publicity re Broadmoor then they may shift Ron back to prison which would be bad.

Ron also wants you to arrange a divorce. I entirely agree with him and please speed this divorce up as soon as possible – if Ron agrees I feel you should issue a statement right away.

Over the next few days, worried about Kate's response, Ron wrote a number of letters to his solicitor asking him to go ahead, to postpone, and finally to pursue the divorce.

In the middle of Ron's crisis Reg was suddenly hit with one of his own. He was told he was being moved to Albany Prison, back on the Isle of Wight. He was distraught. He wrote to Mr Gold:

I'm told I am going to be shifted to Albany Prison which should have been on the 26th October but I got it held up as I appealed. I was told this only yesterday about the move. I would like you to contact the Lifers people at the Home Office to appeal on my behalf. It is a fact that Albany is a prison to house mainly sex offenders and Rule 43 inmates on protection – I do not wish to be in Albany . . . Also I was at Parkhurst for 18 years so have spent far too long on the island. I want you to make it quite clear to the Home Office that I intend to go to the Seg Unit on my arrival in Albany if I go there, and to the Seg Unit too if I should be taken to Parkhurst Prison.

Whilst Reg was awaiting the result of his appeal, there was news of a different nature. In December the *Sun* newspaper proclaimed: 'Reggie Kray is hero in jail siege.' He had come off the exercise field early one afternoon to be told that an inmate called Gray had robbed the prison canteen, taken tobacco, and then barricaded his cell threatening to kill himself. He occupied a cell a few doors down from his own. Reg went to talk to him and eventually persuaded Gray to hand over his knife. The siege ended without any further violence. Reg was later asked to give evidence in court – by both the defence *and* the prosecution. He refused.

Early the following year, following a successful appeal, Reg was told he would be moving instead to HMP Maidstone in Kent. He could not have imagined the terrible event that was about to change his life.

6. LOSING RON

Reg arrived at Maidstone Prison in March 1994 and was allocated a cell on Weald Wing. He was pleased to see his old friend Joe Martin again. The twins had known Joe on the outside. They had also served time with him at Parkhurst. After all his worries over Ron, and the prospective move to Albany, it was good to see a familiar face and have someone to talk to.

By now Ron was out of hospital and seemed to be recovering well. The divorce from Kate was going through and there had been no further upsets or alarms.

Maidstone was a 'B' category establishment with a fair proportion of lifers and other long-term prisoners. It had, at this time, a very relaxed regime. Inmates were allowed to wear their own clothes and cook their own meals. They were generally respectful of each other's privacy and tended to form small tightly knit groups. Without the constant arrivals and departures of other cons, there was a greater sense of stability and more mutual understanding. The prison officers were neither aggressive nor intrusive; for as long as there was peace they operated a policy of non-interference. There was little violence and the atmosphere was better than in any prison Reg had previously lived in. Certain officers were also more than happy to supplement their income; for the right price they would bring in almost anything an inmate wanted.

Reg placed photos and pictures around his single cell. He put up curtains, organized his books and papers, and made the space as personal as he could. He went regularly to the gym and concentrated on keeping fit. His health, apart from his hearing, was good. There were many familiar faces at Maidstone. Old friends invited him to share meals and the occasional glass of hooch. The company was convivial and his surroundings calm.

Although the regime at Maidstone was certainly less strict than many institutions, there were still long periods of solitary lock-up including at least twelve hours overnight, two hours at lunchtime and another hour and a half in the late afternoon. In addition there were regular periods when prison officers' meetings, staff shortages or other occurrences, meant more time behind locked doors.

Reg was allowed about six visits a month and always used them, seeing as many people as he could. Only an hour from London, Maidstone was easily accessible. It was vastly different from the earlier high-security days when visits had been strictly limited and his contact with the outside world minimal. Times had changed. Pay-phones had been introduced in the late 1980s and this made communication a much quicker and more direct process than correspondence. The phones were operated through official cards and these had rapidly replaced tobacco as a major form of currency in prisons. In addition to the weekly canteen, where an inmate could buy up to eight cards, there was also a healthy black market; Reg, like others, made the most of it. Calls could usually be made during any period they were not locked up. The most popular time was the evening when costs were lower. Despite the advent of modern communications, Reg still wrote and responded to letters. It had become, and remained, the habit of a lifetime.

Reg was given a job as a cleaner and from this he earned a small amount, about £5 a week. In addition he was allowed to spend a further £10 out of what was called 'private cash', money that was sent in to the prison for him. Sometimes, like many other inmates, he had no private cash at all. At other times a friend or well-wisher might send a few pounds. Occasionally he had some royalties from his books. At the weekly canteen inmates could purchase such items as extra food, soft drinks, soap, shampoo, tobacco and phone cards.

Reg continued to visit Ron, and occasionally saw Charlie although relations remained strained between them. His visits with Ron were also difficult. After a brief reprieve, when they had been allowed to have a few visits in the Main Hall, the old restrictions had been reintroduced. They were meeting again in a small room and within hearing of the Maidstone escort and Broadmoor staff. Reg often left the visits feeling unhappy and frustrated. Their rare phone calls were closely monitored, as were all their letters to each other. The latter, however, must have been a censor's nightmare. Over the years the twins developed a curious, almost hieroglyphic, form of communication. Reg's once neat and tidy lettering gradually assumed the appearance of an ancient language, a series of symbols, lines and individual shorthand that made it to many virtually indecipherable. Ron's was the same. Starting from the left but slanting progressively, line by line, to the right, they both left large triangles of white space on every page. Through these disguises and distortions they were able to write to each other with some degree of privacy. It became their only means of talking and confiding. There was nothing of a criminal or illicit nature about their letters – they simply contained their private thoughts.

While Reg was at HMP Lewes he had started work on a further project. After finishing *Born Fighter* he decided to write another book purely about his prison years. It was to be called *A Way of Life*. He completed a couple of chapters

and then stopped. In the ensuing years he was shifted so frequently that he never had the opportunity to settle and
resume his writing. In the calmer atmosphere of Maidstone
he decided to finish what he had begun. He saw it as the
most important book he could ever write, a work not primarily about himself but about the real meaning of prison,
its reality and its terrible consequences. Reg was fortunate to
meet up with another lifer called Bill Taylor. Bill was sympathetic and intelligent. He offered to help and while Reg
dictated he wrote down his thoughts and reminiscences.
Over the months they made some progress but work was
halted again by a number of unforeseeable events.

In June 1994, during a visit to the gym, a young inmate
went out of his way to introduce himself. He was called
Bradley Allardyce and was serving twelve years for armed
robbery. Having written a number of fan letters over the
years, without ever receiving a reply, he was keen to make
an impression. Reg was flattered by his attentions. They
talked and over the next few weeks became friends. Bradley
arranged a move on to Weald Wing and quickly established
himself in Reg's life. It was to be the start of another
enduring relationship. The younger man was ambitious
and wanted to be 'someone'; a connection to Reg Kray was
beyond his wildest dreams.

Reg encouraged Bradley to think ahead and to keep out
of trouble. He got friends to see him on visits, made sure
he always had phone cards and bought him new clothes
and trainers. He also gave him a gold cross and chain as a
symbol of their friendship. Reg was still receiving huge
amounts of mail and Bradley helped him reply to some of
the letters acquiring pen-friends of his own in the process.
After his disappointments over Gillett and Paul Marcus, Reg
began sharing his new friend's ambitions. These encompassed, as usual, money and fame but there was one small
difference – these were plans not just for the future but also

for the present. To this end Reg began seeing even more people on visits, following up any business ideas that came his way and promoting his new friend's 'talents' at every opportunity. Bradley, like Gillett, aspired to be a singer but in the meantime he wanted to get his name known and in the papers.

By chance Pete Gillett was also in Maidstone at this time but on a different wing. Although he and Reg remained on reasonable terms the closeness was no longer there. Gillett was unhappy about Allardyce's influence and also the benefits he was receiving. Under Reg's protection, Bradley had a free rein.

Reg rapidly took his new friend into his confidence and the two were soon inseparable. Through this relationship Reg probably found the closest surrogate he could for his twin. There were the same episodic periods of conflict and calm. Rows were followed by reconciliation, antagonism by peace. Peace, in turn, was shattered by further disagreement. Reg was demanding and often impatient. Bradley was moody and manipulative. They were both insecure. In Bradley, Reg recognized many of the characteristics of Ron – his unpredictability, carelessness and vulnerability – and found him both compelling and confusing. All of Reg's serious associations, through these prison years, were reflections and replays of his relationship with his twin. Against Ron's schizophrenia he was powerless but he still struggled to exert some control. He embarked on the same futile cycle of hope and dreams and disappointment, each time believing it could finally be different.

Towards the end of the year Bradley was shipped out to Whitemoor Prison. Reg woke up one morning and found he was gone. It was a shock. He was suddenly on his own again, a depressing but familiar scenario. Bradley claimed at first that he knew nothing, that he had no idea why he had been transferred, but it later transpired that he had arranged the

move himself. He left a number of debts in his wake. Aware
of the probable consequences Reg rang round his friends and
raised the money to pay them off.

The next few months were not an easy time. He felt his
best friend had let him down – and everyone in Maidstone
knew. Reg, searching for occupation to fill the hours, turned
his attention back to the book. Bill Taylor was generous
with his time and they made good progress. The project
helped lift Reg's spirits again. They both worked hard and
within a few months had almost completed the first half of
the manuscript.

Another Christmas came and went and New Year's celebrations heralded the beginning of 1995. There was no sign
in January or February of the shattering event that was about
to blow Reg's world apart. On 6 March Reg reported sick to
the medical room. He had been experiencing pains in the left-
hand side of his chest and was feeling lightheaded and dizzy.
The doctor's examination revealed 'no shortage of breath or
tightness of the chest'. His colour was described as good and
his pulse regular. They could find nothing physically wrong
with him and prescribed 5 mg of Valium.

Nine days later, on 15 March, it was Ron who was suddenly admitted to Heatherwood Hospital in Berkshire for
tests. Reg was allowed to make a phone call. His twin
seemed comfortable but asked if he could visit as soon as
possible. Reg was worried. It was not just a general concern
but something much more distinct and definite. He knew
Ron was seriously ill. He suspected something terrible was
about to happen and asked a Senior Officer, Paul Marsh, if
an escort could be arranged for him to visit that evening. The
request was refused. Reg was upset but there was nothing
he could do. Ron was returned to Broadmoor the same day.
Reg spent a restless night, worried and anxious. He paced
his cell. His thoughts were filled with dread. His fears were
growing by the minute.

The next day Ron was readmitted to hospital. Charlie Kray and old friend Laurie O'Leary went to visit him. Ron was in a small side room watched over by three of the Broadmoor staff. He was subdued and tired but seemed to be holding his own. There was no indication of what was about to occur.

On 17 March 1995, at around 9 a.m., Ron Kray was declared dead from a heart attack. At 9.30 a.m. Reg was called to the office. Pete West, a probation officer, and Paul Marsh were both present. The bad news was delivered. Ron was dead. Reg was devastated. Overwhelmed, he broke down and wept. He asked to make a call to Charlie. His brother confirmed the dreadful news; he had only heard himself a short while ago. In great distress, Reg then returned to the wing. Some of the inmates came forward and offered their condolences. The news had been on the radio. Even before Reg had made his way down to the meeting they had all known but had been reluctant to break the news. Ron's death was already public knowledge.

Without being a twin, it is probably impossible to comprehend the loss. Reg was shattered. It could not possibly be true . . . but it was. It could not possibly be real . . . but it was. There would be no more meetings. There would be no more letters. He would never, on this earth, see Ron again. Faced with his worst possible nightmare, he struggled to carry on. In the company of close friends, Reg drank and remembered. Nothing took away the pain. It just grew worse and worse.

Reg was determined to achieve one thing – to give Ron the best funeral he could. It became his only aim, a defence against the despair he was feeling. He spent the next twelve days constantly on the phone, discussing, organizing and making arrangements. He talked to the undertaker Paul Keays, to the priest who would conduct the service, and to other friends and associates. Reg was warned, by a prison

officer, that what he was doing would not help his parole
chances but he no longer cared. He wanted everything to be
perfect. Ron had once expressed a wish for his coffin to be
drawn by the traditional six black horses with plumes . . .
and Reg wasn't going to settle for anything less. He hardly
ate and rarely slept. Every waking hour was spent in preparation. He had a visit with Charlie but it was not a good one.
Charlie said he thought the cortège would move too slowly
if horses were used; it was six miles from St Matthew's to
Chingford Cemetery. Reg disagreed. He said: 'I'm not going
anywhere, and I don't care if it takes a week.' The matter was
settled. The hymns and prayers were chosen. The service
was confirmed. Everything was ready for 29 March.

In the meantime a very fast inquest into the death of Ron
had been carried out without the knowledge of Reg or
Charlie. The *Independent* newspaper reported:

The inquest into Ronnie Kray, the gangster, was condemned as illegal and 'outrageous' yesterday, after it
emerged that a coroner completed the inquiry within
three minutes in his office at home. Robert Wilson, the
coroner for east Berkshire, carried out the inquest on
Kray, who died on Friday after suffering a heart attack
. . . He faxed a verdict of 'natural causes' to the coroner's office in Slough, Berkshire. Experts argued the
inquest was unlawful, as the coroner had not notified
the public or media. Mr Wilson said yesterday: 'I think
I am to be congratulated on holding the inquest so soon
after the death.' Coroner's rules state that inquests
should be held in public, except in cases of national
security. The press and public should be notified of the
time and place of the inquest. No notification appears
to have been given of Kray's inquest. Deborah Coles,
of Inquest, a pressure group, said: 'It's outrageous. If
the family has not been allowed to ask questions and

the public refused access, this is clearly breaking the
-law.'

With Ron's funeral approaching, Reg didn't know what
to do. Astounded by the speed and indifference of the
inquest, he wondered if he should delay the burial. There
were too many unanswered questions. In the end he decided
to go ahead. He wanted Ron to rest in peace.

Reg was more than concerned about the circumstances
surrounding his twin's death. Ron had collapsed and been
admitted to hospital on 15 March, returned to Broadmoor
the same day, collapsed again and been readmitted to hospital and then suffered terminal heart failure on the 17th.
He had extensive bruising from handcuffs on his wrists and
had undergone a major blood transfusion as well as an
endoscopy. Reg couldn't make any sense of what had happened. Why had Ron been returned to Broadmoor so close
to his death? Why had all his symptoms been dismissed?
Requests were made for Ron's medical records from Broadmoor – but they were all refused. Copies of the statements
from the escort who had accompanied Ron were also
refused. This secrecy did little to reassure Reg or put his
mind at rest.

Dr Romero, a Broadmoor psychiatrist, visited and
although his kindness was appreciated Reg didn't receive
any of the answers he was searching for. He also saw a
Broadmoor senior social worker called Carol Hames who
emphasized that Ron received the best treatment he could at
Broadmoor. Reg had never doubted it. The only other information he was allowed, apart from some police reports,
came in a letter from Dr David Mawson, the Consultant
Forensic Psychiatrist at Broadmoor. It was sent to Reg's
solicitor a few months after Ron's death.

He claimed he had examined the paperwork and discussed the circumstances surrounding Ron's death with Dr

Dilys Jones, the Broadmoor consultant involved in his care. He enclosed a letter she had written to him. In it she explained how on the morning of 15 March 1995 Ron had appeared agitated and breathless and had later collapsed. He had been admitted to Heatherwood Hospital as an emergency. Later in the day, when nothing serious was found, Ron was returned to Broadmoor. She saw him again and noted that he appeared to be in the same condition as when he had left. Shortly after he collapsed again. It was agreed with the duty doctor that he should be urgently re-admitted. Dr Mawson finished his letter with the words: 'I would be grateful if you could let me know if your client is suggesting that he has a potential claim against the hospital. If this is the case, please let me know the basis for it, because it is my understanding that Mr Kray was most carefully attended to whilst at this hospital.'

That was to be their last word. Concern was apparently limited to whether Reg intended to take legal action. Ron's medical records have never been released. In 2000, a forensic psychiatrist called Dr MacKeith was compiling a report on Reg. He wrote to Broadmoor asking to see Ron's medical records. Once again the request was refused.

Reg's greatest agony was that Ron had died alone, with no family or friends beside him. He said in *A Way of Life*: 'I know that Ron must have been terribly lonely, that he had no one to turn to for help . . . I imagine it must have been a time of terrible adversity for him, a time of awful claustrophobia and pain.'

The day of Ron's funeral, 29 March 1995, was memorable. Reg left Maidstone early and travelled with his prison escort into London. Despite previous rainy days, the morning had dawned bright and sunny. At the funeral parlour of W. English & Son he spent a few precious minutes with Ron. He touched his shoulders and face and talked softly to him. In tears he said his last farewell and kissed him on the forehead.

Although overwhelmed by sorrow, he also felt an incredible strength and warmth as if Ron was right beside him.

Following the hearse the prison car passed down Vallance Rd on the way to St Matthew's. It was the first time Reg had been allowed out since his mother's funeral in 1982. Memories of his childhood flooded back. The streets were lined with people. They called out to him and reached out their hands. Along the side of the hearse, created from hundreds of white chrysanthemums, the words TO THE OTHER HALF OF ME were Reg's final tribute to his twin brother.

In the church Reg remained cuffed to a prison officer. Before the proceedings began he was able to talk to some of the mourners and shake a few hands. Throughout the service he sat close to the coffin, his eyes turning towards it again and again as if he could not believe what was actually happening. Throughout the prayers and messages he struggled to keep his composure. His own message, read by a friend, was: 'My brother Ron is now free and at peace. Ron had great humour, a vicious temper, was kind and generous. He did it all his way, but above all he was a man, that's how I will always remember my twin brother Ron.' At several points, Reg looked as if he was about to break down. The final song, 'I will always love you' by Whitney Houston, was too much for him. Charlie and Frankie Fraser offered him support as he left the church.

Outside the onlookers cheered and clapped. Reg climbed back into the blue Peugeot with his prison guard. The long slow journey to the cemetery took almost two hours. Traffic came to a standstill as the cortège passed through London. The roads were full and children ran beside the car. Many people tried to pass gifts through the window, flowers and cards and messages. The crowds were huge. Reg looked at times almost bewildered, the vast turnout more than he could comprehend. The feelings emanating from the street were intense, an almost bizarre mix of support, elation and sorrow. Although he smiled and waved, appreciating their presence, his emotions were in turmoil on this the very worst of days.

At Chingford, after a route had been cleared through the crowd, Reg stopped by the graves of his mother and father, and of his late wife Frances. He laid flowers and kissed the headstones. With Charlie by his side he moved slowly towards Ron's open grave. There was a short service before the coffin was lowered into the ground. Reg stood for a while, a red rose in his hand, staring down. Eventually he let it go. He turned towards Charlie, speechless. It was the end.

Reg, still cuffed to his escort, was led gently back to the car. In just over an hour he was back at HMP Maidstone. Other inmates gathered round and offered support. Many had sent wreaths. They all offered their sympathy. Reg watched the early evening news including the coverage of the day's events; it seemed unreal. His only consolation was that he had given Ron the very best of funerals.

The next day, there was coverage in all the national papers. Although generally derisive in tone they could not resist splashing the story, along with numerous photographs, over the front pages. Their reporting was confused and ambiguous. On the one hand they couldn't afford to ignore what had been such a major event or the general population's interest in it, on the other they refused to condone the 'attention' paid to the death of a one-time gangster or his surviving twin. It was a peculiar juggling act, but one in which the British press is particularly adept. They wrote, embellished, sneered, jeered and generally filled enough pages to ensure the destruction of a small rainforest in South America.

There are some who have claimed that Reg 'lost the will to live' after Ron died. In fact nothing could be further from the truth. The death of his twin, although devastating, made him even more determined to carry on. It had always been Ron's greatest wish that Reg would be free one day. Ron knew his own chances of release were minimal but he believed Reg could regain his freedom. In a touching letter to his brother he once said: 'Reg, when you write our life story start with the Blitz in the war. And the boxing booth with Slash Warner. Reg, you must promise me that if anything happens to me that you will go to China, India, Egypt, Japan, and Hong Kong . . .' These were hopes that Reg wanted to fulfil. They gave him a reason to carry on.

He received thousands of letters and cards of sympathy. He replied to as many as he could. He was grateful for their messages, and uplifted by their support, but was unable to answer all of them. He was still struggling to come to terms with what had happened. Although he felt Ron's presence, and was sure that Ron would always be with him, the physical reality was brutal. Ron was dead and he would never see him again. It was beyond comprehension.

A few months later Reg enrolled on a 'Lifers' Moving On' course, a prison sports regime that helped, in a small way, to distract from his grief. He spent several weeks in intensive training involving swimming, speed-ball, weights, general gym-work, push-ups, pull-ups, and anything that exhausted him to the point where he couldn't think any more. The participants in the course were filmed on video. After its completion Reg was told that, unlike the others, he would not be allowed to have a copy or any prints of the photographs that had been taken because he was 'too high-profile'. A few years later another inmate sold some of the photographs to the national press.

The rest of 1995 passed quietly, the months spent trying to come to terms, trying to make sense of the impossible. While Reg grieved the staff of HMP Maidstone gathered their reports together for his next Parole Review. After twenty-seven years attitudes finally seemed to be changing.

A consultant psychiatrist to the prison, Dr Rose, wrote a considered report about Reg's future:

> His early years of imprisonment were characterized by disruptive behaviour and paranoid attitudes. He has been taking a small dose of a neuroleptic drug Trifluoperazine [Stelazine] for many years but as there has been no suggestion of mental illness for some years now, I have withdrawn the drug with Mr Kray's agreement.
>
> For a number of years he has accepted his sentence philosophically . . . It has been noted in previous reports that no offending behaviour work has been done but I take the view that considering he is 62 years old, and has been in prison for 27 years, the notion that work on offending behaviour is worthwhile would appear to me to be unrealistic.
>
> I have always found him to be extremely respectful and polite and I know that he gives careful consideration to such advice as has been given.
>
> His risk to the public must be minimal, provided that he can disassociate himself from the activities of the criminal fraternity with whom he has been in contact in the past. I consider that he can do this successfully.
>
> He is now fit for a Cat 'C' but I take the view that as he has settled down well at Maidstone it would probably be preferable for him to stay on as a Cat 'C' for a further few months before transferring to open conditions. I consider that he will be fit for release on his tariff date.

Mr R. Boys, the Lifer Liaison Officer, said in his report:

> After so long in the system he knows exactly how to manipulate staff and his situation so as to achieve the

best deal for himself that he can. But he is always very civil in his dealings with staff, and is not seen as a control problem or security risk.

Kray makes no apology for the death of McVitie, believing he was in a kill or be killed situation. Kray would not admit that there was anything wrong or avoidable about his way of life in those days. However, he is adamant and convincingly so, that he has no wish to return to that way of life.

Kray is now three years short of tariff, and as things stand now I see no reason to doubt that he will be fit for release at that time. Currently he does not need Category 'B' security conditions, and my recommendation is that he move on to a Category 'C' now.

Casework Officer Mr Hayes reported:

Kray is pleasant and polite to staff at all times. He continues to cause concern, over his level of drinking of alcohol within the wing.

I can see no reason to oppose a recommendation for recategorizing Kray for Category 'C'. He causes no security/discipline problems within the wing, although I would recommend that he be transferred to another establishment if he is re-catted. Kray would have no trouble settling in at any establishment.

From the Lifer Probation Officer, Pete West:

Attitude to offence: The inmate accepts full responsibility for his actions and does not seek to minimize his involvement. It is quite clear that there has never been any offence based work undertaken. The Lifer Review Board held at Maidstone on 20.10.94 felt that doing offence based work with Mr Kray after so many years would be unrealistic. I do not believe that any work undertaken would alter his perception of or add any insight to the offence.

Behaviour in prison: Mr Kray has no Governor's adjudications and presents no control problems at Maidstone. He is known to drink on occasions and he freely admits this. He keeps very fit through gym work and appears to have a high degree of energy.

Suitability for release: As tariff has yet to be reached and Mr Kray is still Category 'B', it is not possible to recommend release or open conditions. I do though believe it is time for Mr Kray to be moved to Category 'C' conditions if he is to be considered for release around his tariff date.

Without doubt the future release of Mr Kray will arouse passionate opinions from all quarters. To combat the negative side it will be necessary for a planned progression through to release. Mr Kray's actions and activities when in conditions of lesser security will need to be closely scrutinized. I therefore believe that with tariff some three years away that process should be started.

Vicky King, Reg's solicitor at this time, forwarded the following report to the Parole Board:

Turning to the reports completed by staff at Maidstone Prison, I feel that it is appropriate to comment on their brevity . . . they appear significantly shorter and less detailed than the reports on any other lifer dossier that I have ever seen, and I consider this to be quite remarkable given the length of time that he has been in prison.

Despite the brevity of the reports, it is nevertheless strongly recommended that Mr Kray should be transferred to Category 'C' conditions. It is clear that he presents no control problem and he has had no adjudications in the past three years. Two negative comments are made in connection with prison behaviour, which are, firstly, that he knows how to 'manipulate' staff, and secondly, that he drinks hooch on occasion.

Mr Kray tells me that although he does not seek to manipulate staff, given the length of time that he has spent in prison, he knows the system very well indeed. He says that he gets on well with prison staff and other prisoners, and that he has no complaints at all about his situation. He tried to be philosophical about his imprisonment by taking each day at a time and making the best of it.

He agrees that he does sometimes drink hooch, and given the length of his tariff and his subsequent lack of progression through the system to date, I would submit that this is not entirely surprising. However, this is not one of Mr Kray's areas of concern, and there is no reason why he could not address this in Category 'C' conditions whilst progressing towards release from prison on life licence.

Mr West's report states that when Mr Kray was transferred from Blundeston the areas of concern specified were 'lack of insight, shows no remorse, and public notoriety'. In Mr West's opinion, these issues could not be resolved given the circumstances of the offence and the length of time that Mr Kray has been in prison. However, he did not consider that they presented any obstacle to progression or release.

Mr Kray is undoubtedly notorious, and there is nothing he can do to change this. His case has received a great deal of public interest and is still the subject of media attention. Mr Kray . . . has accepted his sentence and cannot be held responsible for the media's fuelling of the public's interest in him and his family.

The majority of notorious prisoners are abhorred by the public, and their release could be argued to undermine the public's confidence in the criminal justice system. This is not the case with Mr Kray. Public opinion of him seems to be favourable, and many consider that he has already served long enough in prison and is not a risk to the community.

Report writers for this review consider that on the basis of Mr Kray's good custodial behaviour and the low degree of risk presented, he should be allowed to progress towards release.

In relation to the next review, Dr Rose considers that Mr Kray will be suitable for release on tariff, and none of the other report writers suggest that there is any evidence that he might pose a risk to the public. In view of this, I would ask again that the Parole Board recommend that Mr Kray is reviewed again after completing one year in Category 'C' conditions. In this way, if reports continue to be favourable, Mr Kray could be in open conditions before expiry of his tariff and be on line for release upon tariff as recommended.

In November, shortly before the Board sat, Reg agreed to be interviewed by the prison psychologist. He had been initially reluctant. They had never met before. Following a brief discussion he refused to continue. The psychologist referred to him as a 'natural lifer' despite the small amount of time left on his tariff. Reg was concerned that the psychologist had done no preparation and was proceeding on the basis of an untrue assumption. When Reg attempted to terminate the interview, the psychologist commented that maybe he would change his mind and agree to being interviewed 'in five years time'. It was an inappropriate and almost threatening comment, implying that Reg, by refusing to be interviewed, would not be released from prison.

In December, with another Christmas approaching, Reg received the result of the Parole Review. It read:

> The Secretary of State has referred your case to the Parole Board which has not recommended your release on licence for the following reasons:
>
> Mr Kray is not suitable for release on licence or transfer to open conditions because he has little insight into the reality of his offending and as such he remains a risk. There is also no evidence of a formal release plan. His conduct is good and he does not present any control problems. Reporting officers are of the opinion that he no longer requires Category 'B' security and recommend that he progress to a less structured prison environment (Category 'C'). The panel endorse this view and feel it is appropriate for Mr Kray to be given a lesser security classification.
>
> The Panel recommend a further review in two years to provide a sufficient period of testing before the next review.

It appeared that some progress had finally been made. With the recommendation of a 'C'-category status, Reg could be moved to a lower-security prison and by the end of his tariff would possibly be in open conditions and close to release. It was not to be. Despite the Panel's recommendation, Reg was not moved for another twenty months, over a year and a half later. The reason for the delay remains obscure.

In the meantime there was more distressing news. Charlie's son Gary was ill. He had been suffering from back problems and these had become progressively worse. He was taken to King's Hospital in Camberwell in January where he spent seven days undergoing tests. The results showed he had cancer. The doctors said it was too advanced to operate. Charlie was told that his son only had about eight weeks to live. Gary was forty-two.

Charlie arranged to take him to see Reg. In February they travelled to Maidstone Prison after provisions were made for a special visit. By this time Gary was very sick and the journey was arduous. On arrival, despite his serious condition, prison officers began an intensive search of his wheelchair. They pushed their hands in and around his body, causing Gary substantial pain. Charlie was outraged. The prison had been informed of his son's terminal illness but seemed completely indifferent to his suffering. It was Gary who diffused the situation – he told his father he was okay, that everything was all right, and not to cause a fuss. In a few minutes it was over. They were allowed through on the visit.

Reg was shocked. His nephew was thin and wasted. Reg stood up from his chair and put his arms around him. There were no adequate words. He held him in his arms and stroked his hair. They spent half an hour together, chatting, talking about old times, laughing over shared memories. The time passed too quickly. When he left Reg could not stop the tears; he knew it was the last time they would ever meet.

The bad news was not over yet. In February 1996, almost a year after Ron's death, Reg was faced with a startling *News of the World* headline: *The Great Brain Robbery*. The sub-title read, *Docs have pickled Ronnie Kray's bonce in a bottle . . . now his wife has half a mind to sue*. It was a gruesome report, made worse by the paper's flippancy. This was the first Reg had heard about it. He had never been told that Ron's brain had been removed at his post-mortem or that it had been sent secretly to Oxford's special neuro-pathology unit for scientific examination. The newspaper claimed a consultant was conducting medical experiments into criminal behaviour and the effects of chemical imbalances on the cells of the brain. Ron's brain was sitting in a jar in some laboratory. Despite repeated requests from Reg's solicitor to both Broadmoor and the authorities, there was no explanation as to why he hadn't been informed. Since that time the scandal of Alder Hey and other hospitals removing organs without permission, or even notification, has come to light. It is not the concept of medical research that offends so much as its bizarre and insensitive secrecy.

Reg arranged for W. English, the undertakers, to go to Oxford. They put the remains in a casket and buried it beside Ron's coffin.

7. CLOSE ENCOUNTERS

In early March 1996 I left Maidstone after my first visit with
Reg Kray. It was almost dusk by the time we drove away.
Darkness fell as we travelled home. The journey seemed
interminably long. I looked out of the window and stared at
the lights. No one said much. I thought about the day's
events, the place, the man, the words that had been spoken
and those that hadn't. We passed silently along the motorway, through the Blackwall Tunnel, and back into Hackney.
Flanagan and Derek dropped me off outside my flat. I got
out of the car and thanked them both. I walked down the
steps, unlocked the door, closed it behind me and gave an
almighty sigh of relief. I was glad the day was over.

Half an hour later the phone rang. It was Reg. I was surprised to hear from him. He thanked me for visiting, said
he'd enjoyed the afternoon and would I come and see him
again? I hesitated. He said, 'Next week?' I apologized, 'I'm
sorry. I can't.' I explained about work and how difficult it
was to get time off. This was true but it was also a convenient
excuse. I didn't feel I really wanted to go back. We chatted
for a few minutes more and then said goodnight. I put the
phone down. I thought that was finally it . . . but I didn't
know Reg Kray.

The day after our meeting he wrote to me. It was a short
and friendly note expressing thanks for going to see him.
That evening he rang again. I received another longer letter

at the end of the week. He wrote about what he'd been doing and asked me about myself. It took a while to decipher his handwriting. I wrote a short letter back. Several days later he phoned once more. Over the next few weeks he continued to write and to ring. He would give me daily updates on events – the good, the bad, the funny, the incredible and the occasionally terrible. Sometimes he would ring once and on other evenings three or four times.

Within the space of a few weeks, from not knowing him at all, he became a familiar voice on the other end of the line. He continued to ask me to visit but I was still reluctant. Three years before, with a couple of partners, I had started a business in media research. The work was demanding with arduous shift systems and long hours, but for the first time I felt I was doing exactly what I wanted. We were building a small but successful company. I was completely committed and didn't want to get involved with anything or anyone else.

There was no real reason why Reg and I should ever have met. That we gradually became friends was perhaps more down to differences than anything we had in common. We were interested in each other and each other's lives. Through all our differing attitudes and opinions there was one sustaining factor – we were never short of conversation. Our experiences were diverse and our characters virtual opposites.

I spent my early years in Southport, a seaside resort on the north-west coast. It was a sleepy place then, a dormitory town for the surrounding cities of Liverpool and Manchester, only briefly enlivened by an influx of summer tourists and foreign students. It was a safe and comfortable environment. Its politics, like its population, was conservative. Nothing much rippled the surface. Even the sea kept its distance. It was a far cry from Reg's childhood. It was a million miles from the hustle and bustle of the East End, distant too from the basic realities of poverty and survival.

My father was deputy-head at the Liverpool School for the Partially Hearing. One of five sons from a small quarrying village in North Wales he had worked hard to educate himself and to provide his family with the advantages he had been denied. My parents met while at work and married a few years later. My brother was born in 1953. Three years later my sister arrived. I was the youngest, born in 1959. The family was far from rich but we never struggled. The ease of our existence was shattered by my father's illness when I was seven. He was diagnosed with lung cancer and despite several operations and some periods of remission, died four years later. My mother was left with the unenviable task of raising the family alone.

I followed my sister into the local grammar school, then called Southport High, in 1970. By this time the Krays had been convicted and were starting their long prison sentences. I have no memory of reading anything about them. While I floundered in the school curriculum, struggling to come to terms with the unfathomable rules of physics, Reg was trying to come to terms with something much more tangible – the high-security conditions of Parkhurst.

My path was a conventional one and I never questioned where I was going or why. I was doing what I thought everyone else did. Scraping together enough exam passes to get me to college, I left home at eighteen and travelled down to London. I spent the next three years living with other students in a house in Stoke Newington, studying for a degree in English Literature at what is now North London University. I made friends, liked the city and decided to stay.

In 1981 I was offered a job with a marketing and publishing company in Covent Garden and began what I thought would be my future career. As I joined the other commuters on the tube, jostling for space and air, I had no idea that Reg had recently been despatched from Parkhurst to Long Lartin. He was beginning a far worse journey of his own.

Several years down the line I began to wonder what it was all about. Working nine-to-five, bored and dispirited, I could not imagine another forty years of the same. In a moment of uncharacteristic impetuosity I resigned and took another job with a small media research company. It offered no great prospects but the hours were unusual, two weeks of night-shifts (including weekends) followed by two weeks off. Although the work was often mundane my fellow workers were interesting, a mixture of artists, musicians, writers and students. Over the next few years people came and went and gradually I crept up the small corporate ladder. With more responsibility and a number of challenging contracts I began to enjoy what I was doing. For Reg there was also change. After eighteen long years at Parkhurst, he was finally on his way to Gartree.

In early 1990 I took a phone call that opened another door. A multinational oil company was looking for four new employees to work overnight in their research department. Was I interested? Along with three of my co-workers I went to talk to them. The pay and conditions were excellent. We could even work from home at the weekends. All in all it was an offer we couldn't refuse. We didn't. Unfortunately, our new and lucrative careers came grinding to a halt barely a year later. A shake-up at the top resulted in a new chairman intent on 'downsizing' the company. There were thousands of redundancies and our department, along with many others, was eradicated. A deal was set up whereby we were returned to our former employer along with the contract. It was not the happiest or most comfortable of situations. In the meantime, Reg had been going through major changes of his own. With barely time to unpack his belongings he had been shifted from Gartree to Lewes, to Nottingham, back to Gartree, back to Nottingham and finally to Blundeston in Suffolk. There he was to remain for a couple of years.

We, on the other hand, had plans for a great escape.

During quiet times at work and over drinks at the pub, we began to dream. Why not start our own business? Between us we now had years of experience. Why work for someone else when we could work for ourselves? What might have stayed a simple pipe-dream, the rather incoherent ramblings of a bunch of discontents, was propelled into possibility when a barrister friend offered to partly bank-roll the enterprise – the rest we would have to borrow from the bank. Faced with the reality we all became a little more cautious and a lot less convinced of our capabilities. Over the next six months we dithered and discussed. We scribbled notes and figures, talked to possible employees and swung dramatically between panic and enthusiasm. What if it all went wrong? We would lose everything. What if it was a success? We had everything to gain. There were phone calls, meetings and sleepless nights. Safety and security battled against courage and enterprise. Eventually we made the decision. We shook hands and raised our glasses. We were about to become a Small Business.

The following weeks were frenetic. While we served out our notice the name was registered and a bank account set up. We found premises that were 'compact' but adequate and, most importantly, not too expensive. Paper and office supplies were ordered. Computers were bought. Photocopier contracts were signed. Approaches were made to prospective clients. We sat and waited for the phone to ring. That was the worst time.

It was a slow start. Sitting in the office, staring at the walls, the full extent of the risk we had taken finally began to sink in. If this failed we would lose everything. Day after day, while prospective clients deliberated, our confidence diminished and our anxiety increased. The phone remained silent. The computer screens were blank. The copiers lay idle. Only the kettle found itself with regular occupation.

When the first contract came in we all heaved an

almighty sigh of relief. When the second, third and fourth
arrived, we knew we had made the right decision. With
money still tight we did most of the work ourselves. Like
hamsters on a wheel we went round and round, the days
passing into nights and the nights back into days. Fuelled by
coffee, cigarettes and adrenalin, we doubled up on jobs and
worked ridiculous hours, driven home to our beds only by
exhaustion. Within twelve months all our hard labour
started to pay off. We moved into larger premises and
extended the workforce. New contracts came in on a regular
basis. With our finances stabilized and a growing reputation,
the future looked brighter. We were far from secure but were
certainly on our way. In the next few years, through continuing hard work, we managed to establish a place in the
industry. With demands on our time partly lifted, we were
also able to resume some degree of social life. And so it was
that I agreed to meet an old friend for a drink and made him
a promise that would change my life.

On 16 March, the day before the first anniversary of Ron's
death, I kept my word. I sent out over a hundred press
releases on the video *Epilogue*, faxing information sheets to
the national and regional press, TV and radio stations, and
numerous magazines. As I came through the door at about
7 p.m. that evening the phone was ringing . . . it was Reg.
He thanked me for distributing the information. There had
been a good response. He seemed amazed by the fact I
had actually done what I said I would do. I asked him why.
He said people often made promises – but rarely kept them.
I thanked him for having such faith in me! Reg laughed and
said he didn't mean it that way. We had a long conversation.
Ron was very much on his mind and he told me a little about
him, recounting some memories of when they were young
and explaining how he still felt his twin brother's presence,
how he still felt close to him. That evening Reg seemed reluctant to leave. Over and over again the pips went and the

phone was disconnected. A few minutes later he rang back. 'I've just remembered something I meant to tell you.' Before lock-up at 8 p.m. he called for the last time. He thanked me yet again for all I had done. 'Goodnight. God bless,' he said. It was his regular evening farewell.

Shortly after its release, *Epilogue* was banned from a major outlet on the grounds that it 'glorified violence'. It was an odd decision. The shelves of the store were stacked with books and videos on every kind of crime from the viciously factual to the fictionally vicious: Jack the Ripper jostled for space with The Terminator; Crippen cosied up to Hannibal Lector; Bonnie and Clyde sat cheek-by-jowl with Mad Max. A store spokesman, oblivious to the double standard, said: 'This is about a man who had a more than criminal record.'

Less than a month after my first meeting with Reg, his nephew died. Charlie was crushed. To help out Reg offered to organize and pay for the funeral. His older brother gratefully accepted. Charlie was, as always, broke. Reg didn't have the money either. It was a matter of love, pride and loyalty. He didn't want Charlie to have to beg or borrow off anyone else. He would rather incur the debt himself. Knowing he wouldn't be allowed to attend the funeral, Reg arranged for an empty car to be in the cortège, a symbol that he was there at least in spirit. He chose the hymns, recorded a poem and ordered flowers. It was just over a year since Ron had died and it was hard to cope with yet another loss. With so much time to think, so many empty hours, it was a relief to be able to do something positive. The service was held again in St Matthew's. Gary was buried in Chingford Cemetery alongside his grandparents and his uncle.

Shortly after Gary's death, Reg asked if I would visit again. This time, knowing how upset he'd been, I agreed and a visiting-order arrived in the post a couple of days later. I went alone and by train. From Maidstone Station it was just a short walk to the prison. He had no other visitors that

afternoon which, as I was later to learn, was unusual. He normally tried to see as many people as possible. Visits were his
only real contact with the outside world; being on the phone,
reading or writing letters, or listening to the radio was not
quite the same. Reg enjoyed direct contact. He preferred to
sit face-to-face. He liked to talk and to listen . . . but most of
all to talk! His old friend Harry 'Hate 'em All' Johnson had
once said that Reg could 'talk a glass eyeball to sleep'! Reg
claimed the reason he 'rabbited' so much was because he'd
been a loner for his first fifteen years in prison.

It was odd to find myself in that room again, even
stranger to find myself alone with Reg. This time he was less
voluble and almost shy. We sat and drank orange squash out
of plastic cups. We talked at first about neutral things – the
video and work, prison life. Small silences punctuated our
conversation. We glanced at each other and smiled. He asked
me where I lived on the Kingsland Road and laughed when
I told him; in the sixties all his suits had been made by a tailor
who had once worked right across the road from my flat. It
broke the ice and from that point on the conversation flowed
more easily between us. I asked him about Gary. He told me
about the happy memories he had, kicking a football around
in Vallance Road when his nephew was just a child, play-
boxing and fighting in the yard, having tea with him in the
kitchen. One of his greatest regrets was that they hadn't
spent more time together; as he and Ron had grown older
they had become preoccupied with their own lives.

Gradually, as the visit progressed, we both relaxed. The
two hours passed quickly. The Reg Kray I met that day was
a little different to the one I had met earlier. He was quieter,
reflective, and much less confident. Looking back, I think
those early months of 1996 were a period of intense loneliness for him. The reality of Ron's death was finally sinking
in. Reg had spent the previous nine months working on the
video, organizing, arranging, writing notes and making

tapes. It had been a labour of love and a way of holding on. Although he was pleased that *Epilogue* was finished, its completion signified an ending. Reg had many friends inside and out of prison but few he felt especially close to. With Bradley away in Whitemoor there was no longer anyone to share his thoughts or his confidences.

When the announcement came for the end of the visit the room was filled with the sound of scraping chairs, the general bustle of coat-gathering and the uttering of farewells. Couples embraced. Friends shook hands and hugged. We stood up and exchanged a rather formal goodbye. Then he leaned forward suddenly and kissed me on the cheek. He said he'd ring when I got home. He was, as always, true to his word.

I suppose that day was a turning point. Some of my reservations slipped away. Through his letters and calls I had already begun to see a different person, someone rather more thoughtful and certainly more interesting than his public persona. I am not sure why Reg pursued our friendship with such determination. He already knew many people. He received over a hundred letters a week and went on to meet many of his correspondents. If he were simply searching for a new secretary, he could certainly have found someone both more available and willing. I was wrapped up in my own work and had little time or inclination to deal with his. Perhaps he found my initial reluctance to visit something of a challenge. He was used to a certain amount of awe and adulation. I provided neither. I wasn't interested in the world of gangsters or the mythology that surrounded them. I hated violence. I wasn't impressed by his reputation. If I was impressed by anything it was simply that he had survived so many years in prison.

Over the next few months I began to visit more often, not every week but fairly frequently. Both Reg and HMP Maidstone became more familiar. Just as he told me his problems

I found myself telling him mine. But it was not just our problems that we shared – we talked as well about the things that brought us pleasure, what made us laugh, our friends, what was important and what wasn't, the present, the past and, with some degree of reticence from Reg, our hopes for the years ahead. He found it hard to think about the future; it was as if he refused to believe in it until it actually arrived. His dream, a simple one, was to live in the country. Although his attachment to London was strong he had no desire to return there permanently. We found it easy to talk to each other. Perhaps this was due, in some degree, to the fact our worlds were so far apart. Just as I had nothing to do with his life, so he had nothing to do with mine. Although not exactly strangers we had only one mutual acquaintance – and he was in the USA. Our secrets were safe. Whatever we said and whatever we discussed remained between the two of us. We exchanged a large number of letters. He usually wrote in the early hours of the morning. While those around him slept Reg expressed his feelings on paper. Sometimes he would write just short notes, other evenings over twenty pages. I began to comprehend the complications of his life, the frustration and angst, the loneliness and despair – they were Reg's constant enemies and he battled against them every day. Despite his worries, he refused to be despondent. The one thing he always tried to maintain was his sense of humour. If it could be laughed at it could be overcome. One of his early letters to me, written at the end of March 1996, described his worries at being 'shanghaied' (moved without warning) from Maidstone.

28th March
Thursday 3–5 a.m.

Rob,
Slept at 9 p.m. – woke 1.30 a.m. – here I am. My stars say distant travel mentally or physically – hope not but

just in case I've been doing best to get all my paper work in semblance of order – been shanghaied three times before – all personal possessions left behind.

I listen to Radio Melody as I write. When I slept at 9 p.m. I said to myself Ron would do the same and say to himself 'Let's go to sleep while they all talk about us'. Ha! Ha!

Glad you are my new friend. Good to talk to you.

New and old friends I saw yesterday are putting on a night for little Paul Stapleton.

You are in my thoughts. 'The only way to have a friend is to be one' – good proverb.

God bless,

Love, affection, Reg xx

Our friendship grew and flourished. It was not romantic; neither of us was looking for that kind of relationship. I was already aware of Reg's bisexuality but it was a while before we actually talked at any length about it. For the time being we simply got on well and trusted each other. Between business commitments I did what I could to help. Reg was always working on various projects, having new ideas and trying to bring them to fruition. It could be anything from a book or a record, to a business deal or an interview, to name but a few. I understood his need to try to achieve; it went some way towards negating the stifling routine of prison life. It was also a method of maintaining his identity. He refused to just give up. Despite his incarceration he remained determined to accomplish something every day. When he had an aim he felt inspired and alive and any achievement, however small, brought him pleasure. It was not primarily to do with money and nothing to do with greed; most of what he made he gave away. Money simply provided him with the means to have a slightly more comfortable life inside and to provide some support for the people he cared about.

Reg's need to keep busy had obvious downsides. One was that others often tried to use him, or at least his name, to attach to some unsavoury enterprise or another. He knew his enthusiasm often clouded his judgement and that his situation prevented him from always seeing the full picture. Some came promising the earth, publishing deals, film deals, various business ideas, all of which rapidly evaporated – although not before Reg had signed a varied selection of photos and books for his disingenuous guests. Reg was no innocent either. He understood exactly what was going on. He tried to use them exactly as they tried to use him.

The majority simply wanted to claim they were a 'friend' of Reg Kray. These usually fell into one of two categories: those who believed the association provided an enhanced reputation on the street (and was therefore occupationally profitable) or those who needed the association as a boost to their own low self-esteem (and was therefore egotistically profitable). Reg often felt like an animal in a zoo, a rare species being permanently prodded and gawped at. He endured it. He knew it was the price he had to pay. Sometimes he even enjoyed it.

There has been much talk about the number of people Reg used to see on any one visit. It's a fact that, at this time, he would get additional visitors in on other inmates' visiting-orders. For him it was simply a numbers game – the more he saw, the more likely it was he might meet someone useful. It was not disadvantageous to the other inmates either; they had a two-hour break from the usual prison routine, were plied with tea, crisps and chocolate, and occasionally made new friends. It was hardly, as some have claimed, a 'criminal empire'. Although the prison officers were aware of what was going on they turned a blind eye. It was just a few people moving around tables. For as long as there was no trouble, for as long as the room remained calm, they had more important things to worry about.

Through 1996 I met a lot of people on visits, some of them genuinely caring and compassionate but most in rapid pursuit of either a reputation boost or a quick buck. Many people would approach him but few were genuine. I heard more empty praise and empty promises in the four and a half years I knew Reg than I am ever likely to hear again for the rest of my life.

It was only when Reg dropped his guard that the real person emerged. I witnessed his many faces: the businessman, the entrepreneur, the sociable host, the criminal, the gangster, the dreamer – he could be all things to all men. Like a mirror image, he reflected exactly what his visitors wanted to see. Reg was the perfect chameleon. He knew instinctively exactly what was wanted and what was required of him. The real Reg, the man behind the mask, was someone very different. Full of private fears and anxieties, he struggled to make some sense of his life.

Another problem Reg faced came directly from the authorities. They were obsessive about the issue of notoriety. Every time his name appeared in the papers another black mark appeared on his reports. Publicity was anathema to them; any kind of media interest prompted the kind of knee-jerk reaction normally associated with serial killers. Despite the fact Reg had nothing to do with most of the coverage he was still often blamed for it. Having said that, whenever Reg had the opportunity (which was rare) to speak out, he would grasp it with both hands. It was mainly to do with trying to put the record straight and partly a desire to stay in the public eye. If he was being talked about then he was not forgotten. After so many years in prison, and so many false hopes, it was a struggle to maintain any kind of optimism about the future.

Reg refused to stop pursuing ideas however big or small. Despite objections from the Prison Service, he continued to respond to the numerous letters he received. He wanted to stay in touch with the outside world and to continue being some small part of it. He found it abhorrent that most inmates spent their free hours watching television. It annoyed and frustrated him. He thought it was a waste, a passive occupation that achieved nothing apart from the killing of time. Time was what he wanted most. Every minute of every day was important. He could never understand how others just wished it all away.

I soon became aware of the precarious path Reg was walking. I understood and sympathized with his needs but realized as well the possible damage to his prospects of freedom. He was existing in a contradiction: to survive he needed to achieve; to achieve was to aggravate the authorities. It was a classic Catch 22. Most of the publicity associated with him was negative and pointless. Nobody was talking about the length of time he had spent in prison, the length of his sentence in comparison with those who had committed far more heinous crimes – including the emerging crop of paedophiles and the IRA – or the injustice of his continuing incarceration. There was no discussion, no serious debate and, worst of all, no apparent interest. If it wasn't 'scandalous' then it wasn't newsworthy. The Reg Kray I read about in the tabloids was a far cry from the Reg Kray I was gradually getting to know.

As I became a regular visitor, shuffling my work schedule to catch a day here or there, I grew accustomed to the routine. The visiting at HMP Maidstone was run on a system of numbers. Visits began at 2 p.m. but booking-in began at 1 p.m. The first visitor in the queue was given a card with the number 1, the second number 2, etc. The search process for visitors could take a long time and if you were far back in the queue it could be half an hour after visits started before you, or the person you had come to see, was able to get into the visiting-room. Because of this most people arrived at the gates early, often an hour or more before booking-in began, and waited outside on the pavement. There was no cover or protection from the elements. In the winter we endured the rain, the snow, the wind and the cold. In the summer we got sunstroke. The queue would snake along the old stone wall, a line of resigned and stoical faces, some already weary from the long journeys they had made.

Faces became familiar and, after a while, friendly. Names were shared and conversations begun. Information was exchanged about parole reports, probation, home leaves and other general prison gossip – who was down the punishment block and why, what a certain prison officer had said or done, how a particular governor had behaved towards someone on the phone. I began to learn about the prison system. I began to learn things I could never have imagined. Even for prisoners far less notorious than Reg, the system created obstacles that wives and partners constantly battled to overcome. Many had solicitors who were either indifferent or incompetent. The women tried to battle through the legal complications alone, seeking advice where they could find it, from the Prison Reform Trust or from other visitors who may have found themselves in a similar situation. This was on top of trying to cope with the major responsibilities of feeding their children, holding down a job, and paying rent and bills. Towards most of these women I felt both sympathy and admiration. They were not stereotypical villains' wives, living off ill-gotten gains, maintaining a villa in Spain until the day they could be reunited; their lives, usually through no fault of their own, were hard and miserable and lonely.

In the queue there was other general news about life, work and aspirations. They were strange fleeting friendships, purely the product of circumstance, but no less important because of that. I can still remember their faces but some of their names are lost to me. They came from all walks of life and had many different experiences. Most tried to make the best of the situation, some coped and others were wretched, but all counted off the months and years.

At the beginning of July 1996 Reg was taken to a local hospital for tests. He had been experiencing pains in his stomach. Prior to his visit, in a letter to Maidstone Hospital, the prison Medical Officer wrote: 'I would be grateful if you would be good enough to send us an appointment for Mr Kray to see you regarding his complaint of intermittent pain and discomfort on the right side of his abdomen. I enclose copies of the recent investigations and I have, as suggested, arranged an abdominal ultrasound to exclude gall bladder and right renal calculus.' Reg told me he expected to go for tests but he had no idea of the actual date. On the day of his appointment someone tipped off the press and they were waiting when he arrived. As Reg had not been previously informed, there were only two possible sources of information – the prison or the hospital. Chained to his escort, Reg ran the gauntlet of the photographers; numerous pictures were printed next day.

Although Reg rang and told me about the morning's events it was still upsetting to read the papers and see the way it had been reported. The *Daily Mirror* claimed on 6 July 1996: 'Gangland killer Reggie Kray was dramatically rushed to hospital from jail yesterday amid fears that he has cancer . . . Jail officials would not discuss his illness, but there were fears that he has a stomach tumour.'

The results of his tests (like so many that came later) were negative. The hospital told him there was nothing wrong and there was nothing to worry about. Reg was relieved. He rang and asked if I could release a statement saying he was A1 fit and feeling fine. He knew the media coverage would result in a huge amount of mail. As he could only reply personally to a small percentage he hoped a suitable press release would answer most people's worries. I faxed a statement to the Press Association.

Reg looked so well it was hard to believe there could be anything seriously wrong. He worked out in the gym, walked on the field, and didn't smoke. His skin was brown from the sun and he seemed, superficially, in good health. He told me he'd been having stomach pains for a while. I got the impression that some prison staff looked on Reg's physical problems as being either psychosomatic or hypochondriacal. These attitudes followed him from prison to prison. In retrospect it is distressing to realize he may have been showing the early symptoms of the cancer that would eventually kill him.

Despite his continuing discomfort, Reg was uplifted by the hospital results and convinced that his physical problems were just the result of stress and strain after Ron's death. The pain returned intermittently. Sometimes he saw the prison doctor but most times he didn't bother. He simply endured it. He wanted to believe, as we all do, that the experts know best.

I was worried about him. Having perceived his major struggle as being against the mental challenges of being imprisoned for so long, the physical consequences had not even crossed my mind. Although he was sixty-two when we first met, I never thought about his age. He was simply Reg. He was not a slippers-and-pipe type of man. Activity and challenge were all-important to him. Without them life was meaningless.

There were usually other people present on our visits but Reg would often ask them to leave before the end so we could be alone. He had begun to confide in me and these were times when he talked openly. Despite having received a recommendation for Category 'C' conditions, there was still no sign of a move. Reg was philosophical; he had learned through the years how slowly the wheels of the prison system turn.

There have been many stories about Reg and Ron. When

other visitors were present Reg was fiercely protective of his twin. He vehemently refuted the suggestion that Ron had been the cause of their downfall. As far as Reg was concerned he had made his own choices and although they may have been at times limited, dictated by Ron's instability, they were nevertheless still his own. He always insisted that Ron had been 'in his right mind' when he shot Cornell. For both the twins it was an important point. At the trial Ron could have used the severity of his illness, his paranoid schizophenia, as a reasonable defence for why he had committed such an outrageous act. He refused. *He* had killed Cornell, not his illness. It was his 'fearlessness' that had enabled him to pull the trigger. To hide behind his illness would have meant damaging his all-important reputation.

By Ron refusing to plead insanity, Reg was unable to pursue a plea of diminished responsibility. The death of Frances and his well-witnessed descent into severe depression and alcohol abuse would certainly have provided mitigating circumstances. Their position as identical twins, and Ron's at this time dominating influence, could also have carried weight for Reg's defence. But no, reputation was everything. They had done what they had done because they were 'hard', the toughest gangsters that had ever lived. Ron would prefer to live in prison with his reputation intact than out of it with his reputation shattered. Reg had no choice. He couldn't let Ron go one way while he went another. As usual, they would stand together.

In public Reg's opinion was always the same. In private he was often confused. Although he understood Ron's motivation, he never completely shared it. He regretted the loss of his freedom in a way Ron never seemed to. Through visits and letters Reg's character became clearer to me. He didn't dwell on the past but was always prepared to talk about it if asked. I wasn't interested in the gory details of his crimes but his past was a part of him and couldn't be ignored. For the most part he preferred to concentrate on the present. Talking about his anxieties seemed to ease them a little and I was happy to listen. We shared many confidences and his trust in me, like mine in him, slowly increased. I was happy with his friendship and wanted nothing more. Reg was alarmingly open, revealing not just his feelings about historical matters but also his current fears and problems. I was careful to be discreet and never discussed our conversations with anyone else.

Although Reg understood that, for various reasons, strangers might try to use him he was distressed that many of his friends were equally capable of abusing his trust. Even some of his oldest associates seemed prepared to exploit his name. Times had changed and loyalties had shifted. There was money to be made from the Kray phenomenon. Reg heard many stories about what associates were saying and doing on the outside. Prisons are full of rumour and gossip. The atmosphere is rife with paranoia. What was true and what were lies? Distinguishing fact from fiction was not always easy.

Despite all his bad experiences Reg remained relatively trusting. He wanted to believe in the integrity of others. To become bitter and cynical was to erode a part of himself. No matter how many knockbacks or how many times he was deceived, he greeted every new acquaintance with an open mind. It was a characteristic I admired. It was also one that worried me. In a society that teems with profiteers and chancers, most of them seemed to beat a path to Reg's door. Whether visitor or inmate, friendly overtures were frequently followed by shady business propositions, an 'exclusive' in the papers or some other less than subtle exploitative procedure. I tried not to get too involved. It was Reg's life and he had to make his own decisions. When things went wrong, as they often did, he would simply shrug and move on. Between us we picked up the pieces.

Perhaps it was the contrast in our natures that provided a balance to the friendship. Reg was open and impulsive; I was closed and cautious. He was trusting; I wasn't. He was extrovert; I was introvert. We were at opposite ends of the spectrum. We were two completely different people but rather than dividing us, our differences brought us together. I liked Reg's candour, his spirit and energy; he liked my carefulness and deliberation. He used to say, 'We make a good team.'

Throughout the early part of this year I came to enjoy Reg's company. His was a world of which I had no experience. It was both strange and fascinating. I was intrigued not just by his past but how he had survived so long in prison. I was also interested in the man behind the myth, the man who was proving to be the antithesis of what I had expected. I never envisaged our friendship growing in the way it did. Nor, I am sure, did Reg.

The summer of 1996 brought a major change. Bradley returned to Maidstone. Despite what he'd done, Reg was pleased to see him and for a while he was happy. All was calm and peaceful. Then, perhaps inevitably, the rows between them started up again and the relationship resumed its rather stormy nature. Reg had given Bradley a gold cross and chain before he left; Bradley returned without it. He claimed it had been lost but later admitted he had sold it for drugs. Over the next few months, symptoms of Reg's former difficulties re-emerged. He became more volatile and suffered manic mood-swings. His frame of mind changed not just from day to day but from hour to hour. He had periods of high elation quickly followed by depression. Some nights when he rang he was full of energy and good humour, on others anxious, angry or despondent. On visits it was hard to know how he might react. His complicated relationship with Bradley exaggerated his insecurities. Although he certainly loved him he wasn't sure if he could trust him. Both

Reg and Bradley were burdened with deep emotional problems and each constantly 'tested' the other's feelings, creating situations where loyalty had to be proved. Just as he had
looked after his twin, Reg looked after Bradley, trying to
keep him out of trouble and to deal with his problems.
Bradley, in return, provided Reg with a purpose to his life.

Prison relationships are, by their very nature, a response
to need and circumstance. There are many different kinds of
love and it is easy to be deprecating, dismissive or contemptuous of relationships that most of us cannot even begin
to comprehend. Faced with ten, twenty or thirty years in
prison, the majority of us would form close friendships with
other inmates, partnerships that could be cerebral, sexual or
simply companionable.

Understanding Reg's personality and motivation did not
mean I could always help him. He was caught up in a cycle
of attraction, conflict, confusion and manipulation. He was
very emotional and never hid or tried to disguise his feelings. It gave him a curious vulnerability, a characteristic very
much at odds with the image of the hardened gangster. Without a second half, a surrogate twin, he always felt his life was
empty. He needed someone to share his existence on a daily
basis – just as he had shared it for the thirty-five years before
his imprisonment.

When Reg rang in a state of anger or frustration I would
attempt, not always successfully, to reassure him. I was
sympathetic but tried to avoid being drawn into his private
rows. I knew by morning it would all have blown over. Reg's
emotional life was always complex. That is not to say I was
forever patient. As those who knew him well can confirm, it
was hard to remain calm when he was being deliberately
provocative. Feeling upset or insecure his worries would
often spill over. If one person had let him down he became
convinced that everybody else would do the same. As if to
prove his point he would deliberately create arguments, pick

fault and criticize the mildest of comments. It was an effective way of losing friends. The few who understood his seemingly irrational and antagonistic outbursts simply waited for the storm to pass; others turned their backs.

Our visits continued on an irregular basis. While we were talking he would sometimes lay his hand over mine, a gesture which I took simply as a token of friendship. When I left he would embrace me and kiss me on the cheek. His confidences grew. We'd discuss many things and he asked for my advice. Sometimes, probably most times, I didn't have any answers but it was at least a problem shared. We often had contrasting thoughts but could still appreciate each other's point of view. Between us we found mutual ground.

It is always good, and in some respects flattering, to make new friends when you least expect it. But these were unusual circumstances. I never looked at Reg through rose-tinted glasses or had any illusions about him. I was never oblivious to what he had done in the past. It was not always easy to reconcile the person he had been with the person he was now. He could have tried to deceive me, to make himself out to be a very different man, but he never did. Some of what he told me I would have perhaps preferred not to know but he insisted on disclosing everything. He seemed intent on revealing exactly who he was.

I began to feel like I was leading two lives, my normal everyday experiences of work, family and friends, and another secret existence. It was not an exciting or thrilling kind of secrecy but a rather disturbing one. Reg was chipping away at my calm and settled future. He was, inadvertently, challenging the things I believed I wanted. Gradually our two worlds were coming together. Their collision would bring major changes.

In the meantime, Reg was facing yet more worries. In August 1996 his older brother Charlie was arrested on drugs charges. He was later remanded to Belmarsh Prison. Reg and

Charlie had rarely seen each other in recent years; he had only visited a couple of times since Ron's death. After his release in 1975, unable to find any kind of career, Charlie had continued to exploit the family name. An easy-going and, by all accounts, charming man he loved the high life and had a reputation as something of a playboy. His expensive tastes had a price of their own.

After Charlie was arrested Reg rang numerous people to try to find out what was happening. There seemed to be little information other than what was in the newspapers. The *Evening Standard* reported: 'Charlie Kray was today being questioned by police on suspicion of involvement in an alleged £80 million cocaine smuggling ring.' Further calls revealed nothing more from friends than a general disbelief. Charlie remained in top-security conditions until the start of his trial ten months later. Despite their troubled history, Charlie was still Reg's brother and he loved him. He also feared for him. Charlie was seventy years of age and the conditions at Belmarsh were harsh even for a young man.

It was a stressful summer. In addition to the strain of Charlie's imprisonment, Reg continued to have problems with his stomach. He also started to smoke again. In October he was seen by the Visiting Gastroenterologist who reported: 'He complains of mid-abdominal discomfort every day which is aggravated by anxiety and emotional upset ... On examination he looked fit and muscular. His abdomen was soft and there was no tenderness or mass palpable. The history is suggestive of the Irritable Bowel Syndrome in a man who is emotional and probably obsessed with his physical condition. I have reassured him that there are no features which would indicate an underlying organic disease.'

As the year slipped into autumn there was at least some good news. Reg had introduced Bradley to a young woman called Donna Baker and on 24 October they got married in the chapel at Maidstone Prison. Reg was best man. It was a

small gathering and at first he seemed ill at ease, as if
surprised and perhaps a little alarmed to find himself at
such a social event. Dressed in a smart suit and tie, looking
immaculate, he glanced round nervously. The last time he
had worn a suit had been to Ron's funeral. This, as the
carnation in his lapel verified, was a happier occasion. He
played with the flower and smoked a cigarette. Gradually he
relaxed. Later, when the short service was over and his confidence regained, he made his best man's speech with feeling and humour. We raised our glasses of orange juice to the
happy couple. The reception was held at the back of the
chapel. Reg passed among the guests, chatting to everyone,
slipping easily into his old familiar role as host.

We talked for a while. It felt strange to meet again in such
unfamiliar surroundings, to see him out of jeans and blue-
striped shirt. He had overcome his nervousness but was
not completely at ease; he still had an edge, an almost self-
conscious wariness. He was pleased about the marriage. He
genuinely liked Donna and hoped she could provide the
love and stability that Bradley needed. Reg wished for him
all the things he had longed for himself – an enduring
relationship, a family and a future. Where he had failed he
hoped that Bradley could succeed.

Donna had brought her camera and lots of photographs
were taken. As the films were finished and changed a prison
officer stepped forward to take the offending material into
custody. They were later developed by the prison service. All
the prints showing images of Reg were removed. The neg-
atives were cut up. Bradley and Donna were told the missing pictures would be returned to them on Bradley's release
from prison. When that day came it was discovered that the
photographs had disappeared. The Prison Service claimed
they knew nothing about them.

Money can buy most things in prison and when Reg had
cash he spent it freely. Despite rumours to the contrary he

did not accumulate vast sums and there were certainly no offshore (or even onshore) bank accounts. His philosophy was that money was to be spent not saved. What could he save for? Every day was already a rainy one. He often relied on the kindness of others and frequently had to borrow small amounts to buy the phone cards that helped him stay in touch with the outside world. Occasionally someone's generosity provided him with the means to live a little better than usual. It was while he was at Maidstone, just before Bradley and Donna got married, that he met his greatest benefactor. His name was Carl Crompton and he had just become a lottery multi-millionaire. He had also expressed a desire to meet Reg Kray. The visit was quickly arranged. Who was Reg to refuse a rich man's dream? The afternoon went well, better than he could ever have imagined. For two hours Carl had Reg's undivided attention. In return, by the end of the following week, Reg had £100,000. He could hardly believe it. Although he had, with his usual opportunistic attitude, asked for a 'loan', the money when it came was not only a much larger amount but had no ties attached.

Reg immediately set about the tricky business of spending it. Bradley only had a few years left of his sentence and, with his impending marriage, Reg wanted him to have something to look forward to. He gave the couple £50,000, enough at that time to buy a flat of their own. In addition he also gave them cash to buy furniture, kitchen appliances, a TV and anything else they might need. There wasn't much change from a further £10,000. With the rest Reg settled most of his outstanding debts, a not insubstantial amount, and to his credit organized a couple of parties in Nottingham – one for the OAPs, with free food and drink, and another for a group of children. He wanted to give me some of the money too but I refused. Although I knew it was legitimate I still didn't want to be a part of it. I had my own business and a good salary. I was independent and intended to stay that way. Reg wasn't trying to buy me – whatever he had, he always shared – but it made me uneasy. I wanted to keep our friendship on an equal footing.

What remained of Carl's gift enabled Reg to buy new clothes, tobacco, alcohol and better food – luxuries that he shared with many other inmates. For the next couple of months he certainly enjoyed himself. It has been claimed that Reg ruled the roost at Maidstone and that money and reputation provided him with everything he needed. The truth is that he was there for over three years and, for the majority of that time, begged and borrowed to make ends meet. His brief period of wealth was quickly over and although it enhanced his standing and provided a fleeting impression of unlimited funds, he was far from King of the Castle. That dubious honour belonged to the dealers. There is only one commodity that enables you to make a fortune while you are in prison – and that is drugs. Whilst Reg did what he had always done, visibly appreciating his temporary good fortune, the real power-brokers went quietly about their business.

Reg became a greater, although not the most essential, part of my life in the later months of 1996. My biggest involvement still lay with the business we had all worked so hard to build up. It was doing well and our efforts were paying off. We were still working long hours and were always exhausted but it was worthwhile; we were making a name for ourselves and building an excellent clientele. We were doing what we had always talked and dreamed about – going it alone and making a success of it. I had managed to extricate myself from the night shift and was now working on days, starting at 7 a.m. and finishing whenever I could get away. This was rarely before 6 p.m. and often much later.

The one thing I had always refused to do was give Reg my work number. I knew I couldn't cope with them both at the same time. I couldn't concentrate on work if I was worried about Reg – and I couldn't deal with Reg's problems if I was worried about work. For as long as I could I tried to keep them separate. It seemed a good idea in principle but it soon came crashing down. Reg became the victim of another blackmail attempt. It had been brewing for a while with numerous rumours and letters, followed by an approach to the press. He felt increasingly stressed. A number of ridiculous stories had recently been published, one claiming he was obsessed with Red Indians, another by a teenage girl who had been to visit him. He felt constantly under attack. Now he was being threatened with an exposure of his bisexuality. An old 'friend' outside was threatening to sell letters Reg had written to him to the newspapers. In them Reg had openly expressed his sexual and emotional feelings.

Under pressure, he made the decision to talk to a journalist. Under pressure, I gave him my work number. We made an agreement that it was only to be used in emergencies. Reg did his interview. He rang me at home in the evening. It had all gone okay. Everything was fine. Everything was sorted. He seemed relieved. For the rest of the evening he was calm and relatively happy.

The next morning I went to work. At 8.15 a.m. Reg rang. It was 'an emergency'. It had all gone wrong. He knew it had all gone wrong. The interview had suddenly become a disaster. He asked me to book a visit and to come to Maidstone. He said he had to talk to me. I told him I couldn't. It was impossible to leave the office; the other phone line was ringing, the fax machines were whirring, deliveries were coming in and going out. It was the usual early morning chaos and I was on my own. He rang off and rang back two minutes later. He had to see me. 'Please,' he said, 'I need you.' He sounded so upset and so bewildered that I couldn't find the heart to refuse.

That day was another turning point. At 9 a.m. when the day-shift came in I made some excuse about a family crisis and left. I wondered, not for the first time, what I was doing. From simple friendship we had shifted to something that seemed infinitely more complicated. Once home I booked the visit, got changed and jumped on the next bus to Victoria station. I arrived in Maidstone by midday and met Donna, Bradley's wife, in the pub across the road from the prison. We waited for the press copy to come through. It was being faxed from the paper to Reg's solicitor and then on to another lawyer in Maidstone who had agreed to drop it off. I thought it had been a mistake for Reg to talk to the journalist but understood why he had done it. As far as he was concerned there had been no choice.

In any prison that is not high-security it is easy for a reporter to see an inmate through the usual visiting procedures. Although prisoners are not currently permitted to talk to the media without previous consent from the Governor, at this particular time the rule was being challenged in court. Until a decision was made no inmate could be punished for communicating with the press. Reg had, unfortunately, been free to say whatever he liked. He had taken full advantage of the lifting of constraints. Already, he was regretting it.

The fax arrived about ten minutes before the visit began. It didn't take more than a quick glance to establish its contents. They were pretty much as expected; the 'interview' was typical tabloid fodder. Reg wouldn't be happy. Donna and I exchanged a look. It was going to be a stormy afternoon.

Inside the visiting-room Reg was jumpy and anxious. I passed the sheets of paper to him. As he began to read his face paled. 'It's rubbish,' he said. He took his pen and began to race through the copy, scoring out words, sentences and paragraphs. 'I didn't say that.' Two bright spots of red appeared in his cheeks. He was so angry that the pen tore through the flimsy paper leaving a collection of ragged holes. The prison officers, alert to the fuss, watched from the podium. Reg felt that much of what he'd told the reporter had been misinterpreted. There were assorted references to Bradley and their 'relationship'. In addition there was the suggestion that Reg felt endangered in his current location. It was claimed that another con had tried to set fire to his cell. The overwhelming impression was that Reg was at risk and unhappy at Maidstone Prison. In fact the converse was true. Reg got on well with other cons and had many friends. The prison regime, although far from perfect, was certainly an improvement on many he had experienced. If these statements were published it would look as though he was making an unprovoked attack both on the prison and its inmates. Reg continued turning over the sheets, muttering, disclaiming, striking again and again with his pen as if he could destroy the words that hurt him so much.

I had to calm him down. Instinctively, I put out my hand and grabbed his. I said simply, 'Reg.' He turned and looked up, startled. He shook his head. I kept his hand in mine and we sat quietly for a minute. Reg was upset, worse than I had ever seen him. For the first time since we had met he seemed utterly lost. Caught in the middle, trapped between a blackmailer and the press, he was fighting a battle he knew he could never win.

Once the initial shock had passed and he was less agitated, I took the sheets and shuffled them back into some kind of order. We slowly went through them together, removing all the blatant inaccuracies, trying to make some sense of it all. I promised to pass the pages back to his solicitor; he would have to do whatever he could.

I felt immense sympathy for Reg that day. I don't believe, as some have claimed, that he was worried about his sexuality being exposed. It was being blackmailed by someone he had once trusted and cared for that distressed him so badly.

Reg began to speak about it all and the words tumbled

out, a jumble of half-phrases, hopes and regrets. He didn't want a conversation. He just wanted to talk. He told me about his relationships in prison, how they had started, what they had meant to him and why. For over an hour he talked and talked and talked, a continuous monologue, as if he might finally unburden himself. He wasn't asking for comment, response or even understanding. He was simply trying to explain. There was no anger – only disappointment. Through the years his emotional affairs had kept him alive and given him a purpose: someone to take care of, to feel for, to share things with, to protect and to plan a future for. They had removed him from his own fears and paranoia. They had given him responsibility. Without them, he said, he would have had no reason to carry on. Without them he would have finished what he started at Long Lartin.

Split apart from Ron, he was lost. His mother's death had been devastating. His close friends filled the enormous space. They gave him hope. He could never turn his back, whatever they claimed, threatened or did. He couldn't hate them. At the same time he couldn't understand them either. For Reg love and loyalty was everything. It was absolute. For most of his companions, however, they were just a couple of meaningless and outdated words. Reg accepted that his relationships brought responsibilities. By defending the bad behaviour of some of his friends he often jeopardized his own safety and standing. Respect is a hard-won commodity in prison. No reputation lasts forever; it is constantly challenged and easily eroded. By protecting another inmate he had to be prepared to intervene, discuss, argue, settle or, in the worst case scenario, to fight. It rarely came to the latter. Reg had learnt the advantages of diplomacy.

When he met someone and became involved his whole outlook changed. Despite the attendant difficulties, the advantages outweighed the disadvantages. He needed to have a close companion. His life felt empty when it wasn't shared. His family, through imprisonment and death, had been destroyed. He tried to create a new one. When close friends let him down, he still refused to turn his back. Once a commitment was made he stuck by it. Even on their release, Reg continued to live his life partly through them. He tried to provide the kind of future he might have had himself; a home, security, money, and support from friends. For as long as the cash and connections flowed they kept in touch. When the bank ran dry so, often, did their interest. Their 'love' was more dependent on cash than emotion. When Reg's financial resources were exhausted so too was their loyalty. Once Reg could no longer raise the money to support them, most drifted away, tried to sell their stories to the press, or embarked on some odious form of blackmail.

Reg was far from unique in having prison relationships. Some younger cons link up with an older man in order to gain certain practical benefits – protection, money, extra food, drugs, alcohol and social position. An older con has knowledge and influence. He often has proficiency and skill. He understands the system and how it works – he also knows how to exploit it to the best possible advantage. Younger cons offer companionship and assistance, often doing routine tasks like collecting food and laundry. Some also offer sexual favours. Prison relationships, like all relationships, are open to abuse. An older con may take advantage of a younger man's inexperience, a younger con of an older man's need and loneliness. Usually a balance is achieved, a series of compromises that benefit both. Many of these partnerships are between fundamentally heterosexual males. They don't consider their activities to be in any way indicative of homosexuality – but simply a matter of limited choices. Most end when one or the other leaves prison.

All Reg's close friends knew the facts, many others too. He could have made a public statement and he seriously considered it. The constant threat of blackmail was casting a shadow over his life. He went so far as to dictate an open letter admitting his bisexuality, but decided in the end it would probably do more harm than good to publish. Some of his ex-partners had wives and children, families who might suffer as a result of his admissions. He also had many friendships that were not of a remotely sexual nature; he knew it could cause untold difficulties for these inmates as well. The statement was never used but it was not destroyed either. After Reg's death the letter appeared in a Sunday newspaper. Although written years before, it was described, incredibly, as a 'deathbed confession'.

This statement has since been used in a number of books as evidence of Reg's 'homosexuality'. The disparity between homosexuality and bisexuality is one that certain authors, for their own questionable reasons, have chosen to blur and confuse. Reg's suspicions that he might never be released were something he had to try to come to terms with. He didn't want to live a life that was bereft of all love and affection. Although he could, and had, survived on his own it was a lonely and unfulfilling existence. Some of Reg's close prison relationships were sexual. Some were not. They were all important to him. Through his disclosures that day, Reg was perhaps trying to explain as much to himself as to me how he had come to face his current ghosts.

Reg's affairs were always fraught with conflict. His long history with Ron, and all its complications, continued to have an impact. He was constantly searching for a replacement. His major prison relationships were with difficult individuals, some of whom preyed on his insecurities and took advantage of his paranoia. He was easy to manipulate. After any kind of argument, a short note delivered after lock-up, claiming depression and hinting at suicide, was enough to drive Reg to distraction. He would pace his cell all night. He would ring the bell and ask for the person in question to be watched by the prison staff. He would ask for reports every half-hour. His fear was a weapon they could use against him. Reg would never lose his terrible guilt over the death of Frances.

In return for his own absolute loyalty Reg demanded the same in return. He tended to love deeply and obsessively, forgiving betrayal or pretending it had never happened. Such was his fear of loss Reg would always find a reason to overlook deceit or treachery. He knew he was being used but preferred to live with that knowledge than to live alone. What Reg dreaded most was abandonment. He had lost his twin, his parents and Frances. The thought of losing anyone else he cared about was a terrifying prospect. He craved unconditional love but that was the kind of love that only Ron and Violet were ever able to provide. Reg lost his twin many years before his actual death; their physical separation, broken only by occasional visits, was not enough to sustain him. He searched for others to fill the void and was drawn towards those who reminded him most of Ron.

Reg was let down over and over again by those closest to him. His hurt and disappointment were obvious. The article that had caused him so much stress was later published. It was not the finest, or the most accurate, of reports but Reg just shrugged it off. Although he had managed to negotiate some changes in the final text his relationship with Bradley was implicitly, if not openly, exposed.

That difficult and emotional afternoon brought us closer together. For the next few weeks Reg wrote at least once and often twice a day. Despite our agreement he also rang every morning at work, many afternoons, and every evening when I got home. Remembering my initial reluctance to give him my work number, he always began his calls with 'I'm sorry to ring you at work but . . .' and would continue to give me some news that he had to share right there and then! Having changed my working hours I was able to visit him most weekends. By now, after ten months, I had met all of his

regular visitors. One of the things that surprised me was how
few of his old friends and associates came to see him. When
I asked, Reg was simply philosophical. That was the way it
was. The years had passed. They had moved on, rejoined
their families (or made new ones) and continued with their
own lives. He was neither angry nor resentful. Just as they
pursued their own hopes and dreams, so did he. They had
drifted apart. Although the past would always be a common
place, it was not enough to hold them together. He related
more to the people he was in prison with than those outside,
the other cons who shared the same daily routine and the
same immediate future.

There were some falling-outs and arguments with his old
pals. Books and articles were appearing with increasing regularity. The rise of 'gangster chic' meant a steady demand for
new revelations. The truth was often abandoned in favour of
sensationalism. Reg had written his own books and could
not complain about others doing the same. His objections
were more to do with the content which through the years
grew gradually more outrageous and drifted ever further
from reality. The myth of the Krays had assumed a life of its
own. Reg used to joke that he had made bestselling authors
out of half the criminal underworld – even though most of
what they wrote was fiction!

Reg had his good and bad days. Some evenings he would
phone me in a cheerful mood and others in a depressed or
anxious one. I was gradually learning more about prison life,
about his past and present, and about his constant worries.
He had learned to cope with the routines, the petty rules, and
the long periods of solitude but knew how easy it was to give
in and to become nothing more than a number. He was also
drinking a lot. Alcohol was so easily available that HMP
Maidstone might as well have installed a bar on each of the
landings. There was a vast amount of spirits as well as hooch
floating around. For Reg it seemed the perfect form of

escape. There were times, however, when instead of making him forget it more dramatically reminded him of everything he had lost.

One of the things I found most disturbing was Reg being encouraged to 'live up' to his reputation by other inmates. While they quietly progressed through their final years of imprisonment, doing courses, keeping a low profile and generally keeping their probation officers happy, they encouraged Reg to do the very opposite. He was expected to be and to do all the things they never dared. When he made bad decisions they applauded. When he made mistakes they praised and honoured him. When he was worried they fed his paranoia. While they slipped soundlessly through the system, Reg remained exactly where he was – and where he had been for half his life. Reg was not a fool but he was inextricably entwined with his reputation. It was what kept him alive, safe, and secure within prison. To lose it was to lose everything.

Through all the trials and tribulations, we not only remained friends but became ever closer. He wrote and rang constantly. In early September 1996, on a visit, he suddenly turned round and said out of the blue, 'I'll never get married again, not after what happened with Frances.' We were alone and had been talking about something quite different. His remark took me by surprise. I looked at him. He looked back at me. I couldn't read his expression. For a moment there was silence. I wasn't quite sure what he was saying. I understood the words but the meaning, or perhaps the motivation behind them, seemed ambiguous. Was he referring to us? It was not the words themselves but rather the way he had expressed them that was disconcerting. I said, perhaps a little over-defensively, 'Well you don't have to worry about me, you're the last person I'd think about marrying.' He took my hand and laughed and the moment passed. We didn't mention it again. On the way home I thought about it. I wondered if something I had said or done had given a mis-leading impression.

Two weeks later, after another visit, Reg rang in the evening. He was unusually quiet. We had a short conversation and he said he'd call me back. An hour later the phone went again. He said, 'Rob, I've got something to ask you.' In that moment's hesitation, even before he began speaking, I knew exactly what the question was going to be.

8. THE BIG QUESTION

Had it come completely out of the blue? I felt some surprise but not as much as I thought I should. Perhaps somewhere in the back of my mind I had even been expecting it. Reg had been ringing with increasing frequency and writing letters every day. We had also started having regular visits on our own. Since his comment about never getting married again he had become gradually more affectionate, often taking my hand during visits and, when we parted, embracing a little longer than was perhaps strictly usual between friends. I was aware of the shift but chose to put it down to the establishment of an understanding as regards our intentions (or lack of them) towards each other. We got on well together and talked about everything. We laughed at the same things. We were comfortable in each other's company. The bond between us had grown progressively stronger. His life had gradually become an integral part of mine. Did I love him? Yes, by this time I certainly did. Was I *in love* with him? That was a trickier question. When you believe that something is impossible it is often easier to close your mind to it. I was happy with his friendship and had never imagined anything more. Even when I suspected his feelings might be changing, it was a suspicion I chose to disregard.

I asked, jokingly, if he was down on one knee. He laughed and swore he was. I then requested, in that time-worn

tradition, to have a few days to think about it. We had already
arranged a visit for after the weekend and I promised I
would give him an answer when we saw each other again.
We said our goodbyes. I put the phone down and stared out
of the window. I suppose, in my heart, I already knew the
answer. I'm not sure if I'm a great believer in fate but such
was the unlikelihood of our ever having become friends,
never mind more, that there seemed an element of destiny
about it. He had taken the chance and risked rejection. Now
it was down to me. I still needed time to consider what it
would mean. He had been in prison for over twenty-eight
years; no one could remain unaffected or unaltered by it. I
understood Reg well enough to know that his feelings were
genuine and that he would never try to deliberately mislead
or hurt me but his emotional life was full of complications.
He was searching for love and stability, for the 'normality'
he had always craved. He had pursued it once with Frances,
the dream of marriage and family, of security, safety and
understanding. He had tried and failed. Ron had drawn him
back into the old familiar web.

Now, for the second time, he was reaching out for the
dream that had always eluded him. It was a different kind
of love, if love can be so simply categorized. This was not a
mad, impetuous flaring of passion but something that began
as a friendship, growing and deepening, changing gradually
into a special closeness, a mutual need and love that neither
of us really expected. If Reg had been less honest, I might still
have married him blindly. But he told me everything. There
were no false pretences. I knew about his past, his time in
prison and his relationships. There were no secrets between
us. I always believed that, in time, Reg could and would
regain his freedom. It might be a long struggle but one that
with perseverance must inevitably be successful. I was not
so much concerned with the practical realities of separation
as with the more daunting complications of his emotional

history. Could we have a future together? There was only one way to find out.

I spent the weekend thinking about everything, going over and over it in my head. I had to consider what marriage to Reg would really mean. The only thing I knew for certain was that it wouldn't be easy. I was not under any illusions about him. Was he a changed man? Only so far as we all change through the years, time and circumstance creating inevitable alterations in attitude and thought. Fundamentally, he remained the same. It was not always easy to reconcile the older man with the younger but the two could not be separated. Reg was not filled with remorse for what he had done. It would be a lie to say he was. He claimed that killing, like being killed, was an occupational hazard of the violent world they had inhabited. Yet his murder of McVitie had not been straightforward. The death of Frances, his deep depression, tranquillizers, alcohol, rage, fear and the manic goading of Ron, had all contributed to the final outcome. I found no justification there – only some reasons for how and why it had actually happened.

I knew, when he was released, that Reg would not return to a life of crime. This wasn't because he had reformed, found God, or become a hugely better person but for the simple reason that he had no desire to return to prison. Like his old associates, Reg would have to rely on the interest of the public and the media, on the enduring fascination with the myth of the Krays.

That was something else to think about. I had spent the last ten years reading, recording and analysing newspaper reports. I knew exactly what I would have to face and the prospect was not a pleasant one. When you marry someone well known your life, like his or hers, becomes a piece of public property. When it came to publicity we were complete opposites. Reg liked attention and I hated it. He had been in the spotlight all his life. It was a part of him.

For me it was something alien and intrusive. I valued my privacy.

There was another practical but still important consideration to be taken into account. I knew that if we married I would have to leave the business. We had a number of Government as well as company contracts; I could not envisage a sympathetic and supportive response to the discovery that Reg Kray's wife was on the board of directors. It might have provoked interest – but not the sort that would be in any way profitable to those who were left to pick up the pieces. We had all worked hard to make the business a success. I didn't want to be responsible for its downfall.

To say yes to Reg would mean leaving one way of life and entering another. It would be final and irrevocable. There could be no going back. To say yes would mean making a leap, not exactly into the unknown but certainly into the unpredictable. There was a kind of irony about it. Reg was searching for stability and security. I was looking at having to leave it all behind. It was a long weekend. I went through the process of weighing the pros and cons. It was, to be honest, no more than an academic exercise, a formality. For all the reasons why I shouldn't marry him, and there were many, one overwhelming reason why I should remained – I had grown to love him.

I travelled to Maidstone the following Monday. An autumnal wind, cold and icy, whipped round the prison walls. There was a short queue. I joined the back of it. There was no one there I knew. Apart from a few polite smiles, we all remained silent. I was glad. It gave me time to think. Did I need to think? I had made my decision but it still seemed unreal. I could change my mind. I could walk away. Did I want to? No. Over an hour to wait.

The queue lengthened. People walked past the prison on the other side of the road. Some were simply curious, glancing and then turning away. Others were more blatant, stopping and staring, scrutinizing the women as if they were exhibits in a curiosity shop. Everything seemed to happen in slow motion that day. Every hour felt like two. The waiting was like an eternity.

Finally, after all the usual procedures, I got to see Reg. He came bouncing into the room. He kissed me. We both sat down. He said quickly, 'Before we talk about anything else we really need to go through these.' From his pocket he produced a handful of scribbled notes. I looked at him. Having spent the whole weekend thinking about his proposal it was a bit strange to find myself staring at a completely unrelated pile of paper. I suddenly thought, 'He's changed his mind.' I tried to catch his eye but he wouldn't look at me. He just carried on talking, passing me messages, taking them back and ripping them up. He chatted away, talking about anything and everything. A heap of debris formed in the middle of the table. We discussed his book, the weather, the state of the economy, and the deficiencies of prison shampoo. After about fifteen minutes he took the last note, unfolded it, examined it and then folded it again. He passed it over to me. He said, 'This one's important.' I took the final scrap of paper. He looked away. I opened it. Reg gave me a sideways glance. I read it. It said: 'Let's get married.'

↗ ↗ ↗

And so it was agreed. And it was also agreed that we would wait until the following summer. Neither of us wanted to rush into anything. I had to find somewhere to live in Maidstone and sort out what was going to happen with the business. I wanted Reg to be sure that marriage was what he really wanted. The next seven months would give us time to be certain we were doing the right thing.

Reg told me he had almost got married before in prison. He was far from proud of his reasons. It was not to do with love, he said, but with money. Ron's two weddings had generated not just publicity but a great deal of cash. It had been a tempting prospect. His old friend Flanagan was keen on the idea of an 'arrangement'. They had pursued the possibility for a few months, along with an agreement for a future divorce – the press coverage would have provided a generous settlement for them both – but in the end Reg hadn't the heart to finish what he'd started. It was one thing to plan such an event, quite another to actually go through with it.

With December approaching there was a lot to do. I began making plans for my withdrawal from work and a move to Maidstone. Christmas was always a sad time for Reg. He felt the loss of his family and the reality of his own situation more keenly at this time of year. Stretching back were twenty-seven Christmas days spent behind bars. His most abiding memory was of Parkhurst where he would stand on the pipes and stare out through the window. In the distance he could see the Christmas lights. It was something he never forgot.

At the end of November Reg wrote me a poignant letter. A part of it said: 'Not long before Xmas – not far away at all – be nice if the snow is falling, tiny snow drops for the kids to see. I thought back to years ago earlier and I can remember so clearly when I was a kid sleighing on a wooden scooter that had ball bearing steel wheels at the front and back and how I raced along the streets just off Vallance Road and how I wondered what I would be doing 40 or 50 years hence and here I am – it is so clear in my memory. I often have such thoughts – time goes so quickly, too quickly . . .'

With no visits on Christmas Day or Boxing Day I saw Reg only on Christmas Eve. It is always an emotional time for inmates and their families, separated at a time when others come together. Although there were decorations up in the visiting hall, the atmosphere was far from festive. We would

Above. Charles and Violet Kray, enjoying a rare break.

Right. Reg and Ron – at home in the country.

Left. Pat Connelly,
Reg and (far right)
Charlie at the Regal.

Above. In Vallance Road.
Reg to the far left, Ron in the
centre, Violet to the right.

Left. Programme for a Webbe
Boys' Club boxing tournament held
in Hoxton on 31 January 1951. Both
Reg and Ron were on the bill.

INTER-CLUB CONTESTS

1. J. BRODSKY *v* P. RUDOLPH
   Webbe (Fed. Semi-finalist 1949) — *Caxton House*

2. RON. KRAY *v* J. O'FLAHOTY
   Webbe — *Lyle*
   (London Youth Champ. 1949)

3. H. THORN *v* J. WIGNELL
   Webbe — *Eastbourne House*

4. L. O'LEARY *v* F. NEWMAN
   Webbe — *Stepney Institute*

5. F. GARDNER *v* L. ELLIS
   Repton — *Lyle*

6. T. GILES *v* G. LEE
   Repton — *Lyle*

7. H. DODDS *v* R. LEE
   Repton — *Lyle*

8. L. REYNOLDS *v* D. WENDEN
   Langham — *Lyle*

9. T. BOGG *v* J. CURLEY
   Langham — *Stepney Institute*

10. J. KENNEDY *v* M. WEBBER
    Lyle — *Stepney Institute*

11. H. MOORE *v* G. WILSON
    Webbe & Army — *Lyle*

12. REG. KRAY *v* Selected opponent
    Webbe (Gt. Britain Finalist 1948, CANLING TOWN
    London School Champ. 1948, PUBLIC HALL
    S.E. Div. Youth Champ. 1948)

13. P. LANGRIDGE *v* Selected opponent
    Webbe

Reg and Frances on holiday, just before they were married.

On their wedding day, 19 April 1965.

Reg's floral tribute to his twin at Ron's funeral in 1995.

The hearse was drawn by six black-plumed horses.

St Matthew's, March 1995. Reg, handcuffed to a prison officer, struggles to come to terms with Ron's death.

Reg showing his boxing skills on the 'Lifers' Moving On' course at HMP Maidstone 1995.

Reg's cell, Maidstone Prison, 1996. Having a drink with Bradley Allardyce.

Our wedding day, 14 July 1997. Inside the chapel at HMP Maidstone.

The wedding party. From left: Ray, Mark Goldstein, Kubilay, Ken Stallard, Donna and Bradley Allardyce, Reg and me, Donna Cox, Danny Brown, Trevor Linn, Len Gould, Barbara and Tony Burns, and (behind) Dave Webb.

The visit that caused problems. In the grounds of HMP Wayland with, from left, Rob Ferguson, Adam Myhill, Huey Morgan (of the Fun Lovin' Criminals), Paul Henry and Jonathan Bloch (manager of the FLC).

A visiting order we didn't get the opportunity to use. Reg was transferred to Norwich Prison Hospital in July 2000.

'Rob, my little one – I have to write because you never listen to me. Ha! Ha!' The beginning of a letter from Reg, April 1999, in response to a conversation about how much he talked!

With Reg, by Charlie's graveside. 19 April 2000.

After Charlie's funeral. A sad farewell, and a final kiss, before Reg was taken back to prison.

Sharing some special time together. At the Norfolk and Norwich Hospital shortly before Reg was allowed to leave for the Town House.

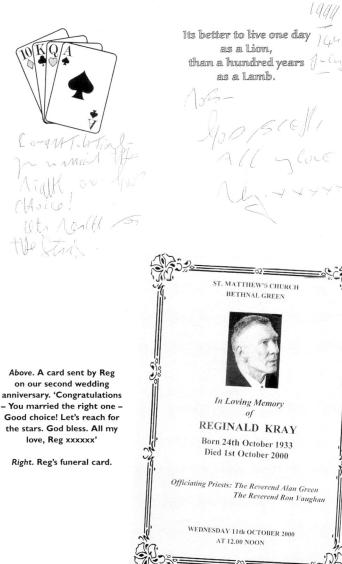

Its better to live one day
as a Lion,
than a hundred years
as a Lamb.

Above. A card sent by Reg
on our second wedding
anniversary. 'Congratulations
– You married the right one –
Good choice! Let's reach for
the stars. God bless. All my
love, Reg xxxxxx'

Right. Reg's funeral card.

ST. MATTHEW'S CHURCH
BETHNAL GREEN

In Loving Memory
of
REGINALD KRAY
Born 24th October 1933
Died 1st October 2000

Officiating Priests: The Reverend Alan Green
The Reverend Ron Vaughan

WEDNESDAY 11th OCTOBER 2000
AT 12.00 NOON

Left. Reg's funeral, 11 October 2000. Chingford Cemetery. With (to the right) Donna Allardyce and Richard Grayston; behind the car, Tony and Tracey Mortimer.

Below. Chingford Cemetery, East London. Reg was laid to rest with Ron.

In Loving Memory

RONALD KRAY
BORN 24th OCTOBER 1933
DIED 17th MARCH 1995

REGINALD KRAY
BORN 24th OCTOBER 1933
DIED 1st OCTOBER 2000

Grant them eternal rest
and let perpetual light shine

both be glad when it was over and the New Year came. Before I left, Reg said, 'Don't be unhappy. We've got so much to look forward to.'

The New Year certainly brought changes. Reg told me he had been passed the name of a good lawyer and had arranged to see him. Although he had an excellent civil solicitor he wanted to talk to someone who had experience in the field of criminal law. With Reg in his twenty-ninth year of imprisonment, approaching his thirty-year tariff, he was sorely in need of some expert advice. The man's name was Trevor Linn. It was arranged that I would meet him after he came out of the early-morning legal visit. As Donna also had a visit with Bradley booked for the afternoon we went to the prison together and waited in her car for the new solicitor to emerge. Time passed and there was no sign of him. It began to rain. We stared out of the window. Across the road a young man in a baseball cap and sweatshirt tried the door of the pub. It was locked. We watched him. He wandered up the road and back, looking around. We decided it couldn't possibly be him. He wasn't even wearing a suit! Our prejudices cost us another ten minutes. The man sat down on the wall opposite. We sat in the car and looked at him. He looked at us. We looked away. No one else arrived. No suited and booted likely candidate made an appearance. Eventually the man stood up and wandered over to the car. He said, 'You're not Rob and Donna are you?' We admitted we were. He introduced himself. 'I'm Trevor Linn.'

It was obvious from first introductions that Trevor was far from conventional, not only in dress but also in attitude. Friendly and open, he was as distant from the stereotypical image of a solicitor as anyone could be. He also had an impressive record in his own field, taking on many difficult and problematical cases with a high level of success. There was no flannel or empty promises. The fight for Reg's release, as he pointed out, was going to be an uphill struggle. No Home Secretary would readily relinquish his hold on one of the country's most famous prisoners.

That first meeting was to be one of many. Trevor went on to represent Reg for almost four years, fighting against the system and against the odds to secure his freedom. As predicted it was an almost impossible task, so determined were the authorities to keep him locked up. It is to Trevor's credit that he never gave up. Battles were fought, some won and most lost, but the war continued. Sadly success, when it finally came in August 2000, was an empty victory.

It was through conversations with Trevor and access to Reg's prison papers that I began to really understand the task that lay ahead. As well as the legal formalities we would have to embark on some form of public campaign. It was important to raise awareness of Reg's situation. Trevor's first priority was to get Reg moved out of Maidstone and into a 'C'-category prison. That Reg was still in 'B'-category conditions after so many years was an obvious travesty. His disciplinary record was good and there was no legal reason why he shouldn't be transferred.

During those early months of 1997 I began to read everything I possibly could about Reg, not just the official papers but all the various books and articles that had emerged through the years. The amount of information was astounding. Year after year the myth of the Krays, like Pinocchio's nose, had grown ever larger. Minor players assumed the mantle of major underworld operatives. Truth was set aside in favour of sensationalism. Rumour and conjecture replaced actuality. Everyone had a story to tell . . . or perhaps, more accurately, everyone had a story to *sell*.

The label of 'gangster' remained attached to Reg for the rest of his life. He represented notoriety, violence, excitement, ambition, success, failure and punishment – the personification almost of a decade. For the various legends to prosper he had to be cast in stone and preserved like a

museum piece. Throughout the long years of his imprisonment, he became more a symbol than an individual. For the
Establishment he served, along with his twin, as an example
of the triumph of law over criminality, of good over evil, a
moral fable of crime and punishment. For the media he
was a larger-than-life villain, an object of equal derision and
fascination, their interest helping to sustain his reputation.
For his peers and fellow criminals Reg was something
else again – the source of a lucrative and legal income. The
'inside story' was not to be missed. That the real inside story,
along with its associated grief, pain and deprivation, was
still being lived was inconsequential. There was money to
be made.

Mixed in with all these factors was another extraordinary
influence. The history of the twins provoked a curious nostalgia. They had ruled the East End in the sixties, a time
when crime less frequently encroached on the innocent and
when violent acts against the old or the young were rarely
heard of. People looked back and recalled an era of doors left
unlocked, of trust and relative safety. It was an age before the
proliferation of hard drugs. The Krays became associated
with another mythology, that of keeping the streets 'safe to
walk'. For the Establishment the whole phenomenon was
appalling. They had locked up the twins and thrown away
the key. It should have meant obscurity but came instead to
mean the opposite. With every year that passed the Krays
became more famous.

There can be no denying that Reg, along with Ron, contributed to the on-going legends. In many ways they were
masters of their own destiny. Their books and the collaboration in the film only added to their problems. Thinking
perhaps that things could not get worse, they embarked on
an autobiographical journey almost guaranteed to seal their
fate. But for them, facing thirty-year sentences, there was
nothing to lose and everything to gain. Money was useful

but it was not imperative. What mattered most was what had always mattered – to be known and to be remembered. To be talked about was to still exist and to *live*, to not be buried without hope or identity in the prison system. They both knew they might never be released.

Reg floundered between the desire to be accepted for who he was and the dread of being forgotten. He had lost almost everything, not just the tangible evidence of his former success but also the deeper more important ties of love and family. All that remained was his reputation. If his time in prison eroded some of his identity, letters from the outside reminded him of its enduring influence. He responded not out of arrogance or conceit but a fundamental desire to communicate . . . and to feel needed. That others might actually care about him, respect him, or ask for his advice was the incentive he needed to carry on. Reg and his reputation, like another pair of identical twins, had become inextricably entwined.

From the seeds of the twins' own recollections came a hundred other offshoots – stories, lies, truths, contradictions and fantasies from anyone or everyone who had ever known, or claimed to have known, them. As the years passed they became trapped in their own mythology. On the one hand it fulfilled the fantasies of those who glorified the world of gangsterism, on the other it confirmed the opinions of those who believed they should never be freed. Opinions on both sides were entrenched and would not easily be changed.

Some of the early months of 1997 were spent coming to terms with the long fight that lay ahead. It was barely possible for Reg to have a fair hearing when so many people held such intractable views. By keeping him incarcerated for over twenty-eight years the authorities had achieved the very opposite of what they had intended; the public's interest had increased rather than faded. Fed by so many books and articles the mythology of the Krays had grown to almost gigantic proportions. What Home Secretary would have the courage to release him?

Reg's own thoughts were full of confusion at this time. On 16 March, on the eve of the second anniversary of Ron's death, he wrote a long letter attempting to make some sense of his own inner conflict:

> Good to have a chat with you tonight and share my thoughts. I seem to have everything but there's an emptiness about my life – rather complex. I seem to search too much and I'm not sure what I look for all the time. Perhaps to know myself or to know others or part of each – what do we all search for?! . . . Bernard Shaw was a wise man. But I believe on his death bed he said words to the effect: 'I never did find what life's all about!' Guess he was great philosopher – so all is open to interpretation. Who can really judge or throw stones . . . the ignorant opinion can be as good as the wise in some respects in life's search – who is really the happier? It is said ignorance is bliss yet it's said it is good to be wise, to seek wisdom. I'm sure of one thing – money is to be spent – other than that I'm not sure of anything sometimes! Hence my conflict of thought tonight – thoughts not in order.
>
> Perhaps I'm too close to the trees – what should I look for on life's path – what mountains should I climb if any?! There's always another hill to climb! . . . Is it wrong to confide in a friend?! Sometimes to bare one's soul can lead to disaster – where does one begin or end? Ron wrote how much he loved life. He was happy at Broadmoor till the latter time just as I am most of the time in jail. But then I search maybe too much – maybe I need advice in this area . . . Perhaps you can give me the advice. Those who hold the keys here – probation

and others have often said, 'How will you cope when out?' They must think I was born in prison. How can a normal society be said to be difficult . . .

Anger is within me tonight . . . it's good to understand or try to but also good to be understood. Wonder why humans live in such conflict? I enjoy lock-up as there are no situations or conflict except in my own thoughts, but then I just argue with myself. Perhaps I'm selfish as Ron would probably like such situations. I pray Ron is at peace. Ron deserved peace and happiness. Ron must have been the loneliest in the last hours – no one to turn or talk to, nowhere to go . . . Maybe you can help unravel these mixed-up thoughts of mine.

The rest of the night I'll go by priority pyramid and do what I have to do, and look to a new dawn – the quicker the day gets here the more eager I will be to start. Yet is that in itself not contradictory to my earlier statement that I enjoy being locked up, my own company, no situations to sort out? Perhaps I have a love hate relationship with life.

It was through his letters that Reg talked most freely, sharing the turmoil he often felt inside. In the quiet hours of the early morning, while those around him slept, Reg poured out his thoughts. This was a very different Reg Kray to the one of myth and legend, no strutting gangster but a very human man filled with doubt and confusion.

His original fears about the circumstances of Ron's death came back to haunt him. He was convinced the whole story had not been told. There were too many unanswered questions. Why were Ron's wrists so badly bruised? Why was he returned to Broadmoor when he was so close to death? Why had the inquest been carried out so quickly? The official version of events couldn't allay his doubts. He tried to get some kind of inquiry but was unsuccessful. He was filled with guilt, guilt that he had not pursued the truth more avidly, and guilt of a deeper inescapable nature – that he was still alive when his twin was not.

In March Reg also had to face the possibility that Charlie would be convicted on a major charge. He was allowed to visit Belmarsh Prison but was upset at the conditions. Charlie looked unwell and Reg was convinced that eight months of the harsh regime had been hugely detrimental to his health. In the presence of five officers their conversation was limited to territory of a purely neutral nature. He couldn't ask the questions he wanted and Charlie could not provide the answers.

8 May 1997 brought the twenty-ninth anniversary of Reg's imprisonment. He had spent almost as long in prison as he had spent out. Only another year and he would complete the tariff that had been laid down for him. But he knew completion wouldn't mean freedom. That dream remained as far away as ever. After three years in Kent, he was faced with the prospect of a move to yet another area. It was now well over a year since the recommendation had been made. Although he wanted to be de-categorized he asked Trevor Linn if, like some other inmates, he could remain in the familiar surroundings of Maidstone. Trevor asked the prison authorities. The answer came back as a resounding 'no'. Reg was reluctant to leave the friends he had made and to start all over again. He was sixty-three and had been moved sixteen times since his arrest in 1968. He was sick of it all. Several other prisons were mentioned and eventually a representative from HMP Erlestoke in Wiltshire came to talk to him. The interview didn't go well. Reg felt they were deliberately antagonistic and had no intention of accepting his transfer. They turned him down a couple of weeks later, claiming he wasn't suitable due to the medical support he required – Reg was still taking a low dose of Stelazine – a fact they should (and must) have been aware of before they even

talked to him. HMP Wayland was then put forward as the *only* alternative. It was a prison with a bad reputation. Other inmates talked about its volatile atmosphere and high level of violence. Reg had spent too many years in similar institutions to want to walk straight back into one. He objected but the authorities held firm. It was there or nowhere. If he stayed at Maidstone he would remain a Category 'B'. There was no option but to accept.

From early spring there was a lot of activity as regards Charlie's trial. It was suggested to Reg that he might stand as a witness for the defence. He agreed to see Charlie's legal representative and the news wasn't good; his older brother was in serious trouble. There were a number of very damaging tapes. Whatever Charlie's part in the whole affair his innocence was going to be hard to prove. Reg had no idea as to whether he had been involved or not – there had been little contact between them since Ron's death. The defence had decided on an unusual, or perhaps simply desperate, tactic; they had decided to call people involved in the criminal world to testify that Charlie was not a villain. Reg, along with many others, was supposed to take the stand and provide a glowing character reference.

At first Reg agreed to do anything that would assist. Over the next few days he began to have his doubts. The more he thought about it, the less convinced he became. Surely his appearance would be more of a hindrance than a help? Virtually all the 'criminal' witnesses they intended to call (including Reg) had been guilty of perjury at some time in their lives. Why should a jury believe they were now telling the truth? It was an impractical and unconvincing line of defence. Reg conveyed his misgivings to Charlie. He felt neither his presence nor evidence would be in any way useful. In fact his reputation and the level of his notoriety might have the opposite effect.

As Reg had suspected the 'references' did not sway the

jury. In June Charlie was convicted and sentenced to twelve years imprisonment. He was returned to Belmarsh and then transferred to Reg's favourite prison – Long Lartin.

↗ ↗ ↗

It had been agreed that Reg would be moved to HMP Wayland after our wedding. In the wake of Charlie's trial, it was hard to make plans. We had thought of June but it was obvious by the middle of May that it couldn't be organized in time. Eventually we set the date for 14 July. By this time I had left London and found myself a small house to rent. This made visiting easier and also meant Reg could ring more frequently as the calls were local. It wasn't long before news about our forthcoming marriage leaked out.

The papers were quick to track me down and I gradually became aware that every time I went outside I was being followed. For a few weeks I inhabited a bizarre world where I was never alone. Stopping suddenly at a street kerb, glancing to the right, a man turned his face away too quickly; it was a movement so rapid and so deliberately evasive that it immediately drew my attention. Later, when I looked over my shoulder the same man stepped into a shop doorway. In a café a couple sat hunched over a magazine. Were they a part of it . . . or was I just becoming paranoid? It seemed that everywhere I went, my shadows went too. Even when I visited Reg they parked by the prison and sat watching the queue.

It wasn't long before the truth was revealed. A reporter on a Sunday newspaper rang and said he had photographs of me taken in Maidstone. He claimed a local news agency had been following me around and had put the pictures up for sale. Would I like to talk to him? No thanks. For a while things calmed down but in June, the original month for our wedding, activity of a different kind began. The owners of the local corner-shop revealed that a journalist had been in asking questions. The pub across the road was then approached. They were asked if they would hire out one of the rooms on the upper floor that overlooked my house. Thankfully they refused. Friends and relatives were also besieged. This was the worst. Simply by knowing me they found themselves the victims of unwanted press attention receiving frequent calls at work and at home. That my own life would be affected was something I had accepted but I had not anticipated how others would suffer.

My decision to marry Reg came as a shock to my family and many of my friends. Some of the latter could not come to terms with it and drifted away. They clearly thought I was quite mad. My family, although disturbed by the implications, remained, on the whole, supportive. It was not what they wanted but they accepted the decision I had made. I know it was hardest for my mother. What parent wants their daughter to marry a man serving life imprisonment? It did not suggest the brightest of futures. She was constantly worried. That my love for Reg brought pain and confusion to others was deeply distressing.

I was facing many upheavals in my life and so was Reg. It was a difficult time. Our personal pressures could have caused problems between us but instead they had the opposite effect. We were drawn even closer together. Reg wrote in the middle of the month:

I feel as though I've lost the incentive to do anything. Music, nothing appeals to me at the moment. I just want to pack and get out . . . this place was good once but I've a lot of bad memories of this place too. Today was the straw that broke the camel's back so to speak. I'm tired of paperwork – letters, press cuttings, my life seems like a scrapbook. I need fresh pastures, though more than that tonight. Everyone I see wants something –

drawings, signatures, photos, whatever they all seem to want – like I'm a computer, and I hate the world of no principles. Even the so-called old school have sunk to the depths. If it was not for you at the moment I would feel totally alone . . . Sorry I'm so down, it's you who should be down if anyone.

The next couple of weeks were not easy for either of us. We met for a few precious hours and talked on the phone whenever we could. Our greatest communication remained in the form of letters. By the beginning of July Reg had regained some of his spirit:

My body is tired but my mind is still too active to sleep . . . Good thing I've you to talk to for comfort or my world would seem pretty empty. It takes away the lone-liness. . . Got people to see about different matters today – life never boring – could do without the necessity though. It would be better to be in a village in Sandwich close to the ponds and the streams – a glass of bitter – somewhere over the rainbow – why can't we!! At times like this a roll-up is my mate. Keeps me company to a degree. Years ago I used to listen to the radio. It taught me to reason, chuck things around as the civil do. Taught me good – I can even out reason you! Pour me another gin please – don't forget the lemon!'

As the big day approached, Reg decided to do something a little out of the ordinary to celebrate. He arranged with our friend John Redgrave to create a laser show around the prison walls on the eve of our wedding. It was not an easy task. Despite the adverse weather conditions John did a remarkable job. Lights flew across the prison walls and rooftops. Silvers, blues and reds danced around the bars. A rainbow hung in the sky and wedding bells swung across the doors of HMP Maidstone. Reg and other inmates gathered round their windows. They laughed and cheered. A riot of colour split the night. It was a spectacular display. It was also a display guaranteed to antagonize the authorities. Prison staff ran from cell to cell ordering inmates to get down from the windows. They were useless requests. A show had been provided and the audience was going to enjoy it.

Reg knew how much the lasers would aggravate not just his jailers but also those who paid their wages. There was an element of bravado in the gesture. For every bit of hope the Establishment had ever offered, they had been as quick to stamp it out. I was concerned about their response but understood his motivation. Always the showman he could never resist marking an occasion. If he couldn't have his freedom he would have the next best thing – a few hours of escapism and some excellent memories!

I spent the evening with Donna in preparation for the big day. The house was filled with the scent of roses; Reg had sent a huge bouquet. We had a quiet night, slipping out only to watch the lasers, mingling with the small crowd that had gathered in the street. I wondered what Reg was thinking. He must have recalled another evening long ago, the night before his first marriage, a time when the future looked brighter and everything seemed possible. So much had happened since. So much had changed.

I had no regrets about the decision we had made. We were not facing the most idyllic of starts but neither did we have any illusions. We'd face whatever we had to face together. There were many who believed we'd fall at the first hurdle, that our relationship stood no chance of survival. Would we prove them wrong? Since the announcement of our wedding it had been open day for all of Fleet Street's amateur psychologists. They posed the questions and they answered them. Why were we getting married? What was our purpose? Love was too simplistic a motivation. Much was made of our differences. Reg was an 'East End villain'; I was a 'middle-class girl'. He had left school early; I had gone to college and taken a degree. He was in prison; I had a career and my own business. He was sixty-three, I was thirty-eight. What could we possibly have in common? Some implied that I was being used, others that I was using Reg. I was an innocent to the slaughter; he was the arch-manipulator. I was the publicity-seeking wannabe; he was the unfortunate victim. As I was quickly learning it didn't do to be too thin-skinned. Words were only words. The opinions of strangers, although often hurtful, were irrelevant.

Through the years we had both loved and cared for other people. I had come close to marriage before but was glad I had stepped back. Having decided I would rather be alone than with someone I didn't feel truly committed to I channelled all my energies into work. It was perhaps inevitable that I would then, when least expected, meet the person who would turn my life upside-down. While I had been preoccupied with business, he had been moved yet again to HMP Maidstone in Kent. There, just fifteen months later, he had received the devastating news of Ron's death. It was through that terrible event that Reg and I had come together, a chance encounter that laid the foundations for a future relationship neither of us anticipated.

While the press dissected our differences, Reg and I celebrated them. Our cultural and educational backgrounds might be distinct and our personalities contrasting, but that only gave us more to talk about. We were chalk and cheese and neither of us was complaining. If it was our dissimilarities that initially united us, what was it that kept us together? Perhaps it was simply that between us we created a balance, each providing something that the other needed. Our characters far from clashing actually complemented each other, my reserve lifted by his openness, his impetuosity moderated by my caution. Our worst traits were softened and our best enhanced. The bottom line was that we were happier together than we were apart.

What makes one person fall for another? Personality, physical appearance, humour, ideas, beliefs, interests? Who knows. Out of a thousand people fitting the criteria only one will generate those intense feelings and seemingly irrational emotions of love. In the end it has little to do with similarities or differences. It is perhaps simply the fact that this person brings something *essential* into your existence, that your life is enhanced by their presence.

I didn't sleep much the night before our wedding. I woke up early and went down to the kitchen to make a cup of tea. It was about 6.30 a.m. Was Reg awake? He usually was at that time. Another hour and a half before he was unlocked and the pay-phones were turned back on. A sliver of sunshine fell across the back yard. Any last-minute doubts or reservations? Yes, of course there were. For Reg too I am sure. The day stretched ahead. I was anxious. It was an ordinary day for most people – work and lunch and work and home. For us it was something different. The next eight hours would change our lives.

We could have stayed together without going through a wedding ceremony. I could have continued to visit, continued to work in the business, continued to talk to him and write to him and provide as much love and support as I could. But to agree to marriage was to make a commitment. It was to say not just that I loved him but that I believed we had a future together and one that would be lived, eventually, outside the prison walls.

I had a light breakfast with Donna, a slice of toast, another cup of tea and a cigarette. I was glad she was there. She helped to calm my nerves. We went over the plans for the day and decided what time we would leave. When I went into the front room and glanced out of the window, I saw two men standing outside. One had a camera. The wedding was scheduled for 2 p.m. They had a long wait ahead.

The phone rang. It was Reg. He sounded equally nervous but was in good spirits. After getting the necessary reassurance that I hadn't changed my mind, he told me all about the night before. After the start of the laser show, officers had banged on his door and told him he would be up on a charge next morning if he didn't get down from the window. As there were no actual prison regulations as regards inmates looking through the bars he ignored their orders – as did the rest of the prison population. They were empty threats. No laws were broken and no charges were brought. He said the memory of the lights would always stay with him. The rainbow had been particularly special. His mother's favourite song was Judy Garland's 'Over the Rainbow'. Reg often found it hard to think about Violet. He knew how much she had suffered and how they, he and Ron, had caused that suffering. The laser lights of 13 July meant many things to Reg, a combination of celebration, remembrance and defiance.

A couple of hours later Reg rang again. He had been called to a meeting with one of the governors, the chaplain and prison security. They told him it had been decided that we could not have any pictures taken at the wedding. Everyone and anyone else who got married within prison walls was allowed the privilege of a few photographs but we were to become the exception. Why? Because they thought they would be sold to a newspaper? Because they were just being deliberately obstructive? Because of the night before? There had been months to make such decisions. Why had they chosen this morning? Reg rang Mark Goldstein and he in turn called the prison. After lengthy negotiations they finally agreed to allow a camera into the chapel – with two conditions. One was that the pictures were taken by a prison photographer and the other that the photographs remained

Crown Copyright. We agreed. If we had thought that was the end of it, however, we were very much mistaken. The Mystery of the Disappearing Photographs was only just beginning.

It was not a restful morning. Reg was completely stressed out, convinced the authorities would create some last-minute impediment to our marriage. It was only as the hours passed by and there were no more meetings or demands that he gradually relaxed. It was not the most conventional start to a wedding day – but then we weren't the most conventional of couples. Just before midday, minutes before Reg was locked up over the lunchtime period, he rang for the last time. 'See you in church,' he said.

We would be permitted two hours, the normal visiting period, for our wedding and reception. To allow for the time it would take to get everyone into the chapel, I had arranged to meet the other guests fifteen minutes earlier. Dressed and ready to go Donna and I watched the hands on the clock tick slowly by. My nerves grew in proportion to the wait. Donna was calm and collected. It was a good thing one of us was. My mind whirled with all the usual fears and misgivings. Was I doing the right thing? Were we doing the right thing? Did I love him enough? Did he love *me* enough? She poured me a drink before we left. Dutch courage. Down in one and time to go.

She opened the door and the cameras flashed. The numbers since early morning had increased. I walked quickly to the car. Someone tried to force a microphone through the window. 'How are you? How do you feel?' It was nothing compared to what was lying in wait at the prison. It was besieged. The gates were surrounded by reporters and photographers. It was a daunting sight. Donna drove past, went to the end of the road, turned round and dropped me off by the entrance. Half-blinded by the lights, smiling inanely, I made a rapid dash down the path and into the safety of the waiting room. Inside, most of the other guests were already gathered. I was glad to see some friendly faces.

It had not been easy deciding on the guest-list, limited as we were to twelve. I left the final choice to Reg. He rarely had the opportunity to spend time with his friends anywhere other than the formal setting of the visiting room. Charlie, the last remaining member of his immediate family, was now in prison; despite their many altercations Reg was sorry he couldn't be there. One old friend who was present was Tony Burns and his wife Barbara. Tony ran the Repton Boxing Club in Bethnal Green and had known the twins since childhood. Reg always had a lot of respect and admiration for him. In addition Reg had asked Mark Goldstein and Trevor Linn, his two solicitors who had become far more than legal advisers and were now close friends. Bradley was to be his best man and Donna was my bridesmaid. Another Donna, our mutual friend Donna Cox, was also invited as were Dave Webb, Len Gould, and fellow inmates Danny, Ray and Kubilay.

It certainly felt strange to be there, standing in the room I had been in so many times before, waiting this time not for a simple visit but for my own wedding. After we had booked in, the prison staff let us go through. We endured the normal search procedure. I passed through the metal detector. I was scanned and frisked. The drug dog sniffed my dress, stared up and stood back. The warders smiled me through the barrier. The other guests emptied their pockets and extended their arms. They were thoroughly searched, thoroughly sniffed, and summarily dismissed. We gathered outside. Instead of the normal short walk to the visiting-room, we were led across the yard, a bizarre marriage procession, a straggling line of intruders. We were propelled through more gates and these were locked behind us. Another path led to the doors of the chapel. God was certainly well protected.

It was quiet inside. When we first arrived I thought the building was empty. It had that quality of stillness that is always found in churches. I stood near the altar. A soft light slipped through the stained-glass windows. There were flowers everywhere. It looked lovely. I was surprised to realize Reg was standing at the other end of the aisle. He was still wearing his tracksuit and trainers. Instead of getting changed on the wing, as was normal, the staff had insisted on taking him straight to church. His suit, shirt, tie, socks, shoes and carnation were lying on a pew. He came down the aisle and hugged and kissed me. I looked at him. We both laughed. I was dressed for a wedding and he was dressed for a session in the gym. I said, 'I didn't realize we were going casual.' He said, 'You look beautiful.'

Ten minutes later he was transformed. Reg emerged from the salubrious surroundings of his changing-room (the toilets) looking exactly like a bridegroom. He played with his tie and smoothed his hair. He pushed his shoulders back and adjusted the flower in his lapel. In that moment it was possible to imagine we were a thousand miles from prison. Surrounded by friends, in a chapel filled with roses, our hopes were as great and our dreams as precarious as any other couple.

We had some pictures taken just outside the doors. The photographer seemed friendly and competent. Someone made a joke about whether he had any film in the camera. Then, with nerves beginning to flutter again, we passed back through the doors, guests took their seats, and the wedding began. I walked down the aisle to a piece of music called 'Amapola'. Ken Stallard, a minister who had also known Ron, conducted the service. He talked of love and the sanctity of marriage. 'Morning has Broken', one of Reg's favourite hymns, was sung. Prayers were said. Ken reminded us of all who could not be present that day but were in our thoughts, all those we had lost but who

remained with us in spirit. Reg and I stood side by side. I felt
a sudden terror, a fear that when the time came I wouldn't
be able to speak. Reg took my hand and squeezed it. He
pressed his shoulder against mine. We looked at each other.
No, it would be all right. We would be all right. Face to face
we made our vows. We looked into each other's eyes. Reg
placed the ring on my finger. I placed a ring on his. We kissed
and embraced. We were finally married.

After the book had been signed we walked to the back of
the chapel where a small reception was to take place. A table
had been laid with sandwiches, fruit and the wedding-cake.
There was tea and soft drinks. The prison officers were out
in force but were quite reasonable and as unobtrusive as they
could be in the circumstances. Senior staff, dressed in suits,
mingled with the guests. Speeches were given and the toast
made with orange juice. We cut the cake. With only an hour
and a half remaining we made the most of it, chatting to our
guests, playing music, sharing what little time we had
together. As the minutes ticked by and we knew the day was
shortly to end, Reg held me in his arms and we danced. He
told me it was the happiest day of his life. It was hard to
imagine that so soon after getting married we would be
separated again. Watching him leave was the hardest part,
knowing what he was returning to. At the door he turned,
raised his hand and waved. Then he was gone.

It felt like a long walk back to the main gates. Donna went
out alone to collect the car. She came back a few minutes
later. The prison staff opened the doors for me. I stepped out
into a blinding sequence of flashes; like a rabbit caught in
headlights I was temporarily paralysed. Somehow I made
it to the car and got inside. We were instantly surrounded.
Photographers crawled over the bonnet, refusing to move.
There were journalists to left and right, front and back.
Donna pressed the horn but no one took any notice. She
revved the engine and tried to go forward. No one shifted.

The flashes continued to go off in our faces. It was becoming frightening. In the end she just put her foot down and accelerated. Most of them got out of the way but one received a glancing blow as we left. I was sorry and hoped he wasn't hurt but I didn't feel responsible – he was clearly aware that we were trying to leave.

We went straight back to the house. There wasn't a further reception. It would have seemed ridiculous without Reg. Instead, we opened a bottle of champagne, and joined by Donna Cox drank a toast to the absent groom. The afternoon felt almost like a dream. It was a day of mixed emotions. I was glad we were married but intensely sad that we were now apart. I knew he would be sitting in his cell alone, reliving the day's events, wondering perhaps – as I did – what the future fates might have in store.

The next morning, feeling a little sorry for myself, I heard a letter drop through the door. I recognized Reg's distinctive writing as I picked it up. The envelope was addressed to Mrs R. Kray. It was an odd sensation seeing it there in print for the first time but it made me smile. Inside he had written, 'By the time you get this letter we will be married . . .'

It was another month before we actually got to see our wedding photographs. Bradley had been moved to Elmley jail but Donna had joined me on a visit to see Reg. The three of us were escorted to a small back room. Inside were five prison officers. The pictures, about eighty in all, had been laid across long tables. We were told we could choose just ten . . . and we had ten minutes to do it in. The rest were to be held by the Prison Service until the time of Reg's release. It was petty and ridiculous. As the prints were Crown Copyright they could not be sold or even reproduced without permission. Under these circumstances what was the difference between having ten or having twenty? All our memories of the day were in those photographs. We knew we might never see them again. While we moved along the tables examining the pictures, the officers accompanied us, scrutinizing every movement as if by some clever sleight of hand one of the prints might find its way down a trouser leg. We eventually chose our final ten. Even then I was not allowed to take them away with me. I was told they'd be forwarded at a future date. That future date turned out to be fifteen months later!

Shortly after the viewing a rumour began to circulate that all our photographs had been sold to the *News of the World*. How could this be when they were supposedly held in the safe-keeping of the Prison Service? Even the photographer was one of their employees. Mark Goldstein made enquiries but the paper was unforthcoming. He informed them that all the pictures were Crown Copyright and therefore couldn't be published anyway. When they didn't appear we wondered if it had all been a storm in a teacup. It was to be another three years before we finally learned the truth.

We were told Reg would be leaving Maidstone towards the end of August and the time passed slowly. Although he had no desire to go to Wayland, once the decision had been made he wanted to get on with it. He was quieter than usual, preoccupied not just with thoughts about the future but also the past. On 8 August Reg wrote, 'I dreamt of Ron. He was young as he used to be – Johnny Nash and others were in the dream too. I've felt sober for a change. I don't mean from drink.'

The one occasion he came a little closer to his old self was on a visit with Tony Mortimer. After being introduced a few years earlier, the two had gone on to become good friends. Reg admired Tony's song-writing talents and they were working together on some new material. For a while at least Reg was able to forget all his troubles.

In preparation for his next parole review, the prison was already collecting papers. They asked a forensic psychiatrist called Dr Sugarman to assess Reg. He provided an eight-page report on 15 August. As regards Reg's background he said: 'I was able to peruse the Inmate Medical Record, and the Lifer Dossier, but actually quite limited information was available about the prisoner's life. The authorized biography of the Kray Twins, *The Profession of Violence* is reputed to be a fairly reliable account, and the prisoner agreed with me that this was so.' Reg had conceded that parts of the book were accurate but even John Pearson himself had admitted getting some of his facts wrong. Reg wasn't happy that a book was being used as part of the foundations for a serious psychiatric report. It couldn't have happened to anyone but him! Under 'Progress in Prison', Dr Sugarman said:

> The prisoner told me that following imprisonment he turned away from life outside and away from crime. However, the Inmate Medical Record reveals a disturbed period in early years, including assaults on others, and self-harm. Later during his sentence there were episodes of low mood and paranoid ideation, although few details are available . . . There are frequent medical reports – medical problems including poor hearing, cataracts, and the irritable bowel syndrome. The prisoner was concerned about chest pains around the time of his brother's death, but he is in fact thought to be in good physical condition.

Under a section entitled 'Interview', it was reported:

> The prisoner is currently sixty-three years of age, and looked if anything, a little older although healthy. He was wearing a loose shirt (not apparently prison issue) open to the waist and numerous gold rings, medallions and other jewellery. It would not be unfair to say he was eccentric. He talked very quietly and politely, making strong eye contact. He talked extensively and positively,

in a philosophical manner. He outlined a view that although he is 'not institutionalized' he explained that he now lives his life in prison a day at a time and has succeeded in doing more with his life in prison than others do with theirs outside. He enjoys answering pleasant letters from 'his supporters' and finds keeping fit 'the best buzz'.

In response to some particular questions, the prisoner was clearly reluctant to make critical comments about others. He made bland philosophical remarks about his situation, and withheld from any criticism of the Home Office or the Home Secretary. He admitted that some people write to him for good reasons and others for 'not so good reasons', but he would not elaborate. He clearly did not wish to have contact with his late brother's wife or others of Ronald Kray's recent associates who live in the Maidstone area.

During the interview there were no obvious features of depression, paranoid psychosis, or any other gross mental illness. However, while generally being polite, sometimes excessively so, there were short periods when the prisoner made strong, even intimidating eye contact, and conveyed a feeling of suppressed aggression or defensiveness, with a paranoid and contemptuous flavour. Topics which triggered this included the death of his brother in Broadmoor, his older brother's recent conviction for drug trafficking (which he claimed was on fabricated evidence) and particularly the issue that he may be at risk of criminal activities if released. He is also sensitive when asked what he felt about possibly being detained as a result of his media profile.

In his final summing up Dr Sugarman gave the following opinion:

'My overall impression is that Reginald Kray is institutionalized with a peculiar reputation, persona and
lifestyle . . . If he were to be abruptly released, then the
combination of financial difficulties, intense media
interest, and the unhelpful attention of numerous individuals preoccupied with the Kray notoriety, may well
lead him into difficulties. The risk would be of alcohol
abuse, recurrence of depressive or paranoid psychiatric
symptoms, and possibly a return to criminal activity.
This might primarily be of a money-making nature
rather than serious violence.

Despite these concerns about any imminent release,
I would support a series of progressive moves through
lower levels of security, which would in fact provide the
degree of support and stability which this ageing prisoner in fact requires.

It was a long and detailed statement. Although not the
most positive of reports, it came at least with a recommendation that Reg should continue to progress through the
system. The negative side was that it also introduced many
concerns that were subsequently adopted by the Parole
Board, providing something of a blueprint for their future
objections to his release.

On 25 August, the evening before Reg left Maidstone, he
wrote two letters to me. A part of the first, reflecting his subconscious anxieties, said, 'I woke about 1.30 a.m. – I'd had a
dream that I was trying to climb out of the top of a tall building and I got to the top but I was hemmed in by bars and
could not get out. I've had this type of claustrophobic dream
before.'

The second was written an hour after:

I leave here with mixed feelings, some of resentment but
I'm glad to be leaving. Hard to believe, especially the

fact it has taken me almost 30 years to get Cat 'C'. Most of all I feel sadness for yourself in that though it is progress for us in theory it is another journey for you. I will do all I can to make up for this. Thanks to you we have some good memories of this place.

Glad I got tobacco. I've no radio though so I can only think which is better. We must look on the bright side of things. It was a good visit today though we should have had it on our own. Think I'll have a think and complete this letter later.

9. HOPE AND HOPELESSNESS

After almost thirty years Reg had finally made it to a 'C'-category prison. He arrived at HMP Wayland just before lunch. It was to be another week before I made my own departure. On the journey down he managed to buy a post-card of Norfolk. He wrote, 'Wish you were here!' and mailed it to me.

His first few days were full of the usual stresses and con-fusions. The staff, unused perhaps to such a high-profile prisoner, seemed overly determined to assert their authority. Allocated a cell on C Wing Reg soon discovered it was the wing with the worst reputation for violence. It was nick-named the Bronx. He was then informed by a prison officer that 'some blacks' intended to mug him for his jewellery. He was given the same story again a few days later by more senior officers. Reg was concerned – not at the prospect of a mugging but at what he perceived as a deliberate attempt to create bad feeling between him and other inmates. Despite his age, Reg was more than capable of taking care of himself. He also got on well with cons of every age, race and religion. Suffice to say no mugging ever took place.

While Reg was settling in I was packing and getting ready to move. We talked every day on the phone. Although he still had reservations about the place there was at least the

consolation of some familiar faces and he was starting to
adjust to the new environment. His old friend Bill Taylor,
who had helped with the manuscript in Maidstone, was on
the same wing. Other friends were scattered throughout the
prison.

I eventually arrived in Norfolk at the end of August. A
friend had found a flat through an agency for me. In a small
block, down a quiet road and near Norwich city centre, it
seemed the perfect place. It was good to be closer to Reg. He
was pleased too and it was only after numerous phone calls,
reassurances that it was a nice area, and a promise to book a
visit straight away, that I finally got down to the mundane
job of starting to unpack. The doorbell went at about 4.30
p.m. I wasn't expecting anyone and when I went down the
stairs and opened the door I got an awful shock. There, standing directly in front of me, was a man in a very familiar
uniform. Dressed in dark blue trousers, a dark blue jersey,
and with the distinctive chain at his waist, there was no doubt
at all that he was a prison officer. Instantly, the most terrible
and illogical thought went through my head – something had
happened to Reg. My stomach did a somersault. What was
he going to tell me? What was he going to say? I stared at him.
I went white as a sheet. A moment later he put out his hand.
'Hi,' he said, 'I'm Gavin. I'm your new landlord.'

I managed to gather a few of my wits together, enough at
least to invite him into the flat he owned. He seemed a pleasant man who obviously had no idea who I was. I chose to
forego the path of revelation. Fortunately, he worked at HMP
Norwich rather than Wayland, which provided a small element of relief. He didn't stay long. He left his telephone
number and said to ring him if there were any problems. As
he left I couldn't help wondering why the fates had con-
spired to place me in such a farcical position!

I knew I couldn't remain in the flat. It felt fundamentally
wrong to be living in a place that belonged to a prison

officer. I made a resolution to move out as quickly as I could. In the meantime I had to come clean. An hour later I rang Gavin and explained the situation. I apologized for not telling him my true identity earlier. He was surprised but extremely civil about it all. He said he would have to inform his senior officers, purely as a formality, but not to worry as he was sure the tenancy wouldn't create any difficulties. In the morning I told Reg what had happened. By that time I had begun to see the funny side of it and he did too. It was so bizarre that all we could do was laugh.

I made my first visit to Wayland a couple of days later. Our good friend John Irving, who also lived in Norwich, drove me down to the prison. I was glad of his company. A new prison meant new regulations, new rules, and new procedures. It was a bit unnerving. I was pleasantly surprised when we arrived. Having grown used to grey stone pavements it was refreshing to find a bright clean waiting room and cafeteria surrounded by green fields. There was even an outside seating area with wooden benches. It was a warm, blue-skied day. We bought coffee and sat in the sun. I felt a sudden burst of optimism. Perhaps here, after so much time, things might finally improve for Reg.

At 2 p.m. our number was called and we picked up the ticket and walked across to the main foyer of the prison. We queued for another ten minutes. Eventually we passed into the glass cage, one set of doors closing behind us and, after a short claustrophobic pause, another set opening in front. From there we walked across an open flower-bedded yard to another set of doors. Once unlocked these led to a flight of stairs. At the top was the search area. Divested of coats and bags, we passed through the metal detector, were frisked and cleared, had our property returned and finally emerged beside another open set of doors that led directly to the visiting-room.

I had expected this procedure to be the same as Maidstone. It wasn't. Instead of having to find a table and wait, Reg was already there. With his usual impatience – defying all the rules about inmates remaining seated while they waited for visitors – he was standing up, hopping from foot to foot, and scanning the visitors as they walked through. I was glad to see him. Although it was only a couple of weeks since we had last met, it felt more like months. He walked quickly across the room and gave me a mighty hug.

Once I'd regained my breath we sat down and talked. He explained what had happened since his arrival and gave us his initial impressions of Wayland. He seemed to be coping well and gradually finding his feet. He had been given a cell on the ground floor, conveniently close to the telephone and the hot-water boiler. Unlike Maidstone, they were not allowed to have kettles in their rooms and could only fill a flask to see them through the long hours of lock-up. There was a reasonable gym and a good exercise yard. The prison, as he'd been warned, was quite volatile. Most of the inmates were serving comparatively short sentences and this created some restlessness. But he stressed he wasn't having any problems; others had been kind and friendly towards him.

The visiting area was very spacious. Each low round table was surrounded by four easy chairs. One of these chairs, the one in which the inmate had to sit, was screwed to the floor; the others could be moved around. There were no internal windows but panels of glass lined the ceiling and sunshine flooded the room. In addition there was the usual bright strip-lighting, so harsh that Reg later took to wearing dark glasses. (He was suffering from cataracts and in a couple of months underwent the first of two successful operations.) Hot and cold drinks could be purchased from a hatch by the door, along with confectionery and ice-creams. The service was friendly and efficient. There was also a play-area for children, a room professionally supervised and full of toys and paints. It made a change from Maidstone where the kids had few facilities; rampaging down the aisles, stubbing toes and running into tables, their afternoons more often than not seemed to end in tears. All in all, the surroundings of Wayland were more comfortable and relaxed.

John, with his customary kindness and discretion, only stayed for about fifteen minutes. After he had left Reg pulled my chair close to his. He put his arm around me and for the first time began to talk at length about the future. There had been nothing to look forward to, he said, before we met; I had given him hope. He told me that he loved me and that this was the first time he had not felt lonely or confused in a relationship. Reg, like myself, was not overly romantic but when he spoke it was from the heart. Sitting beside him that day, listening to him talk, I was sure (perhaps for the first time) that we had made the right decision.

It was less than a week before our long conversations on the phone came grinding to a halt. It began with a faint buzzing on the line. This gradually grew and grew until I could no longer hear Reg at all. British Telecom informed me there were major problems with the lines. They hoped to have it sorted out in a few days. Outside in the street a series of ominously large holes appeared along with an army of engineers. I didn't have a mobile and so had to make the fifteen-minute walk to the nearest phone box at a pre-arranged time. This meant we had to rely on both the phone box being free and Reg being able to get on the phone at his end. It was not an ideal situation and our talks tended to be shorter than normal. On 7 September Reg wrote: 'I felt so sad to leave you all those miles away today on a strange phone. Wish I could have stayed longer too. Since knowing you I could not be without you. My life would be empty. I feel so content since we got married just like a properly important Mr Kray with his wife Rob Kray!! Ha! Ha! I'm serious though. Lou Kane said I've had a spring to my step since being married. I missed talking the day through with you.'

Thankfully, the phones were up and running before too long. In the meantime we made do with one or two conversations a day and lots of letters. On 15 September, after another good visit, Reg wrote: 'You looked more beautiful and radiant today than I have ever seen you. Must be all the laughter we bring each other.'

As Reg grew accustomed to Wayland, the officers began preparing their reports for the next parole review due in spring. Trevor made frequent journeys to Norfolk. He had already begun to organize the representations with our barrister Pete Wetherby. Everyone understood how difficult it was going to be. Neither Reg nor myself had any unrealistic expectations. Release at this stage simply wasn't on the cards. What could be attempted, however, was another move, this time to a 'D'-category or open prison. From there Reg's future would look a lot brighter.

By October 1997 Reg was approaching his sixty-fourth birthday. He knew he was facing an uphill battle and began to have haunting and troubling dreams about the past.

I awoke after dreaming I was in trouble in the East End and I did not like it there or some people in the dream . . . it reminded me how I guess in our subconscious Ron and I were trying to get out and away from the East End and away from most of them there. Ron had more sense of direction on this wish in my opinion. He was first to get my mother a place in the country and I recall he used to say, 'We should have moved years ago'. I once could have bought a beautiful large house in the country near Geoff Allen for four grand which was more money in those days . . . but Frances was against it . . . it never came about. Each time I dream of these way back days it is a bad dream.

There's not a day or night goes by when I do not

regret my situation and wish I was with you but let's
hope and pray it will be so.'

Later that same month he wrote: 'Dreamed of the East
End again – it's always fights and arguments in the dreams
so am glad to open my eyes.' The past, for Reg, was not an
unreservedly happy or glamorous place. He told me he
had often wanted to get away. Even before the death of
Frances, he had tired of the endless East End feuds and
violence. He had good business skills – as he had proved
with the establishment of the Double R Club – but they
were wasted in the petty squabbles and power struggles of
his environment. Ron was not interested in business. The
proceeds were simply a means to an end. For Ron the game
was about power and control. He created conflict in every
area of his life – both personal and professional. To win
was all that mattered. Although Ron talked of retirement he
could not and would not relinquish his position. Reputation,
as always, was everything. And Reg was not an innocent
bystander. He ably contributed to the reputation of the Kray
Twins. As a young man he was equally violent and ambitious. It was only his aims, as opposed to his methods, that
differed from Ron's. Reg imagined a road that would lead
them out of obscurity – and found, instead, only a path to
notoriety.

Trying to understand Reg's life and motivations was like
putting together the pieces of a jigsaw puzzle. What made it
harder was that both Reg and Ron encouraged the myths to
grow around them, obscuring the truth and embellishing
the 'legend'. These provided not just a reason for their
long incarceration but a justification for the decision they
had made at Brixton Prison all those years ago. They could
not languish in prison as simple murderers. They had to be
something more. The truth, as it slowly emerged, told
another story. Although their twinship singled them out, the

Krays were not any more remarkable than many gangsters of their time. Were they more violent than the Richardsons? Were they more feared than Freddie Foreman? Probably not. They were simply different. Their desire for recognition and publicity gave them a unique and ultimately self-destructive profile. By raising their heads above the parapets they not only taunted the authorities but also became the focus of all their attention. Their lust for fame would not go unrewarded.

Under every image lies a living breathing person. Reg's real identity was one that few either saw or wanted to see. Even Reg himself found it hard to disconnect from the alter ego that had been created. Although he frequently questioned who and what he was, he had long ago assumed the public mantle of his reputation. It was that persona that produced respect from his fellow inmates and fascinated the public. Would anyone be interested in another Reg Kray? To admit to confusion and pain, to reveal that he had frequently struggled and suffered through his years in prison, and to confess to regret and disappointment, was to shatter the reputation he was still serving time for – and for which Ron had died.

When Reg talked about always feeling alone in relationships, this was partly the cause. He knew he was rarely loved for himself but only as others wished to perceive him. These perceptions usually encompassed ideas of unlimited wealth, absolute protection and a good deal of reflected 'glory' and 'prestige'. To expose the real Reg Kray was to risk rejection and leave himself vulnerable. On the occasions he did get seriously involved, his trust and confidence were more often than not betrayed. He was used and rejected by many he felt close to. They lied, deceived and blackmailed him. Even when he realized what was happening he remained reluctant to let go – love, even the unrequited variety, was a precious commodity.

Through accepting each other – and all our faults – we found a way forward. Of course it wasn't the perfect relationship. How could it be? But through all the mess and confusion we knew there was something worth fighting for. Love is not a simple emotion. It can't be put in a box and labelled. It is not just about sex or even proximity. Love comes in a thousand different shapes and sizes. It arrives with passion, friendship, need or trust. It can be big or small. It can be wrapped up in tinsel with a red bow. It doesn't matter. All that matters is that it actually exists. At the beginning of November Reg wrote:

Rob – Pinch, punch, first day of the month! I slept at 7.15 p.m. after having tidied up all paperwork etc. Then woke at 10.20 p.m. to a wash, a cup of tea and a roll up. You should smoke to enjoy the occasional fag not for the sake of it. You will enjoy it better too. Thanks for your letter. My world must have been terribly empty and incomplete before I met you, as I know it was when I reflect back . . .

Take care my little one – the world is a much better and brighter place since we met and became betrothed – good word!

Goodnight,
God Bless,
All my love
Reg xxx

By November I had moved away from Norwich to a small town called Watton. Although very quiet it was warm and friendly. I had been warned that people in Norfolk were unwelcoming but found the opposite to be true. During the three years I lived there I was shown nothing but kindness. At Wayland Reg was permitted only three visits a month, compared to six at Maidstone. It surprised me that in a

'C'-category prison, where the inmates are presumably much closer to release, less contact was allowed with family and friends. It was another of those incomprehensible rules of the Prison Service. We always arranged to have at least one visit alone and to try to have some time together at the end of other visits. There were things he couldn't and wouldn't say in company.

Through November Reg remained unsure about Wayland and his place within it. He was never especially happy there. Although generally philosophical about the future he still struggled to rein in his hopes as the parole hearing loomed closer. May 1998 would mark the completion of his thirty year tariff. It was a landmark date. Years ago he had looked towards this moment as an almost impossible destination. Now it had almost arrived, he felt a mixture of emotions.

> 8th November 1997 – 6.45 a.m.
>
> Rob – Been awake since 3.45 a.m.
>
> . . . I find it difficult at times to sort out myself from me in the 1950s, 1960s as to how I am now in personality. Sometimes I slip back as to how I was then . . . it's similar when I try to think back as to how we all were as family – my family, Frances, all of us. It seems as if I've been on two different planets, then and now, which I suppose it is really. Sometimes I feel guilty of my self-survival instinct as though I'm selfish for being a survivor . . . Be nice if we could have a perfect world – but then would it?! Why do we all search so much, that's another question – also at times I feel guilty for being happy.
>
> It's getting close to a world war with Hussein. Hope not . . . must stop these gloomy thoughts and get back to living for the moment. Live for each day – one day at a time.

Take care,
    God bless,
        Husband,
            All my love, Reg
                xxx

                        24th November 1997 – 9.15 a.m.
Rob,
    I will do best to explain. It is combination of facts,
accumulated, not sure really specifically what is making
me so irritable as I had a good afternoon (drinking) yesterday but then today irritable again. It could be a series
of events . . . Then it dawned on me this place is so negative, and most in it, so no real social life. I've tried to be
analytical on all but truthfully not sure what it is –
maybe realization that switch to Gartree was same, no
social life and I'm still in the jungle. Can't get away from
it till out where one is with normal people like milkman
and grocer – also a new dimension now that I could be
released yet so much could happen in between so I
know I'm subconsciously on my toes all the time, never
completely relaxed. Maybe prefer to live like a hermit
till out and ensure, make sure, I get out without it being
jeopardized . . .
    As I write it's like looking in a mirror to find myself.
I've been through these patches before. It's like a personality clash with myself . . . not sure of who I should
settle to be. I think or know that I'm a little gate-happy
for the 8th May . . . I don't usually wish time away but
lately I find myself doing so . . . is all this deep thought
an excuse for something more evident? I don't think I'm
sure myself, hence all this subject matter I write. Maybe
you can figure me out as you usually do?! It would be
helpful. Perhaps when I exhaust theory we can get to the
fact and the root – or you can – even the trying tonight

with you seems to act like a safety valve to some extent.
So let's hope for the answer or answers. I do know I'll
not lose this inner conflict while I'm in jail, that it is part
of a con's life but even more so a lifer's so perhaps we
can only find solution by kicking it around to ease whatever is troubling me. I know I feel a certain frustration.
I guess that's what's making me irritable. I guess it may
be the combined frustration of prison life caught up
with me again as it does from time to time – that must
be the answer.

Thanks for listening. I may post this or save it till
Friday, not sure – indecision is in case it gets in wrong
hands.

All my love, Reg

xxx

The first December in Norfolk passed quietly. Our Christmas gifts to each other were dictated by circumstance. Reg
arranged for twenty red roses to be delivered. He also gave
me a beautifully carved box that had been made inside the
prison. In return there was very little I could give to him.
Prison rules dictated what could and couldn't be received.
At Maidstone I would have sent clothes, T-shirts, jeans, shirts
or trainers. But Wayland didn't allow such items. There
was very little they did allow. As Reg loved music, and
this was one of the few things not prohibited, I bought him
a selection of CDs. It was not the most imaginative of gifts
but he was at least allowed to have them.

We had a visit on Christmas Eve. The room had been dec-
orated and there was even a tree with coloured lights. Reg
turned to look at it again and again. The visiting-hall was
filled to capacity. There was noise, talk and laughter. It was
impossible to be unaffected. Family and friends were gathered for the last time before Christmas Day, determined to
make the afternoon as special as possible. It was like being

in a room full of numerous, connected but individual parties. The children dashed between the chairs, their frantic excitement a reminder of our own distant infancy. Reg was more relaxed than he had been for several weeks but sadder too, as though the festive atmosphere evoked too many sentimental memories.

We talked about what the New Year might bring. There was only one thing on both our minds. Reg leaned forward and took my hand. He said, 'Rob, don't hope for too much. I know what's going to happen.' I looked at him. He shook his head. 'They won't let me out – or give me a move.' I knew he was probably right.

It is the Parole Board that makes the decision as to whether a prisoner is fit to be freed. From a pool of around one hundred people, including judges, magistrates and doctors, a panel of three sits to study the prison reports and assess the risk of release. In the case of mandatory life sentence prisoners the Board then make their recommendation to the Home Office where it can be accepted or overturned. In Reg's case the Home Secretary had not even asked the Parole Board to consider his release, only his de-categorization. The position was clear.

By January all the reports from the Wayland officers had been submitted. They were generally encouraging although most expressed the view that it was difficult to make recommendations based on the short length of time Reg had been in the prison. Had he been moved earlier there would have been greater opportunity to assess his progress. The reports were passed to Reg and his solicitor Trevor Linn. The following are excerpts covering the major points:

Principal Officer Griffin:

BEHAVIOUR IN PRISON
Reginald Kray has settled into the regime at Wayland extremely well, far better than most life sentence prisoners.

He has accepted the restrictions placed on him on a number of occasions without complaint. His response is usually that he will be fine as long as he knows what is expected of him.

A lot has been made of Reginald Kray's public notoriety, both prior to and after being received at Wayland. It is fair to say that this will be hard for him to dismiss. He is a popular man with other prisoners, who attach some importance to being associated with him. Whilst he does not dislike or ignore this attention, he does not court it and, as such, presents very few problems for staff.

ASSESSMENT OF SUITABILITY FOR RELEASE

Release is not an option at this time. Reginald has settled well into the less secure environment at Wayland.

It would be easy for me to state that, due to the short period of time he has served in Category 'C', he is not suitable for open conditions, or if Reginald Kray's behaviour had indicated he could not cope in Category 'C' conditions. This is not the case.

My view on progress is that, if this review had been in six months' time and if the progress being made continues, I would be confident in recommending open conditions.

Personal Officer Burton:

BEHAVIOUR IN PRISON

Since arriving at Wayland, Kray has caused few problems to wing staff. Obviously Wayland has different privileges from Maidstone and he has accepted decisions when items have been taken off him. He is always polite and co-operative with staff and quick to lock-up.

He is still hero-worshipped by many other prisoners

and often has a cell full of people to chat to, although he does not seem to overly encourage this himself.

Kray will always make the best he can from prison and is clever enough never to want for anything. He can be manipulative and devious, but this, as he admits, is his positive attitude to make the most of every day and how he has survived such a long sentence. Because of who he is, there will never be a shortage of prisoners wanting to help him and I am sure that he uses this to his full advantage.

Kray keeps himself very active. He is employed on the General Cleaners' party, uses the gym regularly and spends a lot of time talking to other prisoners and answering the many letters he receives.

ASSESSMENT OF SUITABILITY FOR RELEASE

Given that Kray has only been at Wayland for some two and a half months, it is difficult to assess him as suitable for release, although he has made a positive start here.

It would appear to me, taking into account Kray's attitude and behaviour, he has in fact been suitable Category 'C' material for some time and that, therefore, the closed conditions at Wayland are not different enough to test his readiness for release.

Senior Psychologist D. E. Grayson:

KNOWLEDGE OF THE PRISONER

Before meeting him I had read the documentation available to me, including reports on the offences for which he was convicted and descriptions of the background to them. I have not, however, been through his whole file.

In my opinion, this is a case in which it is important to disentangle the truth from reputation. I suspect that, over the last thirty years, in the popular mind most of the stories of gangland activities have been 'read into' the reputation of the Krays. I recognize that I, too, had loosely ascribed to them at least one notorious violent act committed by another London group during the 1960s.

BEHAVIOUR IN PRISON

Mr Kray appears to have settled well at Wayland. On a day-to-day basis his behaviour appears good and he appears to be a friendly and popular man.

My one experience of him fits with this image. He is a little hard of hearing but I found him to be polite and friendly. I judge him to be more 'at home' talking than listening and I noted that he repeatedly began to respond to my questions well before I had completed them and, at times, this resulted in his 'going off on a wrong tack'. Also I found he would start talking in the middle of what I was saying, sometimes quite moving the topic away as a new thought came into his mind. This sort of behaviour is not unusual on first meeting as, understandably, individuals are eager to get their points across.

Inevitably, I suppose, many prisoners are somewhat in awe of Mr Kray and quite a lot wish to be noticed by him and to be associated with him in some way: he is famous. This attention comes to Mr Kray, he does not have to court it and, as I understand, he responds in a friendly and gentlemanly way. There could be a potential problem here, not necessarily of his own making, if unscrupulous individuals resorted to unacceptable behaviour in order to gain some sort of favour.

From what I have heard of Mr Kray's behaviour here, so far, he seems more keen to make use of any influence he has to help other prisoners than to exploit or use them in any way.

SUITABILITY FOR RELEASE
I do not believe it is possible to form a confident view
on safety in the space of three months, even in circumstances which allow lengthy and regular contact.

Studying the reports it was obvious the prison staff were
generally happy with Reg's progress. One of the most telling
comments expressed by Officer Burton was 'he has in fact
been suitable Category "C" material for some time and that,
therefore, the closed conditions at Wayland are not different
enough to test his readiness for release'. This was partly
echoed by Officer Griffin: 'My view on progress is that, if this
review had been in six months' time and if the progress
being made continues, I would be confident in recommending open conditions.' The review, however, was imminent
and time was running out.

One of the more important reports was that of the psychologist Dr Grayson. Reg, through a history of bad experiences, had a general distrust of prison psychologists. He
was not alone. There is a widespread opinion held among
inmates that these particular professionals cater only to the
whims of the Prison Service and the Home Office. Whether
there is any truth in the allegation is irrelevant. The attitude
is so prevalent that behaviour is automatically altered by it.
Although Reg had agreed to talk to Dr Grayson, he was both
suspicious and defensive, believing that anything he said
would be twisted or used against him. He was reluctant to
discuss his situation openly. Despite the doctor's reasonably
positive report, his refusal to make any kind of recommendation for a move was bound to influence the Parole Board.
In order to gain a fuller and more in-depth analysis Trevor
Linn suggested that Reg was seen by an independent and
reputed psychologist and also by a psychiatrist of equal
standing. Dr Nias, a Chartered Clinical Psychologist, and
Dr Trevor Turner, a Home Office-approved consultant

psychiatrist, were approached to interview Reg. They both agreed.

Despite the emphasis the Prison Service put on psychological reports, no one had ever undergone psychometric testing with Reg. Psychometrics involves the measurement of mental capacities and attributes through the use of psychological tests in intelligence, socialization, and coping strategies. It can help, among other things, to assess the risk of reoffending. Dr Nias interviewed both Reg and myself. His conclusions were as follows:

> The present assessment highlights aspects of Mr Kray's basic temperament. He is very much the extreme Extrovert type. He does not have a neurotic or over-emotional temperament – this should help him in adapting to a new lifestyle.
>
> On a diagnostic test for underlying personality disorder, his score was average so providing no support for previous suggestions of a 'disordered personality'. This is not to say that he has not suffered from mental problems in the past, but it does help to reduce the risk of reoffending. He has a range of appropriate coping strategies at his disposal. This suggests that he has coped well in prison and has not become too institutionalized. This provides evidence for a favourable prognosis. There was no evidence to support previous suggestions of 'denial' as a defence mechanism. On the contrary, he appeared frank and open throughout the present assessment.
>
> On a test of verbal intelligence, he scored above average. As well as being friendly and talkative, he has a wide vocabulary at his disposal. This facility with words may be added to his range of coping strategies in providing a useful resource for dealing with future stressors.

Mrs Kray has abilities to support him and gave evidence of not taking the responsibility lightly. Her personality complements his in certain ways and her intelligence and serious nature bodes well for successfully dealing with future challenges.

The present psychometric approach complements that of previous assessments and provides a number of pointers to support Mr Kray's application for a return to the community.

Dr Trevor Turner also provided a detailed psychiatric report on Reg concluding, 'His current mental state is entirely stable, he has shown no evidence of at-risk behaviours for many years, and he has appropriate insight into his current status. His discharge from prison would involve minimal risk to the community.'

These two reports were added to the papers to be forwarded to the Parole Board. It is doubtful whether their evidence was even examined. The use of independent experts is frowned upon – however high their standing and however better qualified they might be than their prison counterparts. We had deliberately chosen well-respected professionals so the findings would be taken seriously. For either of the doctors to recommend Reg's release had they not believed it to be either safe or appropriate would have reflected badly on their own credibility and reputation. If they had come to the conclusion that Reg was unfit for a return to society they would have been compelled to admit it.

In the hope of gaining some extra support I also contacted the MP Harry Cohen who had previously shown interest in Reg's case. He was sympathetic and wrote a letter directly to the then Home Secretary saying, 'I think that most of the public would agree that although his crimes were awful, he has now effectively served his sentence. He should not be punished beyond that.'

While we waited for the Parole Board to make its decision, Reg's belief that he would get another knockback grew ever stronger. After receiving his quite reasonable reports the attitude of some of the prison staff suddenly, and inexplicably, altered. Although his behaviour remained the same, their attitude towards him hardened. He had two thorough cell spins (searches) in a period of three weeks and was also strip-searched during one of them, a practice that another inmate told him was very unusual. They found nothing. Reg felt they were trying to provoke a confrontation, to push him into a reaction that would adversely affect his review.

In January 1998, for the first time since Charlie's conviction, Reg was offered the opportunity to see him. As he was now a lower category, Reg was the one who had to travel to Long Lartin. He wanted to go but was worried about returning to the prison that held the very worst of memories. His anxiety was tangible. Throughout his twenty-nine years of imprisonment Long Lartin represented the lowest point of his existence. What could he do? What should he do? He asked the same questions over and over. He imagined walking through those doors and being invaded by the paranoia that had once almost destroyed him. To visit was to face his worst demons – to not visit was to let Charlie down. It was a hard decision but, in the end, the present triumphed over the past.

Most of the day was taken up with travelling. It took over three hours to reach Long Lartin and the prison, when he arrived, seemed very different to how he remembered it. Seventeen years had wrought substantial change. It was a relief. He was allowed only two hours with Charlie before he had to begin the journey back. Although they didn't have much time together, the hours they shared were good ones.

When Reg returned he was advised he should apply for a Town Leave. This was, apparently, a necessary requirement for the rehabilitation procedure designated by the Home

Office. It involved spending a short time outside in the presence of a prison officer and was intended to prove that the inmate could cope, or at least learn to cope, with some of the challenges of modern living. Reg submitted his application. It was a nice thought to imagine walking through the streets again.

The Parole Board was due to sit in March although we had no idea of the exact date. There was speculation in the press about the result. The general consensus seemed to be that he had served his time and no further purpose could be achieved by keeping him in prison. Simon Heffer, writing in the *Daily Mail*, said: 'Above all justice must be seen to be done. If a judge decided a man should be punished with 30 years in prison, so be it. Once a man has served those years, and once it is established there is no psychiatric reason for detaining him further, he must be released.' Other papers reported on the psychiatric evaluations and the *Guardian* ran a front-page story outlining their findings. The Prison Service was quick to react, immediately quashing the idea he might be freed. A spokesman said: 'Life-serving prisoners are only ever released from an open prison and we would expect a prisoner to have been at an open prison for a minimum of two years before release. Reggie Kray has only recently been transferred from a Category 'B' prison to a Category 'C'. An open prison would be Category 'D'. So nothing is going to happen overnight.'

Their strong and immediate response was indicative of their intentions. They were not going to let Reg go without a struggle. Despite having served almost thirty years and having his move to a 'C'-category prison delayed by twenty months, they were still insisting on what they referred to as 'normal procedures'. That they had themselves deliberately impeded such procedures was something they chose not to comment on.

During the month of March, although we both felt sure

that nothing was going to change, there was still a small irresistible spark of hope. What if? There was always a chance. A move to an open prison would at least provide a light at the end of a long and very dark tunnel. Reg couldn't resist a glance towards the future. He began to talk about where we might live should something extraordinary happen. If he was transferred then maybe we could find a place to settle in Norfolk or Suffolk. He began to think about life outside. The things that to us seem mundane were to him extraordinary. He liked the idea of supermarkets, of being able to choose. He had never stepped inside such a place in his life. He asked what they were like. Far from being fazed by change, he found it fascinating. Computers, faxes, the internet and mobile phones, although a complete mystery, were advances to be explored rather than feared. Through trips outside, to see Ron or Charlie or even to visit the hospital, he was already aware of the increase in traffic, of motorways and of the faster speed of life in general. Reg was often asked how he would cope with freedom after being in prison for so long. His reply was always the same. 'If I can adapt to an abnormal environment why can't I adapt back to a normal one?' His reply although simplistic was not naïve. Reg was aware that the challenges were of a psychological rather than physical nature. He believed, quite rightly, that the pressures of freedom were less challenging than those of imprisonment. He often wondered what it would be like to simply decide, at any time of the day or night, to go out for a walk, to make a phone call, to eat a meal or take a shower. It is impossible to remain in prison for thirty years and to avoid being institutionalized to some degree but he fought hard to maintain some kind of mental independence, to not be too tightly bound by routines and habit.

On 1 April 1998 Reg returned to the wing after a visit. The time was 4 p.m. He was called to the office on the pretext of discussing his application for a Town Leave. When he arrived he found himself faced with three officers – Governor Martin, Principal Officer King and the internal probation officer. They passed him a piece of paper. In front of them all he had to stand and read the result of his parole review. They sat back and watched. 'The Parole Board has not recommended your release on life licence . . .' It was all he needed to see. He couldn't read anything else. He asked the Governor if it was a 'D'-category knockback as well. Martin acted as if he didn't know the contents. He took the piece of paper from Reg, glanced at it, and said, 'Yes.' They all continued to stare at him. Reg refused to react. He retrieved his statement, said, 'Thanks very much', and left the office. He returned to the wing and got straight on the phone.

By this time there were only a few minutes left before the phones were due to be disconnected. Reg was stunned. He gave me the news and said, 'I'm sorry Rob'. Although we had both expected bad news, when it finally came it seemed worse than either of us had expected. He read out some of the statement but I could barely take it in. I thought I was prepared for the worst – that both of us were – but when it finally happened we were both left floundering.

It was a long wait before the phones came back on at 6 p.m. Hope had been obliterated yet again. It was to be another two years before the next parole review and then, at best, a further two to three years in an open prison. That meant at least five years before we could begin to think about release. Reg would be almost seventy. The mathematics was not lost on him. After an hour and a half alone in his cell to dwell on what had happened, he rang again. He sounded devastated. All the fight and energy had gone. I was equally demoralized. We tried, as best we could, to console each other. He rang me continuously. Other inmates gave him not just their support and sympathy but also the generous gift of many phone cards. As the evening progressed he rallied a little, finding strength through what he always called 'adversity'. It was perhaps the determination, on both our sides, to try to put on a brave face that pulled us through those hours. To give in was to give up. I reminded him of all he had come through in the past, reassuring him that it wasn't the end. He promised, no matter what, that he would keep on going; he wouldn't let me down. I was aware that night of his incredible courage. It may seem, to some people, a strange word to use but courage is not confined to the good and the glorious. Having almost completed his sentence, Reg was suddenly faced with the prospect of at least a further five years in prison; it was like approaching the tape at the end of a marathon and being told he had another fifty miles to run.

The Parole Board's decision was made even harsher in the light of numerous IRA members, many imprisoned for far more heinous crimes, being released under the banner of political expediency. Some convicted terrorists had only served a few years. It was also a time when a number of high-profile paedophiles were given their freedom. Arrogant and unrepentant, there seemed little doubt that they would reoffend. Reg watched them all go free. He never complained about his sentence and always accepted that he must pay the price that society demanded. That debt, however, was beginning to look as if it only applied to him. As opportunity and second chances were offered to thousands of others, Reg continued to be denied. He was not to be allowed the privilege of forgiveness. Simon Heffer wrote in the *Daily Mail*: 'If we as a society believe in justice and the rule of law, we can – whatever we might think of Kray – raise no complaint about his being allowed the liberty for which, over 30 years, he has unquestionably paid.'

So the Parole Board had done their worst, and on April Fools' Day as well. Their timing was perfect. The laugh was on Reg. Except it wasn't a prank; it was a joke of the greatest proportions, perpetrated by a group of faceless officials unwilling or perhaps unable to offer even the tiniest flicker of hope. To compound the misery they had also insisted on the next review being held not in six or twelve months' time but in two years. The message was loud and clear: Reg Kray was not for freeing.

Despite his deep disappointment he tried to stay positive. He knew his future prospects were bleak but refused to wallow in self-pity. He had to find the strength to get through it. When he made his final call he said I mustn't worry about him. It was impossible not to. As the phone went down for the last time and I was left with those familiar words, 'Goodnight, God bless, I love you', I knew he was about to face a very long night.

I couldn't bear to sit and do nothing, imagining what was going through his mind. I rang Trevor Linn to discuss the parole result. We went through it point by point. The document gave four main reasons for their decision: that Reg had admitted drinking alcohol whilst in prison; concerns about 'manipulative and devious attitudes'; a failure to complete 'offending behaviour work'; a failure to undergo a full psychological assessment. The reasons offered were loose and unsubstantiated. They were, in the spirit of the day, almost laughable.

If all inmates were refused parole on the grounds of having drunk illicit alcohol, few would ever leave prison. It was to Reg's credit that he openly admitted it. He could easily have lied. Having never once been disciplined for the offence he was being condemned entirely through his own honesty. The second issue regarding 'manipulative and devious attitudes' was a loose allegation; it came without reference to specific examples. Indeed, Principal Officer Griffin had stated in his report: 'He does not seem to be manipulating beyond the point that is the accepted norm.' Most human beings are guilty of this particular offence – if it can be described as such. Any inmate, like any businessman, politician or lover, will try to make the best of his situation. Reg's admission about the drinking of alcohol contradicted the idea that he was 'devious', an anomaly that the Parole Board unsurprisingly ignored.

The third reason for refusing parole, Reg's failure to complete offending behaviour work, bore all the hallmarks of what could commonly be described as sharp practice. Shortly after arriving at Wayland, Reg had been interviewed by a Lifer Officer who had told him that he did not need to do the course. The dossier given to the Board included the statement from Officer Burton: 'It has not proved realistic, given the length of time that he has served, for Kray to become involved in offending behaviour programmes.' The internal Lifer Review Board held on 20 October 1994 had also claimed that it was 'unrealistic' to undertake offence-based work with Reg after so long. That the Prison Service had failed to offer such courses for the past twenty-nine years was now being used as a stick to beat him with.

The final excuse was the proclaimed lack of a full psychological assessment. In fact the dossier contained two assessments, one commissioned by the Prison Service and the other an independent report by the Senior Lecturer at St Bartholemew's Hospital, Dr Nias. The Board ignored the latter report refusing, or so it would appear, to acknowledge the veracity of his detailed psychometric testing. Such scientific evidence was apparently not applicable unless collected by an employee of the Prison Service.

It was difficult to see what Reg could do to make his next parole review any more successful. He had already agreed to partake in an offending behaviour course but the vague accusations as regards his 'attitudes' were almost impossible to counteract. The admission that he had drunk alcohol would stay on record and future psychological assessments, unless provided by the Prison Service itself, would continue to be disregarded.

I had a long conversation with Trevor. He refused to be downhearted about the result, reminding me, as he so often had before, that Reg's journey towards release was always going to be a long one. Disappointment along the way was inevitable. There were still things that could and should be done. One of the most important was to talk to the media. With their interest at a peak, it was essential to grasp the opportunity to generate debate and test the waters of public opinion. If the public believed that Reg should now be freed it would increase the pressure on the Home Secretary. Trevor himself spoke to the press claiming that the Home Secretary had handed Reg 'a death sentence'. They were dramatic words. He did not realize, as he uttered them, that they would also be prophetic ones.

In the morning Reg rang as soon as the phones were turned on. Sounding exhausted and depressed, he told me his night had been sleepless. The full reality of the decision had finally hit him. Alone, he had descended into despair. 'I had to come to terms,' he said. 'I had to face up to it.' I realized then just how much he had allowed himself to hope. What could I offer in the way of solace? I could only repeat that I loved and believed in him . . . and knew he would never give up. I seriously wondered if this was one blow too many, if he had finally reached the limits of his endurance.

The next few weeks were difficult. Reg's mood swung between optimism and dejection. The main boost to his spirits came from the attention of the media. He had obviously not been forgotten. I gave interviews to several TV and radio stations, as well as the press, trying to expose the injustice of his case. There had been campaigns in the past but their focus had always been vague, the familiar myths too readily reasserting themselves, the same old faces trotting out the same old phrases. As Trevor insisted, we needed to concentrate on the actual issues – that Reg had almost completed the thirty years laid down by the trial judge, that he was not at risk of reoffending, and that his release would not erode the public's confidence in the judicial system.

It was nerve-wracking sitting in front of a camera for the first time. What if I said the wrong words? What if I came across so badly that I damaged Reg's cause? All these things and worse flew through my mind. Somehow I managed to get through the interview and to cover the major points. Although I was glad when it was over, I was also glad that I'd done it. For the first time since Reg's knockback I felt I'd achieved something useful. The evening news programmes ran the story and there were phone polls in London and Norfolk. The results were good. Over 85 per cent of people believed it was time to release him. It gave a boost to Reg's confidence exactly when he needed it.

The amount of mail Reg received also increased dramatically. The support was incredible. Letters poured in from all over the country. The majority of these were not from Kray 'fans' but from members of the public who strongly believed that he was being treated unfairly. They understood Reg had committed terrible crimes but also thought that he had paid the price for them. It was, perhaps as much as anything, a matter of comparisons. Justice had to be the same for everyone. There couldn't be one set of rules for Reg Kray and another for everyone else.

Although the support was gratifying, we still struggled with the knowledge that he was as far away as ever from freedom. I felt a sense of utter powerlessness. The future seemed out of our control. Despite the media coverage and the public response, I suspected that nothing I did would ever make a real difference. We were both hit by crises of confidence. He couldn't believe that he would ever be freed and I felt distressed and guilty that I couldn't do more to help. There were good days and bad but Reg's irrepressible spirit was rarely extinguished for long. We took comfort from each other and at the end of the month, as he approached the

thirtieth anniversary of his imprisonment, he wrote the
following:

> Rob, Thanks so much for your letter. It brought back
> hope when I felt a little like a candle without a flame. All
> this I will explain to you when I see you. Stay strong,
> positive and happy.
>> Thanks for your smile.
>>> God bless. All my love.
>>>> Husband Reg xxxxx

8 May brought a second burst of interest from the media.
Thirty years in prison was certainly something to talk about.
It was just over a month since the Parole Board's decision
and the papers continued to be critical. Richard Stott, writing in the *News of the World*, said: 'The reasons given by the
Parole Board for refusing to release Reggie Kray or even send
him to an open prison are spurious and cowardly . . . He is
a victim of a spineless conspiracy designed to prevent Jack
Straw having to make a decision about his release.' Lord
Tebbit in the *Mail on Sunday* also joined in the debate. His
column, entitled *'If only Reggie was in the IRA'*, continued
'. . . so many murderers are in and out of jail in less time than
it takes to change your socks . . . it does not just look hard, it
stinks of injustice. Poor old Reggie – perhaps he didn't kill
enough people to qualify for parole even after 30 years.'
Simon Heffer, writing again in the *Daily Mail*, called it 'an
affront to the rule of law . . . The latest excuses wheeled out
for his incarceration are comical.'

At the beginning of June Reg had the opportunity to go
and see Charlie again at Long Lartin. This time the visit
would last for a week. It came at a good time, offering a
change of scene and some different company. He was feeling
unwell but thought it was down to the stress of the parole
hearing. Although their differences had never been fully

resolved, he and Charlie wrote to each other regularly. Charlie also rang me every week; he was always pleasant and
friendly. Sadly, we never met until he was seriously ill in hospital. I was glad that Reg was going. He needed a break from
the familiar routines of Wayland and a chance to talk to
Charlie properly. Although he was only going to another
prison it would be an escape of sorts. Reg wrote the following letter while he was away:

Rob –
      Just had sardines and bread, also chocolate. This
place is better than Wayland much more relaxed. Charlie was pleased with food I bought. Someone made a
nice cake for Charlie and I. Charlie got his Enhanced*
tonight.
      Glad Donna is seeing Goombah for his birthday.
Thanks for letter. You are the only person who is on
same wavelength as I. We are compatible all round I
figure. We'll have a good talk you and I next Friday.
There is so much more we have yet to know about each
other which makes it a good adventure.
      I need these days here. I can tell by my stomach I
need a good rest.
      We can go out after 10 p.m. By pressing the buzzer
the door opens so we can use recess and in morning I
can shower about 6.30 a.m. or 7–7.30 a.m. by same
method. Place has changed a little since I was here 17
years ago. I'll speak to Trevor on the 10th June.
Charlie's birthday is 9th July.
      Thanks for all you do for me – you know I love you
so much – the poem you sent me is so beautiful and
apt.

* Inmates, according to their behaviour, are given a status of basic, standard or enhanced, the latter providing extra privileges that vary from
prison to prison.

I'll see Eddie Richardson in gym tomorrow. Not seen him since I was in Leicester with him around about 70–71 year. Nice small cell I got here. Staff from Wayland who brought me were good and sociable – two with a driver in a van. I prefer a van for comfort. Took us five hours – normally takes three hours. Charlie not working tomorrow or any more this week. I forgot to tell you tonight can't phone you till 11.30 a.m.

Goodnight
    God bless
        All my love,
            Reg xxxxx

Reg was happy with the visit and came back more relaxed. For a while the brothers seemed on better terms. The old arguments, although still unresolved, were at least on temporary hold. Peace reigned and everyone was happier for it. The issue of Charlie's books would not remain buried forever but Charlie had neither the power nor the inclination to instigate any changes – he had other things to worry about. His health, like Reg's, was slowly deteriorating.

Sometimes Reg enjoyed the rather frantic atmosphere of Wayland where there was always something happening, always cons dashing through the corridors, always news and gossip. Other times he found it wearing. He used to say, 'I must be getting old!' His illness was starting to slow him down and he found it an effort to exercise or train. His stomach was the source of increasing discomfort. The prison doctor had diagnosed IBS (Irritable Bowel Syndrome) and prescribed Milk of Magnesia and Fibrogel. Neither improved his condition. Shortly after his return from Long Lartin he wrote: 'I dreamt of Ron and woke and all my left chest had a kind of feeling as though it had been pressed on around the area, so I'm going to go special sick in the morning – I was already considering going for a check on my stomach. I woke about 1.15 a.m. and made a cup of tea and had a smoke. I'm going to start walking more and take care of my health.'

That first year in Wayland, despite or maybe even because of the parole result, strengthened our relationship. We had to rely on each other not just for support and understanding but also for the motivation to keep going. The other essential ingredient was trust. Before leaving Maidstone Reg had become increasingly disillusioned with many of his outside 'friends'. His name was constantly being used to promote the dubious reputations of others. I realized shortly after meeting Reg that he was at the centre of many people's worlds – but rarely out of love or affection. A circle of acolytes jostled for his attention, pushing and shoving, each determined to seek a more important place in this bizarre solar system. Lies, rumour and gossip were common currency. Jealousy was rife. The atmosphere was one of perpetual confusion and suspicion. Those who genuinely wanted to help often despaired, stepped back and just gave up. Good people like Frank Haines, Liz and Steph, who had always done their best, gradually lost touch. I was sorry to see them go. I made a conscious decision to stay away from it all and to that end, unless it was unavoidable, neither talked nor socialized with most of the remaining crowd. After our marriage Reg broke away from them. He wanted a new start. His decision was hardly welcome and blame was quickly apportioned. It was as if after years of negotiation, sly manoeuvrings and occasional takeover bids, they had suddenly been thwarted by an unexpected merger.

Shortly after Reg's parole result I received a nine-page letter from Pete Gillett. He was back in prison for handling stolen goods. Reg, after their falling-out, had maintained intermittent contact. It was a long and rather rambling communication in response, or so it seemed, to an offer from Reg to send him £20. I had only talked to Pete on a couple of occasions and was surprised to hear from him . . . and especially at such length. He was still resentful that Ronnie had once called him a 'ponce' and claimed (incorrectly) that ever since that time he had refused to accept any money from Reg. However, he stressed that he wasn't now trying to keep this up and was only declining the offer on the grounds that Reg must be broke as 'if he could really afford it, Reggie would send me more'. He talked about how close they had been and how (as opposed to why) Reg had ceased to trust him. His complaints were detailed and numerous, especially against some of the Krays' former associates. He harboured a wide array of grievances. One of these was against Ron's old friend Joe Pyle with whom he had once been arrested on drug charges. Gillett subsequently received a five-year sentence. He also had a few things to say about Kate Kray. The letter contained various allegations, confessions and expressions of discontent. It ended with the declaration that he respected and supported me for 'taking his place'.

When I received the letter I was not only trying to cope with the parole result but also right in the middle of attempting to respond to it. I barely knew Pete Gillett and was somewhat disturbed at being the recipient of his emotional outpourings. They seemed symptomatic of everything I had been trying to avoid. Knowing that Reg had long ago ceased to confide in him, I wasn't sure what he was hoping to achieve. Reg was equally bemused – and suspicious of his motives. I didn't write back.

Reg began to concentrate on, and consolidate, the friendships that he felt were important. Every three months there were additional and distinctive visits called Family Days. These started at 10 a.m. and continued until 4 p.m. A light lunch could be bought from the canteen and inmates were allowed to walk freely around the room. There were few facilities but the atmosphere was calm and relaxed. As the minimum requirement of visitors was three and Reg had no other close family members (Charlie being in prison), he was allowed to fill the numbers with friends. Donna Allardyce, Tony and Tracey Mortimer, and Adam Myhill, a young boxer, were all regular guests. Reg was permitted to wear his own clothes and, dressed in a casual tracksuit, was more comfortable than in the regulatory blue jeans and shirt. More than anything, he enjoyed the shared midday meal. He usually ate his lunch alone and in his cell. Sitting together, chatting and laughing, eating baked potatoes, salad and rolls, he would look around the table and smile. 'This is just like being outside, isn't it?'

Whatever my general opinion of Wayland, I did appreciate those days. Reg loved them too. They gave us the opportunity to spend a lot more time in each other's company – and to talk without the usual pressures. After one of these visits, in the middle of June, he wrote:

Rob – I hope you are listening to Radio 2, it's beautiful. I feel so content in that I have you. Soon as I banged up I thought about what you said and wrote lyrics for you.

I feel more content today than I ever have – thanks to you. It has taken 64 years to reach a state of content in my frame of mind – you have bridged that gap. Decided to take night off and relax with you. Going to read newspapers now – just relax – enjoy my contentment. Just wish I could do more for you.

God bless,
All my love,
Reg xxx

P.S. I'm writing this as half-light coming through the shaft of my window. Just a thought – I reckon everyone should wake at dawn and sleep at dusk!

10. PILING ON THE PRESSURE

In the early summer of 1998, in the wake of the parole decision, there was a disturbing development. Official papers were leaked to Trevor Linn suggesting that one of the reports had been tampered with and that Reg had been misled by prison officials as to what he had to do to secure his release. The documents suggested that an original and sympathetic assessment of Reg had been altered before being forwarded to the Board. While it had originally been stated that, 'celebrities . . . sought to ingratiate themselves with the Krays', the inference was changed to how the Krays sought to ingratiate themselves with celebrities. References to the fact that Reg had demonstrated that he was in control of his drinking had been removed along with various other positive comments. Most seriously a reported conversation with two prison officers at Wayland, in which they allegedly claimed that whatever they said or did would be of no consequence as a decision on Reg's future had already been taken at a political level, was also omitted.

Trevor wrote to the Home Secretary expressing disquiet and asking for another review – one where *all* the original evidence could be considered. It was not the first letter he had written to Jack Straw but, as with all the others, he received no direct answer. Instead his request was forwarded to the

Lifer Review Unit at the Home Office. They replied that they had made enquiries about the report in question and that there were 'no doubts in regard to its authenticity'. They claimed the Secretary of State accepted it as a 'valid document' and was 'not minded' to refer Mr Kray's case back to the Parole Board. However, they did claim it would be 'helpful' if Trevor could let them know how he had acquired the document!

The *Guardian* newspaper ran a large article entitled 'Kray Cheated of Parole, Says Lawyer'. It concluded with a response from Reg: 'If it reveals anything, it's that Jack Straw and the prison service need no lessons from me on being manipulative and devious.'

It is often hard when hopes have been raised and then dashed to carry on as usual. Although we both tried not to dwell on what had happened, we still experienced all the usual emotions – anger, disappointment and resentment. An injustice had been covered up and there was nothing we could do about it. For Reg it had the effect of increasing his mistrust in everyone connected to the Prison Service. Further events reinforced his belief that he was 'going nowhere fast'. He had been told before leaving Maidstone that he could expect a Town Leave after eight months at Wayland. Several of these leaves were normally followed by Home Leaves where we would have the opportunity to spend some private time together. This was normal procedure for anyone approaching the end of a long sentence. He was disappointed but not surprised when he was called before the Lifer PO and told that his application had been turned down. Eighteen months later a second request was also rejected. This was on the recommendation of the police who claimed that it could lead to 'large crowds and public disorder' which would not be in the interest of the public, the Prison Service or Reg himself. Such concern for Reg was certainly touching! Quite where all these large crowds were supposed to come from was a mystery. An officer could have taken Reg out anywhere, on any day, and the chances of his being recognized would have been minimal. By refusing to allow leave they were denying Reg the opportunity to prove he could cope in the outside world and eroding his chances at the next Parole Board hearing.

The next obstacle was connected to the Board's demand that Reg should take an Offending Behaviour course. Through this he was supposed to address his actions of over thirty years ago. Despite former prison reports claiming that such a course was now unrealistic, Reg agreed to take part. It is usual practice to give an inmate at least a day's warning before the class begins so he can have some time to mentally prepare. Reg, however, was informed that the class was starting when he was on his way to the gym. He went straight there but was turned away on the grounds that he was 'unsuitably dressed'. He was told to return to his cell and get changed. By this time Reg was thoroughly bemused and tried to argue his point. What difference did it make if he was wearing a tracksuit or a pair of jeans? How was he supposed to know about the course if no one had informed him about it? He was told he had an unreasonable attitude and wouldn't be allowed back into the class. He returned to the wing in a state of frustration. A few minutes later he rang me. Angry and upset, he explained what had happened. He had been prepared to do what the Parole Board requested but felt he had been deliberately thwarted. He said: 'It doesn't matter what I do – or try to do – it's always going to be the same.'

It was a further six months before Reg was eventually accepted on another Offending Behaviour programme. It is to his credit that he didn't just give up and walk away. This time he completed the three-day class – but not without sacrifice. On the morning of the final day he was informed that he also had an appointment with the hospital about his stomach. If he attended the hospital he would miss the last day of the course and automatically be failed. He had to make a choice. Having been ill for so long, it was both unfair and unreasonable. The tutor wrote: 'Reg ... demonstrated a high degree of motivation for the course by cancelling an appointment for outside hospital in order for him to complete all sessions. He participated well in all aspects of the group making relevant contributions to discussions that were beneficial to everyone. His ready acceptance of course material and his ability to apply it to himself showed us that he benefited from attending.' Although Reg might have benefited a lot more from going to hospital, the priorities of the Prison Service were obvious. Courses were more important than health. Reg had demonstrated his commitment at the expense of his own well-being. It was a high price to pay.

In addition to coping with all these problems, Reg faced another difficulty. His old friend Paul Marcus had been released and was asking for financial help. Reg was not in the best of circumstances but managed to scrape some money together. This continued for weeks with Reg borrowing small and large amounts from everyone he knew. Reg was worried that if he didn't help Paul would turn to crime and end up in prison again. For Reg it was another of those familiar Catch-22 problems – damned if he helped and damned if he didn't.

The one thing Reg tried to maintain was optimism for those he cared for. He believed that with trust and support Paul Marcus could eventually sort his life out. When Paul fell out with his mother, Reg arranged for him to stay with friends in various parts of the country. They were arrangements that invariably ended in disaster and acrimony. Paul's demands were too great for anyone to deal with. I respected Reg's good intentions but, along with others, he often suffered for them. The constant stress and strain only added to the pressure he was already under. It was all to get worse over the following months.

On 14 July 1998, we celebrated our first wedding anniversary. It had been a year of mixed emotions – love and despair, hope and disappointment. It had also been a year that had brought us closer together. That is not to say we didn't have our rows. We could both be obstinate but I learnt early on that it was pointless to get into a battle of wills – Reg never liked to lose an argument. He was happy, however, to discuss anything and everything; he only became intransigent when others were unprepared to talk. Our differences were quickly resolved and within half an hour peace was usually restored. On the day, Reg sent red roses, cards and a letter. He wrote: 'I don't want you to be down for me. Although many may try to exploit me and have done, I figure I'm still better off than them. The reason why is that I reckon I am loved more! Let's dream together. Happy Anniversary.'

It was hard to believe twelve months had passed so quickly. Reg still rang as often as he could and we probably spent more time talking than most married couples. His first call came at around 8.20 a.m., just after he was unlocked and before he had his shower and breakfast. It was reassuring to hear his voice again. There was always the dread, however irrational, that something bad had happened in the night. He'd tell me what he'd done after evening lock-up, what letters he'd read, who he'd written back to, and even what he'd listened to on the radio. An hour or so later, depending on his cleaning duties, he would ring again. From midday to 2 p.m. Reg was locked up for the lunch period. Mail was usually received late morning and so he went quickly through the next influx of post, taking out the more important letters and putting the rest aside to be read later. He rarely slept well or for long at night so would often take the opportunity of a nap and get his head down for an hour. Sometimes, if his stomach had been giving him trouble, he would sleep for the whole two hours.

It was quieter in the afternoons and I'd get on with my

own labours, completing any freelance work I might have, typing up the latest sheets for *A Way of Life*, and organizing campaign material. After every period of lock-up Reg would phone immediately. The first afternoon call came in at just after two. 'How are you? What have you been doing?' It was impossible to feel lonely with such constant contact. Reg liked to keep busy and that usually meant I was kept busy too. It suited us both. He was always searching for new challenges, for ideas that would stimulate and motivate him. Without one or two projects on the go he quickly became bored and dispirited. I helped him as much as I could. It was a difficult situation because almost everything Reg aspired to was potentially damaging. The Prison Service preferred him out of the public eye – out of sight and out of mind. Although they encouraged inmates to express themselves with creative writing courses, poetry readings and art classes, when Reg put pen to paper he was accused of 'courting notoriety'. He went ahead anyway. After thirty years of grinding routine, he knew it was the only way he could survive. It was a question of sanity.

The second period of lock-up at Wayland was between 4.30 p.m. and 6 p.m. After this, the evening meal was served. Reg usually gave most of his away. He preferred to eat later, having a cup of soup or a sandwich in his cell. The evenings for Reg were a mixture of work and social activities. Sometimes he spent an hour with Bill Taylor dictating more of the book. It must have been hard for Bill to keep up with the pace of Reg's reminiscences and it was good of him to help out and to give his time so generously. I doubt if *A Way of Life* would ever have been finished without his assistance. After Reg had finished working he'd dash down to the phone and tell me the areas they'd covered, the things he'd remembered – some funny, some sad – and how many pages they'd completed. I always liked those evening calls. Reg was usually more relaxed, winding down at the end of the day. Even though it was the time for association, for mixing with the other inmates, he still rang frequently to share his thoughts and any snippets of news and gossip he may have picked up! If he had enough phone cards he would ring round other people too and then call back to tell me what they'd said. Occasionally he played a game of table-tennis or pool but mostly he preferred to chat. His penultimate call came at around 8.10 p.m. The phones were turned off at 8.30 p.m. and there were sometimes queues. He'd claim it was the last call and we'd say our goodbyes and exchange our good-nights. But then, inevitably, he'd manage to ring again, a final thirty-second exchange of words before the plug was pulled and nothing remained but the harsh and insistent dialling tone. That moment never failed to be shocking. I knew that Reg would be walking back to his cell, closing the door and facing the next twelve hours alone – just as he had done for the last thirty years.

The latter months of 1998 were hard for him. Another year stretched ahead before the next parole review. The stresses and strains, on top of his worsening health, all combined to increase Reg's frustration. He was convinced that certain people, including some of his old associates, didn't want to see him released. A constant stream of books, interviews and so-called revelations were providing extra fodder for an ever-hungry and eager Home Office. At the end of August he wrote, 'We have seen some people in their true colours of late. Good to know the score – now more than ever you can see why I have always wished to leave that way of life – Ron hated it too.'

Although Reg got on well with his fellow inmates, there were times when everything got on top of him. Wayland was a prison with a fast turnover – here today and gone tomorrow. Apart from a few good mates, among them Richard Reynolds, Danny Woollard and Bill Taylor, there was little real friendship or loyalty. Advantage was often

taken and principles easily forgotten. After one bad evening
he wrote:

> I listened to tales today of this way of life and I realized
> that there is only one good place. That is out there. It's
> a sickening re-cycle that goes on and so sordid . . . people
> out to score and just a sea of faces – hardly any
> sincerity except when they have a drink or whatever.
> Done a lot of thinking today – tonight – good sober
> thoughts and this is best. I owe too much to you to
> allow for slip-ups. To think I've been so long in this
> way of life – would not like to be at the start. Glad most
> is behind me.

The approach to Christmas was filled with uneasiness.
Charlie was up on appeal, Paul was back in trouble, and
Bradley was waiting to hear if he would be released.
Through all the problems, difficulties and emotional upsets,
the one thing that rarely deserted Reg was his sense of
humour. If all else failed there was always laughter. As
another cold winter in Norfolk threatened to freeze his
assets, he asked if I could send him some warm underwear.
I duly bought and delivered. It took a week for the items to
pass through prison reception. He received them late one
evening and rang and thanked me. They were ski thermal
undies but unfortunately the size was a little less generous
than it might have been. Later that same night, after lock-up,
he wrote: 'Rob – me dear – the long johns would fit a midget
– I just put them on – I look like Rudolph Nureyev!'

There was at least something to dance about. On
24 October Reg celebrated his sixty-fifth birthday and also
his official retirement from work. His cleaning duties were
finally over. After thirty years' hard labour, he was now a
man of leisure. He submitted a request form to Governor
Orton asking for recognition of his faithful service – in

the form of a gold watch! The Governor, with equal good humour, declined on the grounds he was not technically an employee of the Prison Service. Reg, laughing, said to me: 'This lot won't take responsibility for anything!'

There was additional good news a week before Christmas. Bradley was finally released; he had served over eight years. Reg was relieved and happy for him. With a loving wife, a nice home and the luxury of freedom he could look forward to a better and brighter future. Although his own destiny remained ambiguous, Reg tried his best to stay optimistic. Christmas was never the easiest of times.

23rd December '98

Rob – Thanks for making my Xmas for me. Also a good start to New Year. I owe it all to you and so much more. I just wish you and I had met outside. We would have been so happy . . . though as I said I'm more content and happy than I have ever been thanks to you so it's best we count our blessings. It's the lesson in life I've learnt most. We have so much to look forward to in the New Year and we have the challenge of stopping smoking.

I'm just listening to Silent Night on Radio 2. It's beautiful, so Xmas in tradition. If anyone loves it will mean so much to them – maybe, sad to say, some people don't know the true meaning of love.

I had my cowboy meal of beans. Over the years it has helped me sometimes to think I'm a cowboy – always a sunset for the showdown. Maybe if I retain the childlike frame of mind I'll stay younger! There's a lot to do yet and a few challenges – and I'm glad you are on my side. I need you after a lifetime of searching for someone other than my family who are no longer here physically – you are that someone. Thanks for being there.

I love you.
Goodnight.
God bless
All my love,
Reg xxxxx

It is hard to say exactly why Christmas Day 1998 was so much worse than previous ones. It was perhaps a combination of events and circumstances. This was the first Christmas after the completion of his tariff and the conclusion of a terrible parole review. Twelve months before, there had been a sliver of hope. Now, facing another four years minimum, another four festive seasons, Reg's freedom seemed as remote as ever. Age and ill-health added to his despair. It was his thirtieth Christmas in prison.

We talked at length on the phone. He had spent so long looking ahead, looking forward to *this* time – the year, theoretically, when he would be freed – that it was hard for him to come to terms with what was actually happening. He was still in prison . . . and that was where he was staying. He kept thinking back to the years at Parkhurst. At the beginning of his sentence he had never believed that he could or would survive thirty years. Somehow he had endured it. At what price? Frances was dead. Ron was dead. He had lost his mother and father. Charlie was back in prison. He knew he had used the same determination that had shaped his criminality to survive his long imprisonment. His will to live seemed almost shameful. He felt especially bad about his mother and everything she'd endured. For all her love and support she had received in return only pain and grief. After their conviction Violet's life had not been easy; only a few friends stayed loyal. Reg, Ron and Charlie were initially held in three different prisons and the offers of lifts, and any other sort of help, gradually dried up. No one needed to impress any more. The boys were not coming out for a very long time. She had to make the long and always exhausting journeys to Parkhurst, Durham and Chelmsford by public transport. Some people felt free to vent their spleen and the abuse wasn't limited to the vocal – a few bricks also found their way through her windows. His mother spent the rest of her life being punished for the crimes of her sons.

When the phones were turned off that Christmas Day the silence was absolute. All that was left was the memory of his voice, quiet and flat. The only other time I had known Reg to be so down was after the parole review. This was much worse. The long night stretched ahead. We were both alone. He told me later that he went to his cell, locked up, and stood by the window in the darkness. He put his hands through the bars. It was raining.

25th December 1998

Rob –

Thanks to you I had good night – without you I would have been shattered.

I dreamt that a helicopter landed and shanghaied me to another jail, and then dreamt I saw Ron die of heart attack. They were bad dreams. At lunchtime I slept a short while and felt terribly lonely and empty – I did thinking and said a prayer . . . and I shed a few tears which made me feel better.

Now we must start every day as a new year as you said tonight. My thoughts are with you. Hope you have good night and we have good day tomorrow.

Goodnight,

God bless,

All my love,

Reg xxxxx

We emerged rather shaken from the Christmas period. Reg, as always, tried to get himself back on his feet and to put it all behind him. We have to look forward, he said. He knew there was nothing to be gained from regrets or despair. Despite his best attempts, he never quite recovered. It was as if something had splintered inside him. He had faced too many demons. He had not given up but a part of him had given in.

There was at least some consolation on entering 1999 – we were another year closer to the next parole review. There was encouraging media interest. In February the *Sun* newspaper ran a front-page article claiming Reg was 'fit to be free' and an opinion poll in which its readers voted overwhelmingly that Reg should be released. It gave him a bit of confidence. The major regional newspaper, the *Eastern Daily Press*, ran a follow-up story shortly after. Since Reg had moved to Wayland they had followed his progress closely. They asked me for a response to the *Sun* poll and I said, not without anger: 'This is a Government that claims it is tough on crime . . . but it seems to be a government that is just tough on Reg Kray. If this Government thinks it reflects the feelings of the people it should look at how people reacted to this poll. They are behind Reg and think he has suffered enough.'

Mail was still coming in from the public and the extra publicity created another surge. Hundreds of letters began arriving every week. I wrote back expressing thanks for their support and asking them to forward questions and opinions to their MPs and the Home Office. Many of them sent the replies they received from their MPs back to me. Coming from so many different MPs the responses were eerily identical – same phrases, same sentences, same paragraphs, and on numerous occasions, even the same *entire* letter. Instruction had obviously descended from above. All responsibility was shifted to the Parole Board. Without its recommendation (they claimed in unison) the Home Secretary was unable to authorize Reg's release. There was nothing they could do about it. What they all knew, but failed to acknowledge, was the fact the Board was unable to even consider Reg's release without permission from Jack Straw – permission that had been categorically denied.

Whatever the result, we were both grateful for the effort and determination that so many members of the public showed. Every correspondent made an important contribution. Every letter was a further reminder to Reg that we were not fighting alone, and a further reminder to the Home Office that he had not been forgotten.

February was also the month of that least-wanted of birthdays – my fortieth! I could remember as a school-girl looking ahead and imagining what I'd be doing when I reached that distant age of grey-haired decrepitude. Of course I would have had a career, got married, had children – followed all the conventions. At forty I would be sitting in my slippers, knitting cardigans and waiting for my teeth to drop out. Had anyone had the power to look into the future, I would not have believed it.

We had a visit booked for the afternoon. During the morning he had forty red roses delivered. In the post there were cards including two from Reg and a short letter. He wrote: 'Have happy thoughts on your birthday, the day you get this note. We could be together some time in the not too distant future, then we can have the luxury of time on our side.' It is hard to look back and to recall reading those words. Neither of us knew just how quickly time was slipping away.

Reg was waiting when I arrived, standing up as always, shifting from foot to foot and watching the visitors as they passed through the door. He dashed across the room. He gave me a hug and a kiss and wished me a happy birthday. We sat down. There was a large envelope on the table. He picked it up and passed it to me. Inside was a pretty mock-Fabergé egg. It had been made in the prison by another inmate. About three inches in height and hinged at the side, it opened to reveal two photographs – his and mine.

It was a quiet day at Wayland. The visiting hall only filled up at weekends and Christmas. There were probably about twelve tables in use, occupying less than half the room. Reg and I sat talking. Speaking quietly, inches from each other, we were oblivious to anything or anyone else. It happened with such speed that we were both taken by surprise. The rear doors opened suddenly and disgorged half a dozen prison officers. Aware of the disruption, I glanced round. They seemed to be coming straight for us. I barely had time to think before one of them had slammed into the back of my chair and thrown me forward. Reg grabbed hold of me. They passed us by and surrounded a nearby table. There was shouting and struggling. The inmate was overpowered and dragged, kicking and screaming, out of the room. His visitor was also escorted, although by more moderate means, out of the visiting area. It seemed unreal, like a fictional sequence from a Tarantino film. After it was over there was complete silence in the room. Everyone understood why they'd been taken – some kind of transaction, probably drugs, had been picked up by the cameras – but no one understood the necessity for such force. Reg still had his arms around me. I became aware of the children. Some had sought comfort from their parents but others continued to stand apart, solemn wide-eyed infants receiving their first lesson in gratuitous violence.

It was all part of the way of life Reg had come to detest. The day-to-day squalor was bad enough but when it spilled over into visits he found it unbearable. That this had happened on my birthday made it even worse. Gradually, the conversation around us restarted. Although everyone tried to make the most of the hour they had left, the atmosphere was inevitably altered. Voices rarely rose above a murmur. There was no more laughter. None of the children returned to the play area. Everything was subdued. We were quiet too. What had begun as a celebration ended in solemnity.

Temporary escape was broken, as it so often was, by harsh reality.

Leaving Wayland that February afternoon I was more determined than ever to try to change things. Fortunately, interest in Reg's plight was increasing. I was approached by Anglia TV about a half-hour documentary and then later by an independent production company wanting to make a longer programme for Channel 4. I've never believed in the adage that all publicity is good publicity but at this point it seemed there was little to lose and everything to gain. I discussed the proposals with Reg and Trevor. Reg left the final decision up to us. We both agreed that we were happy to co-operate with anyone prepared to take a serious look at the issues. We weren't looking for a whitewash. All we wanted was a factual and open investigation as to why Reg was still in prison, an exploration of the reasons proffered by the authorities, and an examination of whether those reasons were justified. For so many people Reg Kray was just a name from the past, a name synonymous with crime and violence. The man behind the myth had completely disappeared. After thirty years in prison he had ceased to be anything other than his reputation. The most important question of whether it was *right* or *just* for his sentence to continue indefinitely was never being asked.

In these documentaries Reg was not permitted to contribute or to speak for himself; both producers asked permission from the Home Office for an interview but were turned down. Article 10 of the European Convention on Human Rights says: 'Everyone has the right to freedom of expression. This right shall include freedom to hold opinions and to receive and impart information and ideas without interference by public authority.' Unfortunately this right had not yet been extended to British subjects. Under the rule of British law, Reg was not allowed to talk to the media. Jack Straw, although perfectly free to speak, chose to forgo the privilege. When asked for his opinion he refused to comment.

Reg was not the only lifer without answers. A joint report by the HM Inspectorates of Prisons and Probation published in 1999 reported that about 60 per cent of inmates jailed for life were being kept in prison around six years beyond their tariff. The failure to prepare lifers for release was described as having 'serious natural justice implications'. The inspectors also expressed concerns about the inconsistent quality of many of the prison assessments.

We had no editorial control over either of the documentaries. I was interviewed and allowed to put my point of view. After that, it was down to the producers. They made their own decisions as to whose opinions they wished to include. Anglia, who had a much shorter time-slot, concentrated more on local angles and local responses. Although not especially in-depth, it asked some pertinent questions and was a well-balanced piece. AVP, who were making the programme for Channel 4, interviewed a wider range of people. The end result was interesting but not quite what we'd expected. There was a lot of emphasis on the past and little on the present. On first viewing I thought they had concentrated more on the crime than the punishment. It was perhaps an unfair judgement to make. Without direct access to Reg himself, it was difficult for them to provide an accurate portrayal of the man he had become. The good thing about both documentaries was that they raised public awareness and opened the subject up for debate.

There was an inevitable downside. Although the authorities were unable to prevent Reg watching the Anglia programme, shown early in the evening, they categorically refused permission for him to watch a video of the Channel 4 documentary broadcast after lock-up. As he had not directly contributed to either programme he had not broken any rules and could not, legally, be penalized. They made it clear, however, that they were not happy about the publicity. The only unofficial punishment they could inflict was to deny him access to a discussion of his own case.

They were not alone in their discontent. Pete Gillett was also unhappy – for different reasons. He wrote to Reg complaining about his exclusion from the Channel 4 documentary. Claiming he was a 'veteran of such programmes' and, as such, should have been consulted, he accused Reg of deliberately omitting him because he was worried about what he might say. Gillett's accusations were unfounded. The makers of the programme did in fact go to talk to him but chose not to include him in the final documentary.

By this time there was little left of their original friendship. They hadn't met for years. Gillett berated Reg saying he 'wrote nothing of importance' and asking him to provide more information. Reg found the request, as he had found his letter to me, suspicious. Despite their rift Gillett was still insistent that Reg should express some feelings for him: 'It's a bit strong that I have to force any emotional commitments from you. You can't even say "Pete I like you a lot, as a dear friend."' Gillett's letters were full of rumours, allegations and gossip. He claimed in one that he had 'heard' I disliked Bradley – because I suspected the nature of his relationship with Reg. If he had hoped to create a stir he was sadly disappointed. Reg had revealed the nature of *all* his relationships to me, whether sexual or otherwise, long ago. No amount of malicious gossip could come between us.

Another voice from the past resurfaced in 1999. John Pearson, the author of *The Profession of Violence*, wrote an article for *Esquire* magazine, promoting the new edition of the paperback. He announced that 'when writing about violent criminals there is always the risk of ending up as hard core in a flyover'. Despite his concerns, Mr Pearson had survived over thirty years without undue injury to his bodily parts! With perhaps just a touch of vanity, he claimed his book had been mainly responsible for the mythology that had grown around the Krays. He expressed regret for 'making heroes out of murderers'. In what must have been a strain on his conscience, he had just produced a spanking new chapter.

It has to be said that *The Profession of Violence* was actually a well-written and researched book. Although there were some inaccuracies, it provided a fascinating insight into the lives of the Krays, their personalities, and the environment in which they lived. His postscript identified how after so many years in prison they had actually become 'national celebrities', a phenomenon understandably abhorred by the authorities.

It had been a long time since Reg had met his erstwhile biographer. After reading the article, he decided he would like to see John again. It was the first of several visits, a reacquaintance that he enjoyed. It was not often that he saw a face from the past. They discussed the old times and the new, sharing their memories and their hopes for the future. John expressed the opinion that Reg had served his time and should now be out of prison. He said he'd like to write another book, reassessing the trial and making the case for Reg's release. It was all very encouraging. We agreed to give any assistance we could and Reg introduced him to his solicitor and also to friends. The new book was published a year after Reg's death. I found it a disappointment – although by that time the situation had obviously changed. In addition the rumour mill had grown to such proportions that separating fact from fiction was a major enterprise for anyone who had not been especially close.

In the summer of 1999 both Reg and I were thankfully oblivious to the horrors of the future. Indeed that summer was a happy one. On 27 July Wayland organized what they referred to as a 'Lifers' Day', an opportunity for life-sentence prisoners to spend some extra time with family and friends. This was slightly different to the usual Family Day in that the afternoon, weather permitting, was to be spent outside in the grounds of the prison. There would also be the opportunity to talk to various officers about reports, sentence plans or other subjects of relevance. Wayland had never held such an event before and it was something of an experiment.

I know there are critics who will be horrified at the idea of any prisoner 'enjoying' such a day as I'm about to describe. They will perceive it as soft and lenient, a wishy-washy liberal experiment that erodes the principles of British Justice and rewards criminality. I would just like to explain that *all* of the men who took part were approaching the end of long sentences. These hours spent with their families, with their partners and children, were the first periods of semi-normality they had experienced in ten to thirty years. Most of their time was spent behind bars. Their days were grotesquely repetitive. Their nights were spent alone. This opportunity probably did more to remind them of the consequences of their actions, and everything they had sacrificed, than all the previous years of incarceration.

The visit started at 9.30 a.m. Our party consisted of Reg, myself, Bradley and Donna, Paul Marcus, Chris Rowlands and his young son and his pal, and Reg's old friend Georgie Woods. The morning was spent in the visiting-hall, drinking tea and chatting. Reg was on good form. Surrounded by friends, he felt relaxed and happy. At midday we all made the move outside. It was a strange feeling to walk out of those doors with Reg – even if it was just to step onto the prison field. I realized I had only breathed fresh air with him on one previous occasion, the day of our marriage when we had spent five minutes having photographs taken at the chapel. Now we could look forward to three and a half hours of what felt almost like freedom. A small marquee had been erected with tables and chairs inside. Lunch consisted of a cold buffet or hamburgers and hot-dogs. There was tea, coffee and soft drinks. It was all simple inexpensive fare but much appreciated. It felt good to sit around a table, to eat and to talk, and to just enjoy the moment.

After lunch we went out onto the field. It was a glorious afternoon. The sun was shining and the sky was blue. The children played football and rounders with their dads, jumping up and down, laughing like any other kids in a park. For many it was the first time in years they had been with their fathers outside the visiting-room. There was a good atmosphere. Everything was calm and easy. We kicked a ball about and walked around the field. We sprawled in the sun and talked. Later, while Reg gave some boxing tips to his friends, I met a few of the officers and governors. They told me they were pleased with Reg's progress. There was *no* reason for him to be refused a move to an open prison at his next parole review. They were encouraging and enthusiastic about his prospects. No one raised any complaints. No one suggested there were any problems. Everyone was optimistic. It was all very reassuring.

We returned periodically to the marquee for a cup of tea or coffee. On one occasion there was some music playing. Reg took my hand and asked me to dance. We had a slow waltz between the tables. Gradually, other couples joined in. It was one of those funny and touching moments. There we all were in the middle of a tent in the middle of a field in the middle of a prison, dancing. It was simultaneously strange and wonderful.

The hours passed too quickly. As the afternoon was drawing to a close, our friends discreetly disappeared. We lay quietly together on the field. Reg closed his eyes. I stroked his forehead. The minutes, like our friends, slipped away. Reg told me he had forgotten what it meant to be so relaxed. He said he hadn't felt so free in over thirty-one years. When the final call came we stood up and gathered our things together. It was hard to believe it was almost over. Reg put his arms around me. He said, 'I'll never forget today.'

neant a lot to me . . . When I had my head on your
you massaged my forehead – most I've been relaxed
e years – like being in paradise.'

ther event, of a different character, also occurred that
er. Reg was called to the office and informed by a
or that a decision had been made to shift him to
oint Prison in Suffolk. He was told it would be a 'pos-
move. However, as Highpoint was the same category
ayland, it was hard to conceive of the transfer being in
way progressive. Trevor Linn was concerned. Reg was
in six months of his next parole review. At the last
ew comments had been made about Reg not having been
Wayland long enough to be properly assessed. By moving
n to Highpoint he would face the same problem all over
ain. When Trevor made enquiries and asked for an expla-
tion, the answers were vague. Despite what had been said
Reg, they now insisted no final decision had been reached.
revor persisted. A week later the transfer was dropped. No
eason was ever given.

It didn't bode well for the future. The odd behaviour
of the Prison Service suggested some machinations behind
the scenes. Reg's conversations with senior officers also set
alarm bells ringing. He received not just criticism over his
decision to ask for further independent assessments but
open hostility. Trevor had made arrangements for Dr Mac-
Keith, a forensic psychiatrist, and Dr Gudjonsson, a psychologist, to provide additional reports. They were both men
of impeccable credentials whose integrity could not be called
into question. Like their predecessors, they could not afford
to make recommendations they did not believe in. It was
perhaps their status as admired and highly esteemed professionals that bothered the authorities so much.

Both experts spent long periods of time with Reg and
produced extensive and detailed reports. Dr MacKeith
wrote: 'In my opinion Mr Kray is suitable for transfer to an

We walked back to the marquee
The farewells were terrible. Having
extraordinary day it was painful to sa
remember the look in Reg's eyes; what
about to be taken away. The dream was o
around the corner. We embraced, saying
lost for words. The officers hurried peopl
back and watched us go. We walked slo
leave. At the gates we stopped and turned
seemed a tiny figure. He raised his hand. The
us through. It was over.

The effect on Reg was profound. He ha
something he suspected he would never feel ag
of freedom. This was quickly followed by a sens
was simultaneously elated and depressed. Altho
to have shared time with people he cared abou
knew it might never be repeated. After being retur
cell for early-evening lock-up, he spent what
described as 'one of the longest hours of my life'. C
and alone, his thoughts were not just of the day but o
years that had passed him by.

Later we talked at length. As if he wanted to fix th
in his mind forever, he went over every detail. Although
tially cheered by the recollections, as the evening wore or
became more subdued. The night stretched ahead. I was co
cerned about him. He decided just before lock-up that
would ask if his friend Bill Taylor could sit with him for
while. Bill was what is known as a Listener, the prison equivalent to a Samaritan. As a fellow-lifer he had an understanding of what Reg was going through. After he left, Reg
wrote me a letter. 'I spoke to Bill Taylor till 9 p.m. He is a
good person – helped a lot. I've so much mixed thoughts on
the whole day and night – also got pain in right side near
right temple. Having black coffee, listening to Radio 2, old
song "I've got you under my skin". Glad all were happy on

open prison. It is noteworthy that such a recommendation was made in reports preceding the tariff date but has strangely and without explanation disappeared from prison service reports since that date yet his behaviour has not deteriorated.' Commenting on Reg's reluctance to co-operate with the prison psychologist he said: 'Like many prisoners, Mr Kray is understandably suspicious of prison psychologists who owe a duty to the prison service as well as to the inmate. He co-operated well with Dr Gudjonsson although subjected to a gruelling process of assessment which required concentrated application to tasks which he did not find easy.' He concluded that there was now a 'window of opportunity' for a well-managed release into the community. Dr Gudjonsson was of a similar opinion. He wrote: 'On the basis of the present assessment it would be appropriate that Mr Kray spends a period of time in open conditions (Category 'D' prison), before being released on licence. My view is that he is ready for transfer to an open prison where his behaviour in a more open setting can be tested out.' They both expressed a willingness to consult with the prison healthcare service and prison psychologists about their findings. The offer was turned down.

We remained doubtful about the outcome of the review. The antagonistic attitude of the prison officers seemed indicative of its likely result. That any outsider, however well qualified, could hold a relevant opinion was obviously viewed with an attitude approaching outrage. Reg was accused of trying to sneak out of the back door. In fact he had simply laid himself open to independent and unbiased investigation. Had Dr MacKeith and Dr Gudjonsson decided that Reg was unfit for release we would not have been able to withhold that information from the Parole Board. Under such circumstances, I suspect, the Prison Service would have shown a little more enthusiasm for further discussion!

While all this was going on, Reg tried to keep busy. That

small seed of dread was growing inside him again. How would he face another knockback? How could he cope? He was sorely in need of distraction, of anything that would take his mind off the impending decision about his future. This arrived in August in the form of the American band Fun Lovin' Criminals. Reg had been writing song lyrics for some time and the group expressed an interest in putting his words to music. It was Rob Ferguson, a good friend who ran a music and technology business in Bedford, who arranged the introduction. We were grateful to him – not just for this opportunity but, more importantly, for all his unstinting support. Lead singer Huey Morgan and the manager Jonathan Bloch came to visit. They got on well with Reg. There was talk of singles and perhaps even an album. It gave him the lift he needed. The music business is always precarious and he was not oblivious to the fact that it would probably come to nothing. It didn't really matter. For as long as the possibility existed he could still look forward to it.

The reaction of the Prison Service was predictable. Reg, by seeing 'famous' people was once again accused of courting notoriety. He was told it would go against him in his reports. One can't help wondering if that future Wayland inmate, Jeffrey Archer, faced the same difficulties. When he received a visit from a well-known politician or writer did the prison officers complain about it? Did they express extreme concern about his motivation? Did they put in writing, as they did with Reg, that he should 'think carefully about the damage such publicity could cause'? I doubt it. The two were, of course, serving different sentences for different crimes. Reg Kray had killed a man. Jeffrey Archer, leaving aside his assaults on the English language, had only lied, deceived and destroyed the trust of every person who believed in his integrity and voted for him as a Member of Parliament. Whatever the guilty deeds, prison rules and judgements should surely remain the same for everyone.

With little hope as regards his future, Reg worked remorselessly for an achievement in the present. It wasn't just a case of bolstering his reputation. He needed to move *towards* something. The doing was more important than the final result. His response to success or failure was always the same: What can I do next? For as long as he had an objective, something to aim for, his life wasn't pointless. He also spent many hours answering letters from other inmates. Usually he just sent a note but if the inmate seemed upset or worried he would write a longer letter. He corresponded with friends outside as well. Although once he had enjoyed reading and responding to mail, now he often found it an effort. He slept badly and felt continuously tired. The problems with his stomach were not improving.

In October Reg celebrated his sixty-sixth birthday. As the day fell on a Sunday Reg decided to have a visit on the Monday instead. This was for two reasons. The first was that the visiting hall was always crowded at weekends and the second that the weekends had early lock-up. It was the latter that bothered him most. Visits usually ended about 4 p.m. The visitors left first, the inmates remaining in the room until they had all departed. This took about twenty minutes. By the time Reg had gone through the search routine and returned to the wing there was barely enough time to fill his flask with hot water, make a quick phone call and collect his food before he was locked up at 5 p.m. It would be another fifteen hours before the door opened again. To pass straight from the pleasure of a visit into that long period of solitary confinement was unendurable.

Reg's birthday was, of course, also Ron's. It was now over four years since his death. Reg was constantly aware of his absence. He passed the day quietly, going out for a walk on the field, listening to music, writing letters and making a few phone calls. He rang and reassured me that he was all right. He said, 'Don't be sad for me.'

Reg lost several old and dear friends that year including Georgie Woods, who had spent the special Lifers' Day with him. But in November he lost the very closest of them. His name was John Copley. They had first met in Lewes. John was six years older and a fellow lifer. An intelligent and well-travelled man, Reg found him both interesting and perceptive. They wrote three or four times a week for ten years. Reg valued his judgement and often asked for his advice; he felt able to confide in him. By this time John was in Kingston Prison in Portsmouth where they had a special unit for the over-65s. He suffered with heart problems and was on constant medication. His health was rapidly deteriorating. John knew when he was taken into hospital that he would never come out and sent me a note asking if Reg could call. Reg got permission from the governor to ring from the office. John died a couple of days later.

Rob,

I have a great sense of loss after the passing of our friend John. I had a cry and have tears as I write this letter. John died on the same day as Ron, the 17th. I knew before you told me that John had died. I will miss John's letters so much, just as I did and do Ron's. Mail time will not be the same. John like Ron had a hard but sometimes good life – just as I have had.

I feel bad about the last phone call to John as I said such a stupid and mundane goodbye of cheerio – I don't seem to have my head together in situations lately, but it was difficult with PO and Governor calling time on the call and I find it difficult to be warm and natural in their presence. John's last words were for me to take care of you. He said, 'Take care of Rob'.

I really wanted John to see all come together just as I did Ron. But I reckon they will know. We must think of John, of the good times he had in New York and Canada. Remember he was a good friend and still is.

> God bless
>> All my love,
>>> Reg xxx

It was a sad way to end the year. John's death left another irreplaceable gap in Reg's life.

11. FALSE HOPES, FEARS AND FAREWELLS

It was impossible not to feel enthusiasm for the New Year. It was, after all, a brand new millennium. There was a general air of hope and anticipation. There was a sense of expectancy. Reg felt it too. All over the world, as fireworks exploded and nations celebrated, countries were giving amnesties to their prisoners. This was going to be a better year wasn't it? We could put the disappointments behind us, all the false promises and deceptions. Surely something good was about to happen?

Our optimism was quickly tested. It was only a couple of weeks before we suffered the first blow. On 10 January Carlton television began a two-part documentary on The Krays. It's main protagonists were Freddie Foreman, an old associate of the twins, and Albert Donoghue – the man who had given evidence against them at their original trial. Broadcast just before Reg's forthcoming parole review, their 'revelations' and allegations of past crimes couldn't fail to be damaging. Constrained by prison law, Reg could not publicly respond; he was not permitted, as everyone who contributed to the programme knew, even the slightest of replies.

It was hard to understand Freddie Foreman's motivation. Was it simply money? Reg had always, up to this point, respected his loyalty and principles. He had also been a good friend to Ron. Whatever his reasons, the repercussions of the documentary were immediate. Within a couple of weeks the police had contacted Wayland. They wanted to question him about the allegations. Had he wanted revenge, it would have been the perfect opportunity – he knew enough about Foreman to cause him problems of his own. But Reg was not prepared to go there. He refused to talk.

At this point many people, including old associates, came forward and expressed their astonishment. They described Foreman's actions as 'disgusting'. Frank Fraser was one of the most vociferous. In his book *Mad Frank's Diary* he said: 'The timing of the programme was at a crucial time when Reggie Kray was seeking parole. Fred is too experienced a street person to believe that this error of judgement was due to a brainstorm of foolishness. It was far more serious than that. With the Establishment desperate to find any reason to keep Reggie locked up, this was a gift to them on a silver platter. Did Freddie never consider this, or is he that naïve? Freddie may be a man of various character features, but in no way is naïvety one of them.' Although it had been several years since Reg had any direct contact with Foreman, he was still shocked and dismayed by what he had done. Respect is a word much bandied around in the tight-knit community of old villains. If showing respect constitutes kicking a man when he is down then Freddie Foreman certainly showed it to Reg.

Although many voices were raised after the initial screening of the documentary, accusations against Foreman were rapidly withdrawn. Reasons were given and excuses made; outrage quickly gave way to self-interest. Frank Fraser was one of the few who stood by Reg. It made him less than popular. He bore the brunt of others' criticism but refused to back down. He continued to visit Reg in Wayland and his support and encouragement were appreciated. Prison is a lonely place at the best of times – to find yourself suddenly under attack by those you had trusted is not the most gratifying of experiences.

It has to be said that amongst some of the old faces there flowed a steady undercurrent of resentment. They seemed less than enthusiastic at the prospect of Reg's release. While he stayed in prison they remained the shining lights on the media 'gangster' circuit, the next best thing to the Krays. Should he ever walk out of those gates they would be immediately overshadowed. It was hardly something to look forward to. Tony Lambrianou, who stood trial with the Krays and later formed a close friendship with Foreman, was openly critical of the twins. He complained about the length of his sentence (fifteen years) and blamed Reg and Ron for not standing up in court and taking full responsibility. After his release, although he made a comfortable living playing the part of the hard gangster, he whined perpetually about the consequences of his own actions. Lambrianou was not an innocent bystander. He knew exactly what was planned for Jack McVitie the night he was killed. He voluntarily led him to his death. He also knew that Ron had murdered George Cornell. He chose to stay with the Krays because he was criminally ambitious. He participated in all the day-to-day activities, reaping handsome rewards from fear, violence and extortion. It is true, of course, that he was little more than a gofer, a sprat in a pool of sharks – but a sprat, as it turned out, with eyes bigger than his stomach.

Reg had no time for Tony Lambrianou. It wasn't because of his bragging or his reinvention of the past. Lambrianou had served a long sentence and Reg didn't resent his attempts to grab some recompense for all the wasted years. What he *did* resent was his pretence that he had always stood staunchly behind the twins and taken his punishment 'like a man'. As Reg was all too aware, Tony Lambrianou had given a statement immediately after they were all convicted claiming he was 'under duress' when the killing took place. In an attempt to get his own sentence reduced, he had given evidence against the twins. His appeal was turned down. This was not generally known for a long time. It was only publicly revealed in 1999 when official government records were released. Reg could have talked or written about it long before but he didn't. He let Tony Lambrianou continue to pretend he was someone he wasn't.

As if all this was not enough it was only a matter of weeks before another damaging documentary hit the television screens. Just over a year before, in January 1999, Dave Courtney had asked if he could visit Reg with the editor of Front magazine, Piers Hernu. The magazine was serializing one of Reg's books. Courtney first came to the public's attention when he organized the security for Ron's funeral. Young and ambitious, not unlike the Krays in their early days, he shared their desperation to *be* someone. He also shared their love of publicity. Reg liked him. Dave was competent, confident and amusing. Since Ron's death, although never close, they had continued to stay in touch.

I met them at Wayland and we sat chatting and drinking coffee while we waited to go in. It was then, for the first time, they mentioned that a documentary was being made about the magazine with BBC2. A camera crew had apparently accompanied them to the prison. They didn't say much else about it and, when they talked to Reg, gave the impression that it was nothing to do with their visit. The truth was very different. A year later, a few weeks after the Carlton documentary, the programme *Between the Covers* was broadcast. It told a merry tale of two enterprising characters, Dave and Piers, going down to Wayland Prison to secretly interview Reg Kray. Armed with numerous items of undetectable equipment, recording devices and photographic gadgets, they bragged about passing freely through security and into the visiting room.

Halfway through the programme Reg's solicitor Trevor

Linn rang. He said: 'Are you watching this?' Neither of us
could believe it. We were only a month away from Reg's next
parole review and another nail was being firmly hammered
in. There was no indication given as to whether Reg knew
what was happening but the inference, because of his previous association with Courtney, was that he must have been
in collusion. It was disastrous. It made Reg look like he was
deliberately flouting the rules and mocking the Home Office.
It would be wrong to claim that Reg had a huge regard for
either – he didn't – but he certainly wasn't interested in
deliberately antagonizing the people who were about to
decide his future.

After the visit, the dynamic duo were filmed cracking
open a bottle of champagne on the bonnet of their car. It was
a moment of smug self-congratulation. A good day's work!
A job well done!

Later, Courtney claimed that none of the equipment was
working and it was simply a joke, a big James Bond-type fantasy that we were all supposed to enjoy. Sadly, the documentary didn't quite manage to clarify that point. Reg's role,
or lack of it, was far from obvious. While others revelled in
the publicity, Reg was left to pick up the pieces. There were
so many questions. Why had Dave failed to inform him
about the content of the programme? (He had not only spent
two hours on the visit but a whole year had passed between
recording and transmission.) Why hadn't Reg been warned
about the stunt? Only Dave Courtney knows the answers to
these questions. I don't believe that either he or Piers had any
malevolent intent but under the circumstances I think their
actions could be seen as both stupid and thoughtless.

Courtney rang me a couple of minutes after the programme ended. He didn't understand why I was upset. He
told me that all his friends thought it was 'really funny'.
They might not have been laughing quite so hard if they had
spent the last thirty-one years in prison. The Governor of

Wayland Prison was equally unimpressed. Reg was hauled before him the next morning and asked for an explanation. What was he supposed to say? Yes, he knew Dave Courtney. Yes, he had met Courtney and Piers Hernu on a visit. No, he didn't know what they had planned. No, he hadn't known about the documentary. He was in a no-win situation. The presumption was that if Dave Courtney was an associate, Reg *must* have known what he was doing. When he insisted that he didn't, the allegation was then turned on its head. If this was the case then Reg obviously had extremely bad judgement – he had allowed someone he considered trustworthy to come into the prison, to dupe him and then publicly abuse and ridicule the system. If he made such bad errors in prison, he would surely make even worse outside. How could they recommend his release under such circumstances?

It was hard to believe that one documentary, never mind two, had appeared so close to the parole review. All the participants of both the programmes were aware of his situation. In addition to his deteriorating physical condition, Reg had to face another unpleasant truth – his life was up for auction. While his former associates bargained and bartered, that life was gradually slipping away. The doctors stood by their claim that he had Irritable Bowel Syndrome and treated him accordingly. Milk of Magnesia, enemas and paracetamol became part of his daily diet. Nothing helped. His discomfort increased. He stopped going to the gym or exercising. The pain grew worse and worse. Eventually he was taken to hospital. A number of tests were carried out. The doctor came to the same conclusion as the Prison Service – Reg was suffering from IBS. They also diagnosed diverticulitis, an uncomfortable but rarely life-threatening inflammation of the intestine.

Our feelings were a mixture of relief and frustration. We both wanted to believe that the diagnosis was correct but it did little to help Reg's suffering. Nothing they prescribed helped to ease the pain. He returned to the prison doctors again and again. They continued to dole out the same ineffective medication. Even on visits, the time when he was usually most relaxed, Reg was in distress. Reports began to circulate in the press that he was seriously ill and might be suffering from cancer. It was a shock for Reg to read it in the newspaper. Although he'd been told this wasn't the case, a small part of him wondered if it might be true. In order to try to put his mind at rest I asked the West Norwich Hospital for confirmation of their results. The Specialist Registrar wrote the following letter back to Reg on 3 February 2000: 'I can confirm there is no reason to believe that you have stomach cancer, or indeed, cancer anywhere. We have never at any time considered or suggested an operation as there has never been any need for one.' Despite this reassurance we continued to worry. At the beginning of March I arranged, through Mark Goldstein, for another specialist to see Reg at the Wayland medical centre. He did a thorough examination and his conclusions agreed with those of the hospital: 'I think, on balance, his symptoms are more related to anxiety about his abdomen than to any real pathology. I am sure he ought to try stopping all medication and let Nature resolve things spontaneously. I have strongly reassured him that there is nothing abdominally for him to be worried about.' Everywhere we turned the answer was the same. Reg was *not* fatally ill. Had he been released on the expiry of his thirty-year sentence we could, and would, have taken further medical advice. Caught early enough the disease might have been treatable. He might have survived.

As things stood, we could only try to find ways of easing his symptoms. The obvious route, if the medical experts were to be believed, was to improve his diet and reduce his levels of stress. Neither were very realistic options. Reg did what he could. He cut out dairy produce, milk, eggs and cheese. He stopped drinking tea and coffee. He tried to stay calm. There were no positive results. In fact the opposite occurred. His pain and discomfort increased every day. Where once he had prided himself on keeping fit, it became an effort even to take his daily walk. He knew in his heart that something was very wrong.

Avoiding stress proved to be impossible. By March most of the new parole reports were in. With a Home Secretary of limited courage, two bad documentaries, and an obvious sea-change in the attitude of the officers, we should not have been surprised at their content. The overall recommendation was that Reg should spend 'a further period' in 'C'-category conditions. The reason provided, with oddly similar phrasing, was that he needed further psychological assessment. Several of the officers, coincidentally, referred to the psychologist Dr Gudjonsson in their reports as 'Dr Johnson'. Whether this was a collective inability to write a name down correctly, or an utter disregard for his opinion, is hard to say.

Only one senior prison officer refused to toe the party line. He wrote: 'Mr Kray's risk to the public in my opinion is low with chances of him reoffending very minimal, which makes him suitable for open conditions.' His recommendation was quickly qualified by the comment that Reg's refusal to 'co-operate' with the prison psychologist could not be ignored. The findings of Dr Gudjonsson were disregarded. His intensive psychometric testing of Reg was dismissed without comment. Although he had actually *created* some of the major exercises generally used in analysis, his interpretations of his own tests were considered to be worthless.

As reports were drifting through, Reg was called to the office and introduced to the prison psychologist who was taking over his case. This young woman was now in control of his future. She told Reg that in order to be released he needed to take an additional number of courses. Top of her list was 'Enhanced Thinking Skills'. It had been two years since Reg's last parole review. In all that time not one prison officer, governor or official had suggested that Reg should take anything other than the Offending Behaviour course. That in itself was looked on as little more than a hoop-jumping exercise. Reg had gone ahead and done it. He had even sacrificed a hospital appointment to complete it. When she suggested he would benefit from doing Enhanced Thinking Skills Reg replied that she might benefit even more from doing it herself. It was not a wise thing to say but was spoken in a moment of anger and frustration. He felt that, even after thirty-two years, they were still looking for reasons to keep him inside.

Despite having no close contact, and no one-to-one interview, she managed to produce a three-page report on Reg for the Board. She concluded that: 'Although Mr Kray is now an elderly man and has served just over 30 years in prison, he has not satisfactorily addressed areas of concern and met the targets set. In addition he is still exhibiting aggressive behaviour towards staff.' Aggressive behaviour? There wasn't a single report, in this review or the last, that described Reg as anything other than courteous towards staff and inmates. Reg's 'aggressive behaviour' actually translated as a single retort to herself. She recommended, not surprisingly, that Reg should remain in 'closed conditions'.

In June 1999 Reg had been given two new external probation officers. Martyn Elliott and Harry Matthews were based in East London and had over twenty years' experience. They made several journeys to Norfolk and as well as intensive talks with Reg also visited me at home and talked to us together at Wayland. In response to our concerns about the Enhanced Thinking Skills course (ETS) they contacted Dr Linda Blud of the Prison Department, Offending Behaviour Programmes Unit. They later wrote in their parole report:

Reginald Kray was resistant to this course, primarily because he questioned its relevance at this point in his sentence, and saw it as a further hurdle added at the last minute. We have spoken with Dr Blud who suggests that Reginald Kray does not fit the normal profile of course participants who are usually serving shorter sentences where there is a degree of impulsive behaviour in their offending . . . She has also told us that this course is available in Open Conditions. In our view this course might have more relevance and significance for Reginald Kray when he can associate it with resettlement and release planning.

Aware that the theme of notoriety was constantly being put forward as an impediment to his release, they also raised the point that it was impossible to say how far Reg actually contributed to it himself; newspaper articles would be written irrespective of his co-operation. Having dealt with many inmates released from HMP Wayland, they commented that not *one* of those prisoners had ever said they knew Reg or sought to gain any status from it. They assessed the likelihood of Reg reoffending as 'negligible'.

On meeting I had been relieved to find them well aware of Reg's problems. One of the major difficulties discussed was in planning for the future. They understood how hard it was for Reg to look forward without any indication of when or even if he would be released. Their final recommendation was that Reg should be recategorized and transferred to a 'D'-category prison where his responses could be properly tested. 'In our discussions with him and his wife, he was absolutely clear that failure to succeed in Open Conditions would have a detrimental effect on his eventual release. To his credit, he welcomed that challenge and the opportunity to move forward.'

Looking at the collective reports it didn't take much

imagination to predict the outcome. Apart from the probation officers, every recommendation was against a move to
a lower-category prison. The dossier made for depressing
reading. In the two years since the last review they had
passed from active support to virtual condemnation. This
was despite the fact there had been no disciplinary procedures against Reg, his behaviour had not deteriorated and
he had completed the course they had asked him to do. Their
obsession with psychological assessments seemed little
more than an enterprising means of justifying rejection.

It is right that society should be protected from dangerous people. Where there is overwhelming evidence that an
inmate will reoffend then decisions can hardly be taken
lightly. If an individual's release will erode public confidence
in the judicial system then that issue must also be addressed.
Neither of these factors was relevant to Reg's case. In fact the
opposite was true. As an ailing sixty-six-year-old ex-gang-
ster, who had already served over thirty-two years for the
killing of a fellow criminal, he had neither the intention nor
the inclination to return to a life of crime. The public, far from
being averse, was generally in favour of release. Retribution
had been achieved. It could not be said that his punishment
had been inadequate.

All that remained now was to wait for Reg to have his
pre-Board interview. The Board was due to sit in a matter of
weeks. We knew what to expect. There would be no sur-
prises. We also knew, despite our lack of hope, that the result
when it came would be devastating. In the meantime, for as
long as the decision remained unmade, there was always
possibility. In that tiny space between expectation and
reality lurked the tiny chance of a miracle.

There were other worries to contend with. Charlie's
appeal had been turned down and he'd been moved to HMP
Parkhurst on the Isle of Wight. As news of his brother's illness began to filter through, Reg was faced with the prospect

that Charlie might die in the prison where he had started his own endless sentence. Although Charlie never complained, friends expressed concern at his worsening health. They said his legs were badly swollen, he could hardly walk and he had lost a lot of weight. Reg asked for permission to visit. After a short spell in hospital Charlie had been returned to Parkhurst. It was only a matter of days before he was readmitted. This time the prognosis was drastic enough to warrant a call to Wayland Prison.

With a heavy heart Reg made the long journey down to the south coast and crossed the water, as he had done so many times before, on the ferry. Pursued by the press, the trip was not uneventful. He was photographed at every opportunity. Who had informed them he was even travelling? They seemed to know his every move. As only a limited number of people (and neither Reg nor I were one of them) knew exactly when he would be leaving and what route would be taken, the leak must have been an internal one. On arriving at Parkhurst the van passed through the main gates but then quickly exited again and continued to St Mary's.

Reg was led, handcuffed and chained, into the hospital and on to Newport Ward. As soon as he entered the room, he realized how ill Charlie was. It was an emotional reunion. They talked for half an hour. Four prison officers remained with them. Two, on bed-watch, were part of a team that stayed with Charlie twenty-four hours a day. As I was later to learn, it is hard to have an intimate conversation when all your feelings and sentiments are being shared with complete strangers.

After the meeting Reg was escorted back to Parkhurst and put in Charlie's cell. It was on a wing that had once been part of the psychiatric unit. He had spent three years there with Ron. They had not been the happiest times. Reg rang me every day. The news got progressively worse. Charlie had advanced heart disease. On heavy medication and in regular need of oxygen, he was not expected to live longer than a few months. Even at this late stage there was talk of returning him to prison. It was an inhumane but hardly unexpected reaction from the Home Office.

I travelled down to Dorset to stay with Wilf and Ros Pine. Their invitation was a welcome one. I was grateful for their hospitality and kindness. Wilf was already making daily trips to see Charlie. Reg was visiting whenever he could. Due to staff shortages this was less often then he would have liked. On 24 March I crossed the choppy Solent for the first time. Wilf and I arrived at St Mary's in the late morning. Charlie's condition was instantly evident. Lying in bed, he looked pale and gaunt. Although we had often spoken on the phone we had never met before; these were hardly ideal circumstances. He insisted on getting up and into his wheelchair. His breathing was badly impaired and every movement was an effort. We went into the day-room where there was a little more privacy; the ever-present prison officers kept a discreet distance. Wilf disappeared onto the balcony. Charlie and I were left together. We sat and talked.

In the afternoon Wilf and I went to visit Reg. Standing outside Parkhurst, it was hard to believe how long he had once been imprisoned there. The building loomed over us, large and oppressive. We booked in and waited. Inside security was tight. All our possessions, apart from a bit of loose change, were consigned to a locker. When our names were called we were thoroughly searched; our shoes were examined, our bodies frisked and our open mouths shown a level of attention more suited to a dental surgery. Eventually we were allowed through to the visiting hall.

Reg was sitting alone at the far end. With his head down he appeared lost in thought. He turned as we came in and jumped to his feet. I was aware of how tired he looked. He asked about Charlie and we passed on the little news we had. Wilf stayed only for a short while. After reassuring Reg that he'd continue to go to the hospital every day, he left us alone to spend some time together. Reg told me he was coping. Charlie's friends were keeping him company and making sure he had everything he needed. They were a good crowd. He said he wouldn't mind returning to Parkhurst on a more permanent basis. At first I thought he was joking but it soon became apparent that he wasn't. He told me that if he got another knockback, and if I could deal with another move, he'd ask to be transferred there. I looked at him. I realized what he was saying. He believed a refusal this time would mean he was never leaving prison – and that he'd prefer to spend what remained of his life in the secure surroundings of a place he had once been used to. After the devastating experiences at Long Lartin, his mother had described his return to Parkhurst as a 'coming home'. I felt cold. I experienced one of those moments that are often described as someone walking over your grave.

Over the next few days I tried to push it out of my mind. These were difficult and emotional times. Reg was gradually coming to terms with Charlie's illness; there were so many memories and regrets. On 29 March 2000, he wrote, 'Writing in the half light of TV in my cell – I miss being near you.' I missed it too. Although proximity wouldn't have meant any more visits, it was hard to be so far away. He rang every morning and evening. On one occasion he was more upset than usual. He had been told that Freddie Foreman had arranged to visit Charlie. After his contribution to the Carlton documentary, Reg neither wanted to see nor meet him again. Worried that their visits might coincide he informed the prison officers that he didn't wish to go to St Mary's that particular afternoon. The last thing Charlie needed was a row and Reg was not convinced that he could hold his tongue should he come face-to-face with Freddie. He thought it best if he just stayed away. Although Foreman had treated him badly, it was not the time or the place for recriminations.

I saw Reg again the following weekend. He looked exhausted; there were dark shadows under his eyes. It was, coincidentally, 1 April, two years to the day since his last parole knockback. Bradley and Donna joined me on the visit. Reg was pleased to see us all but was obviously stressed and agitated. He pointed out a few of the other inmates, Charlie's friends, and reiterated how kind they had been. It was a relief to know he had support and sympathy inside the prison. The visit passed quickly. Bradley and Donna gave us time alone at the end. After they had gone I bought us both a cup of tea and we sat and talked. Reg had something on his mind. Despite his trips to the hospital he said he had not been able to talk to Charlie properly. He felt past differences still lay between them. He couldn't make things right but he craved some form of mutual understanding and forgiveness. When the time came to leave, although I had no choice, I felt like I was abandoning him. Charlie probably only had a few days to live and Reg would have to face the inevitable alone.

On the evening of 3 April Reg was rushed to St Mary's. Charlie's condition had deteriorated. He left Parkhurst in the pouring rain. It was dark. He couldn't remember the last time he had been outside at night. As he stepped out of the car he was confronted by a series of blinding white flashes; the press, once again, were lying in wait. The officers pulled him into the hospital.

Reg sat with his brother for over an hour. Charlie was breathing heavily through an oxygen mask. His eyes were shut. The time for talk had passed. There would be no final conversations, no shared thoughts and perhaps, ultimately, no real understanding. Maybe it didn't matter. Charlie knew he was there. Their peace was of a different kind.

Reg was taken back to Parkhurst. He passed a sleepless

night. His only consolation was that Charlie was not alone. As well as visiting every day Wilf was now staying overnight, making sure that if Charlie woke it was always to the face of an old friend. Ron's lonely death had never ceased to haunt Reg. It wasn't until the following evening that he was allowed to return to the hospital. His brother was dying. All Reg could do was watch. He held Charlie's hand and said a few words. When he left he knew it would be for the last time. This farewell was a final one.

Later that night three officers went to Reg's cell. They broke the news that Charlie had passed away at a quarter to nine. His last wish, that his long-term girlfriend Diane should be with him at the end, was granted. Charlie had died peacefully holding her hand.

Reg was transported back to Wayland the next day. It was an eternal journey. He was distraught. Charlie was the very last of his immediate family. Now they had all gone. Everything was made even worse when, five days later, a Sunday tabloid printed what purported to be an 'exclusive interview'. His feelings, and sense of loss, were splattered over a double-page spread. I would like to state categorically that this was not an interview that Reg participated in or had any knowledge of. He had neither talked nor had any intention of talking to the press. The article, despite its headline, admitted partway through (and in small print) that all the information had been provided by a close friend. That much was obvious. Some of the sentiments expressed were very familiar to me. I had no doubt that a conversation with Reg had been recorded and then sold on. It was more than opportunistic; it was contemptible.

Upset and confused, Reg's suspicions fell unfairly and temporarily on Wilf Pine. Wilf was understandably dismayed. In such a situation it is hard to prove your innocence. However, this was something he battled, successfully, to do. It was a matter not just of reputation but of loyalty and friendship. The person who was actually responsible had sold many other stories.

Over the next week Reg coped in the only way he could, by keeping busy and organizing the funeral. The date was set for 19 April. Wayland allowed him a special visiting order and I went in with Paul Keays of W. English & Son, the undertakers from Bethnal Green. He had also overseen Ron's funeral. Together they went through the order of service, the prayers and the hymns. Diane had some readings that she wished to be included. Reg ordered the coffin and confirmed the burial arrangements. Paul was kind and considerate, doing everything he could to ease the situation. We had no idea that he was seriously ill himself. I was saddened to hear of his death later in the year.

Another major issue was security for the day. Although the police would be present Reg preferred to make doubly sure there were no problems. He refused to ask for Dave Courtney's help; after the BBC2 documentary the bond of trust had been broken. While at Parkhurst Reg had got to know a friend of Charlie's called Peter Grayston. He had a brother, Richard, who was involved in the business. Reg met him for the first time nine days before the funeral. They got on well and it was agreed he would manage the security.

Reg asked me to organize some of the cars. He also wanted to ensure that special friends were around him in the church. St Matthew's didn't have a large capacity and seats were quickly filled. At Ron's funeral he had found himself distanced from people he wanted to be close to. I arranged for three of the rows to be roped off and reserved. I had his suit cleaned and pressed and took it, along with a new white shirt, tie, socks and shoes, into the prison. Reg wrote on 16 April: 'Thanks for all you have done for the day. We have been through so many trials and tribulations together. Guess there will be more to come.' He could not have imagined just how true those words would be.

On 18 April Reg was taken to Belmarsh Prison in London where he spent the night before the funeral. I travelled down with friends the following morning. Worried about traffic, accidents or possible delays on the motorway, we left at the crack of dawn and arrived in Bethnal Green at 7.30 a.m. We found a café and had a light breakfast. Nobody was hungry. We drank mugs of tea and stared out of the window. There were faint glimmers of sunshine. I knew that Reg would be awake and preparing for the day ahead. He was to be transferred to Bethnal Green police station before travelling again to the undertakers.

At just after 10 a.m. we made our way down the road to W. English & Sons. Already the police were in evidence, an accumulating presence on the streets. A crowd had started to gather outside the funeral directors. We went inside and waited. There were a few familiar faces. In one of the smaller back rooms a table had been laid with sandwiches and soft drinks. The staff were very kind. It was another hour before Reg finally arrived. We heard a murmur gradually rising to a roar from the people outside and minutes later he was led, handcuffed to a female officer, into the room. There were hugs and embraces. He looked thin and drawn but insisted he was fine. A stiff whisky was surreptitiously poured into a glass of Coke and passed to him. He drank it down in one. Before leaving for the church Reg asked me to go with him to the Chapel of Rest. The prison escort accompanied us. Although they temporarily removed his cuffs, they remained in the room with us. Reg laid a photograph beside Charlie's coffin, a picture of the three of them in happier times. He took my hand and said a silent prayer. We leaned against each other. I was aware of the stillness, the scent of the flowers and Reg's terrible sadness. But above all, I was aware of the presence of strangers. Even in grief, he was not allowed a moment's reprieve. His emotions, like everything else, remained the property of the state.

Six months later I would find myself in that tiny room again. This time Reg would not be at my side. There would be no calming words. There would be no hand in mine. There would be no comfort.

When the moment came to leave we parted reluctantly. We were not allowed to travel together. The cuffs were reattached to his wrist. Reg was escorted back outside. I rejoined the others and we walked to the car. There were a large number of people gathered on the streets. They provided a sympathetic and vocal welcome. Their support meant a lot to him. As the cortège took the long route to St Matthew's, Reg was able to see again the parts of the East End he held forever in his thoughts. We went along Bethnal Green Rd, Vallance Road (where he had spent his childhood) and past Pellicis café before finally arriving at the church. The police presence was huge. With hundreds on the streets, along with a motorcycle escort and helicopters in the air, East London resources must have been severely stretched. There was no necessity for such extreme, or expensive, measures. The message, however, was as loud and clear as it was meant to be – Reg was a dangerous criminal and warranted the most extreme of precautions.

Inside St Matthew's we were reunited. I sat to his right. To his left was the officer he was handcuffed to. Two other prison officers sat behind. All around were his closest friends. The presiding priest, John Scott, had previously expressed his reservations about Reg being handcuffed in church. He found it, understandably, un-Christian. His complaints fell on stony ground. Reg was accepting of the situation. He would rather be shackled than not allowed to attend at all. Many people came up to talk to Reg and to pass on their condolences. Some he hadn't seen or heard from since Ron's funeral. As Freddie Foreman came forward to shake his hand, Reg had a moment of hesitation. Then, moved by how genuinely upset Freddie seemed at Charlie's death, he knew the time for anger had passed. Although he could never forget, he could at least forgive.

It was a moving service. Father Ken Rimini gave his address with feeling. He had known both Charlie and Reg for many years. His sentiments were expressed with understanding and compassion. It was not, as he said, his place to make judgements. Reg's recitation of the poem 'I am not there' was also played; he had recorded it in his cell at Wayland prison. After hymns and prayers, as the pall-bearers prepared to take Charlie away, Reg stood up. He took a step forward and placed his hand briefly on the coffin lid. As Charlie was taken from the church, Reg and I walked slowly behind. Once outside we were separated again.

The prison car followed the hearse on the long journey to Chingford. At the cemetery a path was forged through the crowds and Reg laid flowers on the graves of his parents, Ron and Frances. We stood together as final prayers were recited. After Charlie's body was lowered into the ground, Reg dropped a red rose on the coffin. He had time for only a few moments' contemplation before being led gently away by his escort.

↗ ↗ ↗

By the middle of May, Reg's own health was rapidly deteriorating. In addition to his stomach problems he had developed other uncomfortable symptoms. On visits with friends he would summon all his energy, making every effort to act as normal. It did not escape their notice just how unwell he looked. Alone, we would relax. Reg would lean his head against my shoulder and close his eyes. On 16 May he wrote:

Rob,
    I slept 7.30 p.m., woke at 12.30, made cup of tea, had two roll-ups. Put my lamp on and radio by earphones.

Straw is on a crackdown on crime – bet there is more to follow by him.

My windows are wide open – nice cool breeze. I like thinking in the early hours. Took a paracetamol. I reckon it's pretty obvious where inflammation is – my kidney!

You looked so lovely on the visit yesterday. I would just like to lay next to you and relax. Lately I just feel as though I just want to relax especially in your company. I reckon we should have a couple of visits soon just you and I. You have such a lovely smile you know.

Good on Radio 2 – music as I write. Big orange mist from lamps close by my window, giving off a glow. I can see TV still on in cells opposite me. I watched the rubbish for six years in Parkhurst special block. I reckon that's why I can't stand it now.

You are a good steadying force on my thinking and temper.

Well, good looking, I'll close now to have another cup of tea, a smoke. I'll write again soon.

God bless,
  All my love
    Reg xxxxx

Due to the death of Charlie, the Parole Board interview had been postponed. No new date had yet been set. Reg informed them he was ready to go ahead. He wanted it over and done with. The waiting was awful. In the meantime, aware that his refusal to work with the prison psychologist could be detrimental, he made the decision to see her. Charlie's fate had shaken him. He didn't want to die in prison. At their meeting she presented him with a list of assessments he would need to complete. These included the following: *Intelligence Test (WAIS III); Enhanced Thinking Skills (ETS) Semi-Structured Interview; Social Response Inventory; Mini*

Situations Inventory; Personality Questionnaire; Interpersonal Reactivity Index; Locus of Control; Long Questionnaire; Social Problem Solving Inventory; Consequences; Sentence Completion; Psychological Inventory of Criminal Thinking Styles (PICTS); Perspective Taking Questionnaire; Psychopathy Check List Revised (PCL-R). In addition he would also have to do the full Enhanced Thinking Skills course. Following this she expressed the likelihood that Reg would be considered for a group work programme and then, finally, that he would need to demonstrate he was applying the learning consistently over time before he could be considered for open conditions. Faced with similar demands I wondered if even the Governor could make it out of the gates.

Reg threw in the towel. Her opinion that it would be in his 'best interests' to remain at Wayland was the final straw. If he started her interminable list of assessments he would be there for the rest of his life. Whatever the outcome of the review he wanted to move on. He was prepared, if required, to do the ETS course but not under her supervision.

At the end of May he was taken to the hospital wing of Norwich Prison for X-rays. This wasn't anything to do with his own declining state of health but because another inmate, on the same wing, had been discovered to have tuberculosis. Many of the older cons, like Reg, had not been inoculated and were considered to be at risk. Fortunately, he got the all-clear.

By June there was still no word from the Parole Board. Reg finally completed the last chapter of his book. It was no small task bearing in mind the emotional and physical pressures he had been under. He closed with the words: 'This will be the sixth book I have completed and now I will take a long rest. I feel at peace with the world so I cannot complain.'

As summer approached, Reg grew more restless. He felt a desperate need to get away from Wayland. He began to talk again about the future. Closing his mind to the prospect he might never be released, he dreamed of new starts and better days.

3 June 2000

Rob,

I slept early but decided at 10.30 p.m. to stay awake for a while. I just took another Stelazine. Hope you had a good night with your friends. I miss you so much, but let's hope all will come together when we leave this area so we are eventually together. Not looking for big company, just you and I most of the time.

I've got windows wide open – earphones for my cd on. Seems such a long night. Just had 2-3 glasses of water and lemon juice. More I drink of it more I want.

I'm not much of a letter writer lately. All my emotions have been put to pen so many times over the years. Be glad to speak to you at a.m.

God bless,

All my love, Reg xxxxx

It wasn't until 3 July that Reg finally got his parole interview, a long and inexplicable delay despite the circumstances. He rang me afterwards. He had little idea of how it had gone; tired and anxious he had simply answered the questions that were put to him. The Board itself would sit, consider the reports, and make its decision on some undisclosed date during the following few weeks.

The very next day Reg was taken again to hospital. His continuing illness appeared, at last, to be causing some concern to prison medical staff. Having diagnosed a minor kidney infection they seemed surprised by the absence of any improvement. The antibiotics had been ineffective. His symptoms had not subsided. Reg was not recovering. They opted for a second opinion. A hospital ultrasound was able, temporarily, to put their minds – if not ours – at rest. There was no indication of anything 'serious'.

Reg was returned to Wayland. His health didn't improve. It grew only worse. For all his pain and discomfort he was rarely prescribed anything stronger than aspirin. The arrival of summer was a mixed blessing. Although Reg enjoyed the longer lighter days, he found the heat and humidity hard to endure.

12th July 2000

Rob,

It is so hot in the cell even though I have window open. It takes me all my time to write just a couple of letters these days. You and I both need a complete change and some good news as a stimulant. With my complaints it's made me feel right low, but I'll get there. I'm laying on my bed trying to hide away from the heat of the sunshine. It's going to be too hot this season of summer for me. I prefer it cool. I'll just try to take it easy rest of the night and try to get my stomach right. Sorry it's not a more cheerful letter.

Goodnight,

God bless, All my love

Reg xxxxx

P.S. Let's be more optimistic and look forward. We will have a lot to look forward to, especially a move for both of us. It will be like a breath of fresh air, you see.

Less than a week after writing this letter Reg phoned and told me something I will never forget. He had just spent a wretched night. Feeling desperately ill, he had reached for the emergency bell. He rang again and again but nobody came. Whoever was on duty that night had no interest in offering help or assistance. Reg was left alone. Eventually, he just gave up. Sick and in pain, he waited for morning.

On 27 July the authorities finally conceded there might be an undiscovered problem and moved Reg to Norwich Prison Hospital. Here he could be kept under observation. I arranged a visit for the following day and, along with Bradley and Donna, made the short trip into Norwich. We were alarmed by Reg's appearance. He looked ashen. He was in obvious pain and spent the whole visit clutching his stomach. I went to the desk and asked if someone from the medical department could come over and provide some pain relief. I knew they had been giving him paracetamol and stressed that he needed something stronger. It was half an hour before a nurse finally arrived and passed over two white tablets. They were, unsurprisingly, paracetamol. Reg held them in his hand, shook his head and said he couldn't swallow them. Donna went and got a glass of water and I broke the tablets into little pieces. Eventually, slowly, he was able to take them. I was angry with the staff but held my tongue. I didn't want to create a scene. Reg was in their care and he would have to deal with the consequences if any offence was taken.

Reg had never looked this bad before. The physical pain was also affecting him psychologically, making him extremely depressed. He was quiet and solemn, far from his usual self. When the call signalling the end of the visit came he stood and put his arms round me. We held each other in a long silent embrace. Goodbyes were never so hard. I felt afraid for him.

We didn't talk much on the way home. We all had the same thoughts. As soon as we got back I tried to ring the prison doctor. It wasn't until the Monday that she eventually returned my call. She seemed blasé about the situation and stressed that there was absolutely *nothing* to worry about. They now suspected Reg had a urinary tract infection. He would be taken to the main hospital for examination by a urologist the next day. Despite her confidence, I remained worried. An infection didn't explain any of the other long-standing symptoms. The tests were duly carried out but no immediate conclusion reached. He was told he would have to wait a week for the results. I was glad that at least one of his problems was being investigated and relieved he was now in close proximity to a proper hospital.

Just a day later, on the morning of 3 August, the phone rang earlier than usual. As soon as I heard his voice I knew that something was wrong. Reg told me he was on his way to hospital. He had been violently ill and throwing up blood. I promised I'd be there as quickly as I could.

12. A ROOM WITH A VIEW

It was only after Reg rang off that I realized I didn't know which hospital he was going to. In a panic I called Norwich Prison but got no reply. I then rang Wayland. They told me they couldn't give out any information over the phone – I had to go there in person. Although I understood their caution, it was still incredibly frustrating. I ordered a taxi and went directly to Wayland. Once there, and recognized, the officers were kind and helpful. After a few calls they were able to tell me he was at the Norfolk and Norwich and also the name of the ward. I thanked them and dashed outside.

It was an interminable journey, the longest half-hour of my life. I felt desperately worried. On arrival I went straight to reception. Within minutes I was taken to see him. He was in a tiny room lying on a bed. The prison escort was also present. Reg gave me a hug. He said, 'I can't believe you got here so quickly.' We talked until he was taken down for his endoscopy in the early afternoon. This would involve sedation, followed by the insertion of a tiny medical camera into his stomach. It wasn't the most pleasant of procedures. I went with him while he was wheeled on a bed through the hospital, down lifts and along corridors. The prison officers couldn't have drawn more attention if they'd tried; cuffed and chained, he became the focus of everyone's curiosity. The restraints pulling on his wrist were an additional discomfort to the terrible pain he was already experiencing. I am not blaming the escort. Their orders came from above. Pain and incapacity were irrelevant. Rules could not, and would not, be broken for anything as mundane as common mercy.

After the procedure, I talked to the specialists. They had not got the results they hoped for. Dark liquids in his stomach had obscured their view. They took him for an immediate X-ray and this revealed a large blockage in his intestine. It was suddenly all systems go. An operation was scheduled for the next day.

I returned with Reg to the small room he had been allocated. We sat together on the bed. His two-man escort settled down on a couple of chairs. Reg was exhausted. He had passed from being told there was nothing wrong with him to being informed he needed a major operation. It was too much to take in. I put my arms around him. Within ten minutes he was fast asleep. I realized it was the first time I had ever really held him outside prison.

The following morning, at 10 a.m., Reg was taken down. He appeared calm but grasped my hand as he was wheeled along the corridors. I went with him as far as the theatre. We kissed and said goodbye. 'I'll see you soon,' I promised. I went back to the room and waited. There was no indication of how long it would take. I felt a combination of relief and dread; relief that he was finally being treated, dread at what they might find. I tried to stay hopeful. Reg had always been so fit and strong. Surely he'd come through. I had to be positive.

The first hour passed slowly. I paced the floor and stared out of the window. The second hour came and went, then the third and the fourth. Still there was no news. It became increasingly evident that something was wrong. I was grateful when Reg's old friend Wilf Pine arrived. Although unwell himself, he had driven straight from Dorset to Norwich. We sat together, both knowing there was bad news ahead. It was almost six hours after he had gone for surgery that we were told we could finally see him.

First the surgeon came to speak to us. The look on his face did not offer any comfort. He told us Reg had been through a long and difficult operation and had lost a lot of blood. They believed he might have suffered heart failure during the operation. As a result he had now been placed in intensive care. He said we shouldn't expect too much, that the next twenty-four hours would be 'telling'. The tone of his voice suggested we should prepare for the worst. He went on to inform us that a large growth had been removed from Reg's intestine and that a sample would be sent to the pathology lab. He claimed the obstruction did not look cancerous but he couldn't be sure. I listened and nodded and thanked him.

A nurse accompanied us to intensive care. It was in the lift that realization suddenly hit. I felt the cold shock of fear and disbelief. This couldn't be happening. I wasn't sure if I could keep on standing. I started to shake. The tears began to fall. I didn't want to cry. I couldn't afford to fall apart. This was the time he needed me most.

The room was small and dark, like a cocoon. Wired up to numerous monitors, surrounded by tiny flashing lights, Reg seemed adrift in the monumental complexities of modern medicine. I sat beside him and held his hand. He opened his eyes and smiled. I told him he was doing well, that everything was fine. While he rested Wilf interpreted the jumble of numbers and lines. Having been through many operations himself, he reassured me that Reg was quite stable and that the figures were good. Our main concern was for his heart – we were not to know there was a more lethal enemy lurking in the shadows.

After Wilf had left, I curled up in a chair beside Reg. I stayed with him throughout the night. The doctors and nurses checked on him frequently. Outside the room, his prison escort guarded the door. It was only their chains that had been temporarily removed. I watched him sleep. I prayed that he would get through these hours. Occasionally he opened his eyes and we talked for a little while until he dozed off again. I stared at the screens and the monitors. I listened to him breathing. Just before dawn, I laid my head on the bed. I woke half an hour later to find Reg stroking my hair. He said, 'Thanks for being here, Rob.' There wasn't anywhere else I wanted to be.

The next forty-eight hours were critical. Thankfully there were no setbacks and Reg grew gradually stronger. It was an immense relief when they said he was well enough to leave intensive care. He was to be transferred to Horsford Ward on the ninth floor. This was a ward specifically dealing with heart problems, a place where he could be closely monitored with regular ECT tests.

On the day that Reg was due to be moved the communications manager Mark Langlands spoke to me. The hospital had been inundated by press and media requests for information. Although the hospital was releasing regular if minimal bulletins about his condition, he asked if I'd like to do a press conference. It was entirely up to me. If I wanted to talk to them direct, it could be arranged. My initial reaction was absolutely not. I couldn't think of anything worse. But when I thought about it, I knew it was something I *had* to do. Reg was seriously ill. Although he had pulled through the operation, his future was still in the balance. We needed the media to start talking. We needed a debate. We needed them to put the questions that the Home Secretary was unwilling to answer. Was Reg ever going to be released? Was he ever going to be allowed any hope?

I don't remember much about the conference at all. Having barely slept for a couple of days, I was extremely tired. The cameras flashed and the queries came. I told them what I knew – that Reg was out of intensive care, that a growth had been removed and we were awaiting the results.

I also told them what I wanted – for Jack Straw to find it in his heart to show some compassion. Surely, after thirty-two years, punishment and retribution had been duly carried out. Revenge might be sweet but was it still appropriate? I talked briefly about the parole review. Trevor Linn had asked for a postponement shortly before Reg had been admitted to hospital. Aware of how ill Reg was, he had requested a delay of not more than six weeks so his medical condition could be properly assessed and an accurate diagnosis and prognosis given. We both felt it was wrong for a decision to be made in the current circumstances. If the Board were to sit and turn Reg down again, it would be the final blow.

I was glad when the conference finished. Although Reg was theoretically over the worst, it was still hard to be apart from him. I wanted to get back as soon as possible. There is nothing worse than being sick and alone. The surgeon's words remained constantly in my head – what they had removed did not *look* cancerous. I repeated it like a mantra, over and over. All the emphasis remained on the condition of his heart. Having survived the operation, and its aftermath, Reg had every chance of recovery.

It was a relief to escape and take the lift to the ninth floor. Reg had been allocated a small room next door to the main ward. With the press preoccupied by the conference, staff had been able to quietly move him from one part of the hospital to another. When I walked in he was lying in bed with an oxygen mask over his face; he looked as vulnerable and fragile as in intensive care. Two prison officers were already in residence, seated one on either side of the room. Reg was weak but still improving. He was able to talk for a while before slipping again into sleep. I stayed beside him, glad he was resting and thankful that he had pulled through.

The ward staff were the very best we could have asked for. Understanding, kind and considerate, they did their utmost to make Reg as comfortable as possible. It was here that he began his recuperation. Every day he grew a little stronger. A series of ECT tests were inconclusive as to whether he had actually suffered heart failure. There was, at least, no evidence of lasting damage. He was not permitted to eat after the operation and was only allowed a small amount of fluids. Although very thirsty he was limited at first to 60 ml of water every hour. Apart from this he was quite comfortable. Able to sit up and chat, he soon regained his former spirits. By the weekend he felt well enough to start seeing visitors.

In the meantime, the hospital offered me temporary accommodation across the road. They had some overnight rooms. It was a godsend. I was able to stay with Reg until late in the evening and return first thing in the morning. My greatest fear was that something would happen in the night and I wouldn't be there. I now had the reassurance that I was only a phone call and a short walk away.

I was surprised to discover that Horsford was far from a subdued ward. In fact the patients were probably the row-diest crowd ever encountered in a hospital! We could often hear them laughing through the walls. It was a good sound. Their banter and good humour was better than any medi-cine. When they discovered who their neighbour was, they sent a card wishing him well. The gesture was not lost on Reg. He really appreciated it.

He welcomed the attentions of HMP Norwich with less enthusiasm. Every day a governor from the prison came over to the hospital to assess his condition and to make a decision as to whether the handcuffs should go back on. He was given a temporary reprieve based on the number of drips and tubes that were already connected to him. It was made clear, however, that as soon as these were removed the cuffs *must* be reinstated. I was informed by a senior officer that there was pressure from 'above' (and he stressed *high* above) to chain Reg again as soon as possible.

One of Reg's major concerns was that he might be sent back to Wayland. While he should have been resting, it was always on his mind. He was not afraid of going back to prison; he just couldn't bear the thought of returning to that particular place. He had begun to feel trapped, convinced he would never be released while he remained there. The daily visits from Norwich Prison governors increased his distress. He was convinced the Home Office would shift him out of hospital and back into the system as soon as they could.

Reg fought against his illness, determined to get better. The doctors came every day and examined him. For a short while the signs looked good. The brutal scar on his stomach was starting to heal. He was even able to eat a little. Appetizing as hospital food is, he was grateful when a local friend, John Brunton, brought him a flask of home-made crab soup. Reg said it was the best thing he'd tasted in years.

We were feeling reasonably hopeful by the time the consultant received the pathology results. She came into the room carrying a small sheaf of papers. From the expression on her face it was obvious the news was bad. She perched on the edge of the bed and looked solemnly at us both. I took Reg's hand. I could hardly bear to listen to her. She didn't prevaricate, for which I was grateful: the tests showed that the growth was cancerous. Reg's hand tightened round mine. He didn't say anything. She went on to explain that he would need to be seen by an oncologist, a cancer specialist who could decide what method of treatment would be appropriate. There were various possibilities including radiotherapy and chemotherapy. Before she left she asked if we had any questions or if there was anything else we wanted to know. I couldn't speak. I looked at Reg. He shook his head.

The prison escort was outside the room. She asked them to wait and give us some time alone. We were grateful for that. Thinking he was over the worst, it was even more devaslating to hear the truth. Cancer is a terrible word. It arrives, so often, attached to hopelessness. Reg's mother had died of it. So had my father. We both knew exactly what those six letters could mean. There were things we wanted to say but how do you talk when you know there are two people waiting to come back in, two captors whose very presence takes away any chance of privacy or confidentiality? We only had ten minutes. We said what we could. We held each other. We made the most of the little time we had together.

The rest of the day passed slowly. There was nothing more we could share in the presence of strangers. Reality was slowly sinking in. In the early evening, while Reg was sleeping, I left the room and went down in the lift to the lobby I bought a coffee from the vending machine. Outside the main entrance was a small car park. At its furthest end was a low elbow-high wall. The main car park lay beneath. I walked across and leaned on the wall and looked down. This was the place I always came to, a place where I could usually be alone. There were a couple of window-boxes filled with pink and scarlet geraniums. I smoked a cigarette, sipped the coffee and watched the occasional car come and go. My thoughts that night were full of fear and dread. Eventually, I made the calls I had to make; I rang his solicitors and close friends and gave them the bad news. It was just as hard to say the words as it had been to hear them.

I stayed with Reg overnight. While he slept I considered the future. There was a fight ahead, two fights in fact, one against his illness and the other against the Home Office. If the former was out of my control, the latter certainly wasn't. He had spent over thirty-two years in prison and was now suffering from cancer. Surely the time had arrived for some small show of mercy.

Reg became more anxious over the following days. He found it increasingly hard to suffer the presence of the prison escort. He not only had to find a way to deal with his illness but also to endure the indignities it brought. It was an additional discomfort that these were constantly watched and witnessed by the guards. At night the officers inadvertently disturbed his sleep; he woke to their coughs or their talk or the rustle of their newspapers. In such a small room it was impossible to move without creating a disturbance.

A continuing worry was that Reg would be returned to prison. We talked to senior staff from HMP Norwich and they confirmed our fears. Even if Reg were undergoing treatment he would still be transferred back into the system as soon as he had recovered sufficiently. It was a frightening prospect. I thought of what it would mean for him – being sick, enduring cancer treatment alone, returning after each session to an empty prison cell. The majority of people facing such an illness have their family and friends to turn to for love, comfort and reassurance. Reg would only be allowed three visits a month. How could he survive? He would go back to prison knowing he had cancer and that he was probably facing another parole knockback. The treatment might give him time but all that time would be swallowed up by his continuing incarceration. There would be no reason to keep going or to keep fighting.

There was only one hope and that was for compassionate parole. If Reg were released from prison his chances of recovery would be vastly improved. At this point we were still in the dark as to the severity of the disease. Cancer had been found but its extent was unknown. His assessment for therapy would be made after he recovered from the operation. During these days our close friends offered endless support and encouragement. Everyone knew someone who had cancer, someone whose story gave hope if not of complete recovery then at least of temporary reprieve. It was something to cling to.

We were asked by the hospital if we'd like to see a Macmillan nurse. We were, in all honesty, rather indifferent and agreed more out of politeness than anything else. Sandra, however, proved to be a revelation. She was helpful, friendly and understanding without ever being intrusive. She also knew about every treatment that was currently available.

I was in constant contact with Reg's solicitors, Trevor Linn and Mark Goldstein. While Trevor began the preparations for an application for compassionate parole, Mark dealt with the media. Although we had always appreciated everything they had done, I will never forget their hard work, support and kindness during this period. Other good friends, like Donna Cox, sent regular messages for which we were grateful. Reg saw a few people on visits – Bradley and Donna Allardyce, Joe Martin, Tony and Tracey Mortimer, Johnny and Rose Squibb, Adam Myhill, Richard Reynolds, Billy Knox (who flew back from Nigeria), Dave and Brenda Whitmarsh, Patsy Manning, and of course Wilf, who came as often as he could. Flowers, cards and letters poured in from all over the country. The hospital switchboard was swamped with calls.

A few days after Reg was diagnosed with cancer I was told that a journalist from a Sunday newspaper wanted to talk to me. Although many reporters had made similar requests this one was a little different – he claimed to have photographs of Reg taken in hospital. I didn't see how it could be true but, along with Wilf, I went to meet him. This was the same paper that had printed the purported 'exclusive interview' with Reg after Charlie's death. We met just outside the main doors. After mutual introductions he produced a large brown envelope and withdrew a number of black and white prints. He passed them to me. The pictures had been taken in the room on Horsford Ward, shortly after Reg had left intensive care. With an oxygen mask over his face he looked, as he had indeed been, extremely ill. I felt sickened by them. The reporter claimed they had been sent

anonymously and that no fee had been paid. I didn't believe
him then and I know for certain now that he was lying. My
initial instinct was to walk away but the reporter had come
with more than just a set of pictures. He wanted to make a
deal. In exchange for permission to print the photos they
were offering to run a major campaign backing our application for compassionate parole. It would run for several
weeks, on double-page spreads, putting increased pressure
on the Home Secretary to make a decision. I felt caught
between the proverbial rock and a hard place. We needed all
the publicity we could get but the price was Reg's privacy. I
suspected they would run with the pictures whatever my
response. Having gone to so much effort to procure them, it
was unlikely they wouldn't eventually publish. The decision
had to be mine. I couldn't even discuss it with Reg. With two
prison officers permanently encamped in the room, it was
impossible to have a private conversation. Wilf believed
there wasn't any real choice. In the end I was forced to agree.
What was more important – privacy or freedom? Eventually
I signed the piece of paper agreeing to publication. I didn't
feel good about it. I felt disgusted.

   The pictures appeared the following Sunday. These were
slightly different to the ones I had been shown. By this time,
fortunately, I'd been able to warn Reg. During a brief period
when the prison officers were absent from the room, I told
him what had happened. He didn't blame me for the decision I had taken. It was still a shock for him to see the actual
photographs. The article suggested he was close to death.
Still in recovery from his operation, it was the very last thing
he needed to read.

   The pictures created problems for the hospital. The staff
came under suspicion. Had one of them taken a camera into
Reg's room? They were all, unfairly, put under scrutiny. The
prison authorities were also less than happy. Despite the permanent bed-watch, someone had managed to surreptitiously

take a series of snaps. I spent the morning staring at the paper. There had to be a clue as to who had done it. I thought at first I must have been absent from the room but on closer examination discovered one particular picture that showed Reg lying on the bed with his left arm by his side and his hand in mine. That was the strangest feeling, knowing I was there when the photographs were actually being taken. That was also the point when I realized who must have taken them.

The next few days were difficult. Reg was faced with the knowledge that someone close had sold him out for a handful of cash. He knew who it was. It didn't help his recovery. He couldn't understand why they had done it I didn't have any answers for him. He wasn't angry. He wasn't even bitter. He was just hurt and confused. At any other time he might have coped but in his current state the blow was cruel and terrible.

Reg tried to concentrate, as best he could, on getting better. He found it hard to be confined to bed. He missed his daily showers but always insisted on keeping clean and shaving every day. He made a few phone calls and wrote some letters but most of his time was spent simply in recuperating and getting the rest he needed. Although sick and anxious he tried to keep a positive attitude. He appreciated the efforts of the medical staff, and the kindness of the nurses and auxiliaries. He never complained. He faced his illness the same way he had faced his prison sentence. He tried to make the best of it.

One morning, desperate for a proper wash, Reg managed to persuade the nurses to take him for a shower. It was not the easiest of missions. Attached as he was to so many drips and drains the enterprise was a major one. They could have refused but they didn't. Realizing how much it meant, they took the time to help. Some tubes were temporarily disconnected and others were waterproofed. Finally, wrapped in a dressing-gown, carrying soap, towel, sponge and tooth-paste, Reg set off towards the bathroom. I watched him walk slowly and unsteadily down the corridor. As if he were embarking on some major expedition I felt a sense of trepidation. Flanked by a couple of nurses, and escorted by a rather bemused pair of prison officers, he epitomized the victory of mind over matter. Ten minutes later he was back. Soaking wet and laughing, accompanied by a nurse almost as drenched as her charge, he proclaimed himself clean and happy! I will never forget the way he was that day. The physical effort exhausted him but mentally he was exhilarated, determined and hopeful. Suddenly anything was possible.

He was further cheered by a visit from his old friend Frank Fraser who made the journey from London. Reg was pleased to see him. Frank, as usual, was the only one of the old faces who showed any real concern. He had always been vocal in his support of Reg's release and had frequently visited him in prison. His good humour lifted Reg's spirits and they spent a couple of happy hours together.

Every morning the hospital consultants came to examine Reg and monitor his progress; they looked, prodded and investigated. They talked and made notes. By the middle of August initial optimism was gradually turning to concern. He was not getting any better. If anything, his condition was deteriorating. By now Reg had lost his appetite and could barely eat. The pain was getting worse. It was all going wrong. Finally, they made the decision to operate again. We knew what they suspected . . . that the cancer had spread. But nothing was certain. We tried to stay hopeful.

An operation was scheduled quickly. On the day it was carried out I waited in an empty room with Wilf and Bradley. It felt like a lifetime had passed since his first operation but it was only a few weeks. We didn't talk much. We stared at the blank magnolia walls preoccupied by our private thoughts. Prepared for a long wait it was a surprise when after only a couple of hours a prison officer put his head round the door and told us that Reg had left theatre. He said he was sitting up in bed and looked well. We all felt a rush of confidence. Perhaps things were not as bad as we'd imagined. Encouraged, we waited for one of the surgeons to come and talk to us.

Our expectations were soon dashed. Whatever we might have thought, whatever we might have imagined, the truth was ten times worse. We sat silently and listened. I can't even recall what he looked like . . . only his words remain in my head. What he said was brutal and terrible. There was no hope. There were no possibilities. There were no curative treatments. There was no further surgery, no drugs, no medication, no intervention that could prevent the inevitable. The cancer had taken hold. His bladder was virtually destroyed. His kidneys were failing. Reg was dying.

It is impossible to describe how I felt at that moment. There are words – desolation, desperation, despair, panic, rage, emptiness, fear – but all of them are hopelessly inadequate. Alone they are useless, together they barely start to express the beginnings of grief. When the surgeon had left we slumped forward in our seats. There was nothing left to say. Wilf and Bradley put their arms around me. Together we cried.

It was only fifteen minutes before Reg returned. He was delivered to a different room on a different ward. Oblivious to what had been found, he was bright and cheerful. Had we heard anything? Did we know how the operation had gone? As if by silent and mutual consent we stayed silent. None of us could bear to tell him. The doctors would come soon enough. By not speaking out, by not uttering those fateful truths, we held them away from us, hoping they might disappear, hoping a miracle might happen.

When the news was broken, Reg responded calmly. He asked the question we had been incapable of asking. How long did he have? They didn't know. All they could say for certain was that a kidney drain was needed if he wished to prolong his life. It was his choice. If the drain wasn't inserted he would, in a matter of days, drift into longer and longer sleep and eventually into death. It would be painless and peaceful. If he chose to have the drain his life expectancy would be increased but so too would the potential for pain. I knew which option Reg would choose. He hadn't come this far to leave without a fight.

Later that evening, as we were both trying to come to terms with the terrible prognosis, one of the doctors asked to speak to me. We went outside the room. He said he needed to discuss what would be done in the event of Reg suffering a heart attack. I looked at him blankly. He explained they needed agreement on whether he should be resuscitated or not. His personal opinion was that he shouldn't, taking into account the circumstances, but they required a definitive answer from Reg himself. I couldn't believe what I was hearing. Having just been told he was dying from terminal cancer, Reg was now expected to say he willingly agreed to forgo any attempts at revival. I could imagine how that would make him feel. It was more likely, I thought, to provoke an attack than prevent one. I said he couldn't ask that question – it wasn't fair after everything Reg had been through. At the very least they could wait until the morning. He had enough to cope with on this particular night. The doctor, however, was persistent. It had to be agreed. It was a matter of policy.

He went into the room and began to talk. Reg looked confused. I interrupted and explained that it was just red tape. There was nothing to worry about and there was nothing wrong with his heart. It was a situation, I assured him, that we would never have to face. I went to sit beside him. It was not the doctor's fault. I understood that. What I didn't understand (and still don't) is how anyone, anywhere, could have decided that such a question was both reasonable and compulsory.

If there was one thing Reg wanted it was to die a free man. Trevor was unable to submit his application for compassionate parole until the medical reports were forwarded. These finally arrived on Friday 25 August and, along with the legal representations, were faxed to the Home Office the same day. He was informed that we would probably get a response by the following Tuesday. It was a Bank Holiday weekend and everyone was away. We prepared ourselves for the long wait.

On the Saturday morning, while a nurse was attempting to take yet another blood sample from Reg, the door opened and I was told I was wanted on the phone. I went to reception and picked up the receiver. It was the Governor of Norwich Prison. After a brief preamble, he said he was pleased to inform me that Reg had been granted his compassionate parole. I heard what he said but it sounded unbelievable. I felt stunned. I felt like I was dreaming. *Compassionate parole*. We had some kind of conversation, a polite exchange of words, but nothing I remember clearly. I thanked him and put the phone down. My heart was racing. I could barely breathe. The door to Reg's room was six steps away. I wasn't sure if I could even walk. Before I had gathered my senses the phone rang again. The woman on reception smiled and passed it over to me. It was Mark. The news had been on the radio. Reg's release was already public knowledge. The Home Office, desperate to publicize the extent of their humanitarian and forgiving hearts, had not even bothered to ensure that Reg was the first to know.

I walked slowly back to our room. The prison officers, already apprised of the situation, were standing outside. They had not said anything to him. I opened the door and went in. The nurse was still there. I sat down beside Reg. I didn't want to tell him until we were alone. The next few minutes were an eternity. The skin of his inside arms was blackened and bruised; the daily collection of blood was becoming increasingly difficult. Although the needle was inserted again and again, Reg never complained. While he endured the pain I sat beside him, holding his hand while I searched for the right words. Every second was an agony. Eventually, she was successful. She took the sample, packaged and labelled it, and left.

And then, as gently as I could, I told him. The phone call had come through. After thirty-two years it was finally over. His compassionate parole had been granted. The papers had been signed. He was a free man. We looked at each other with incredulity. I could barely believe what I was telling him; he could barely believe what he was hearing. This was the moment he had waited so long for. He put his arms around me. Close to tears, we embraced and kissed. It was unreal, almost impossible. He was free. Nothing could detract from that simple single fact.

In reality the news was simultaneously wonderful and terrible, bittersweet, a truth overshadowed by an awful certainty. We both knew it and we both made a choice; we chose to make the best of that single gratifying moment. To be free was everything. The rest was just the future. We would face it when we had to. We were aware that Reg would never have got his compassionate parole unless the authorities were convinced his death was imminent. The medical reports had confirmed that fact. The Home Office had just reaffirmed it. Their gift of freedom was easily given. They thought it was finished. But nothing was over yet.

The prison escort left that afternoon. It was the first real symbol of Reg's freedom. He had finally gained not only his liberty but also some much-needed privacy. The relief was immense. I have no complaints against the men and women who acted as bed-watch but their presence was always, by its very nature, intrusive. When Reg and I had needed to speak, we had not been able to. Every hope, fear and word was constantly witnessed. Although they were, on the whole, kind and courteous, we were still far from sorry to see them go.

For the rest of the day we talked. The room was finally ours. For the very first time we could speak freely. In the early hours Reg suddenly asked if there was anything I wanted to know. We looked at each other. I shook my head. There were many parts of his life I might have wished to understand a little better but the time had passed for questions and answers. When sleep finally overtook him, I curled up in the chair beside his bed. For the next five weeks, day and night, I stayed beside him. After spending so long apart, we were grateful for the time we had together.

Reg had been moved onto a busy post-operative ward. Instead of waiting for the nurses, we developed our own daily routine. Early each morning I would help him to wash and shave. He was losing weight and was often very tired. He found it hard, as anyone would, to be unable to do the simplest of tasks. I would make us both a cup of tea before the consultants came round. They would proceed with the same examination and ask the same questions to which they always got the same replies. There was no progress. There was only one thing Reg wanted now and that was to leave hospital. Until he was able to eat, however, he couldn't be discharged. He remained on a permanent drip, receiving intravenously all the nutrients and fluids essential to his body.

The following weeks, apart from X-rays and tests, Reg spent sleeping, talking and listening to music. Bradley and Donna often sat with us. On a couple of occasions someone came in to cut his hair and give him a proper shave; it broke the routine and made the day a little different. When he felt well enough Reg enjoyed having other visitors although he tired quickly and found it hard to talk for long. The situation with visitors rapidly became a major problem. A number of acquaintances and complete strangers began turning up at the hospital on a daily basis. Although he would not see strangers, Reg found it hard to refuse anyone he knew. This put an additional strain on him. Sometimes his eyes would close and he would drift off to sleep even while they were talking. Although he appreciated their kindness, he needed to rest. It was impossible to do this with a constant stream of people coming in and out of his room. I was worried and even the doctors expressed their concern.

In the end, we had to make an arrangement with the hospital that no visitors, unless previously arranged by Reg, would be allowed in. His health had to take priority. Reg asked security to deal with any uninvited guests and to explain the situation. I know that many of them understood but a few took it as a personal slight. It was never meant that way. He had many friends and cared about them all but it wasn't possible to see everyone.

After Reg's death, I was accused of 'preventing' people from seeing him. To quote Freddie Foreman, who had not visited his old associate once in the previous four years, 'We was all kept away – by Roberta, obviously. She was in charge, in control of everything.' I think Reg might have had something to say about that! Although physically impaired his mental faculties were far from damaged. He continued to make his *own* decisions about who he wanted to see – and when. He frequently used the pay-phone, which could be wheeled in beside his bed, to make calls. It is sad to note that it was only after terminal cancer was confirmed that many of his old associates and relatives showed any interest in meeting him again.

Another event occurred around this time. A photograph of our wedding was printed in a paper. As we were only in possession of ten prints ourselves, and this wasn't one of them, we were rather bemused. Having spent over three

years trying to retrieve the pictures from the Prison Service
it was surprising to find one suddenly splashed across a
Sunday tabloid. The following week a second paper published several more. Despite a written statement, in which
the prison authorities stated quite categorically that we
would not be allowed any further photographs of our own
wedding until Reg was released, their promise of holding the
photos in 'safe-keeping' was beginning to look a little empty.
It was distressing that photos of huge sentimental value to
us both had mysteriously found their way from the Prison
Service to the *Sunday People* and the *News of the World*. Mark
Goldstein rang the latter and asked if they would forward on
the prints they had. A few days later they delivered an album
with a set of over twenty pictures.

Reg fought hard to try to get himself well enough to leave
hospital. As time passed it became obvious that he was not
making the required progress. Every movement became
more of an effort. Although mentally he was still alert and
lively, physically he was growing weaker. One morning,
when it was quiet, Reg told me he wanted to organize his
funeral. It wasn't something that I wanted to talk about but
he was insistent. He asked me to ring his solicitors, Mark and
Trevor, and ask them to come down as soon as possible. In
the meantime I provided him with pen and paper and he
proceeded to make notes. He said it would be easier for me
if everything was in place. He chose the hymns and prayers
and made a list of his pall-bearers. It was this list that was
later to cause uproar. Reg chose, quite naturally, those who
were closest to him. Although there were some friends
who due to age or ill-health could not be included he was
happy with his final decision.

Mark and Trevor came the next day and Reg went
through the arrangements. They stayed for a couple of
hours, wrote down his instructions and gave the necessary
reassurances that all would be done as he wished. He was

pleased that everything had been sorted out and he didn't need to think about it any more. His peace of mind was short-lived. Less than a week later, having mentioned his choice of pall-bearers, someone suggested they should consist (like Ron's) of the old faces. The idea had never entered Reg's mind. There had been so little contact in recent years. They had all, long ago, gone their separate ways. With no visits and no letters, the occasional Christmas card was the only indication they had ever known each other.

It soon became obvious that some rather distasteful lobbying was taking place on behalf of certain people who believed it was their 'right' to carry his coffin. Reg felt upset and pressurized by the suggestion that this was what 'Ron would have wanted'. Reg was, apparently, obliged to have a proper gangster funeral – with proper gangsters in attendance. That Reg had, for the past twenty years, abhorred being labelled simply as a gangster was a detail of little importance to them. He told the person who had raised the subject that he would think about it. He discussed it with me that evening. I felt desperately sorry for him. Already so ill, this was a further unwanted and unneeded burden. What should he do? It was a question I couldn't answer. All I could suggest was that he followed his instincts and did what he thought was right. Who did he really *want* for his pall-bearers? Why had he originally chosen the people he had? No one else could speak for Ron and say what he would or wouldn't have wished. I told him I would abide by any decision he made – but that the decision must be his.

Reg made the choice to stand by the four friends he had initially picked. These were Bradley Allardyce, Mark Goldstein, Tony Mortimer and Adam Myhill. It was not intended as a rejection of his old associates or his former life. It was simply a matter of the heart. Through the difficult years, through the parole knockbacks, the disappointment and despair, it was mainly the love and support of his more recent friends that had given him the courage to continue. He would not, even for the sake of 'gangster tradition', turn his back on them now.

It was around this time that Reg suddenly expressed a desire to go outside. Tired of his hospital bed, of being constrained, he longed to breathe fresh air again. It was not an impossible request. We discussed it with the staff nurse and security. They were sympathetic and understanding. The medical practicalities were surmountable but a more pressing problem would be the media. They had more or less surrounded the hospital. We had to find a place where he was safe from intrusion. A few locations were put forward and eventually we settled on the small internal courtyard, a peaceful area filled with flowers and plants, and accessible from several wards. With no direct access from outside the hospital, it looked the best solution.

Plans were made and late one morning Reg was helped into a wheelchair. He struggled into a jacket and a blanket was placed across his knees. We went quietly through the corridors, down in the lift, swiftly across the foyer, through another ward, and eventually arrived at our destination. It was the first time Reg had been outside in six long weeks. He had chosen the perfect day. The courtyard was very still. It smelled of summer dust. The sky was cloudless, a strong unbroken blue, and the sun was shining. For a moment it was possible to believe that we weren't in a hospital but in some secluded garden far away. No one spoke. Reg raised his face and closed his eyes. He breathed deeply. I knelt down beside him and placed my hand on his arm. It was the last time he ever felt the sun on his face.

On our return, twenty minutes later, Reg was quiet. Lost in thought he was helped back to bed. For the rest of the morning he slept. In the afternoon he began to talk again about leaving hospital. He knew his time was running out. He had gained his compassionate parole but remained, in different ways, a prisoner. Anchored by tubes and drips, he was still without the freedom he craved. I talked to the consultants but their position was clear – they couldn't discharge Reg in his present condition. They were, however, sympathetic to his plight and were prepared to do everything they could to stabilize and help him.

If Reg was to achieve his dream it was essential to find somewhere, not too far from the hospital, where he could spend what remained of his life in comfort, privacy and freedom. A few people offered places but none were suitable. Eventually John Brunton suggested the Town House, a small hotel about ten minutes' drive away. I went with him one morning to take a look. The manager showed us the room. It was the honeymoon suite, pleasant and with reasonable space, but what attracted me most was the view. The lawn ran directly down to the River Wensum, a wide expanse of silvery water with an occasional boat drifting by. It was an idyllic scene. If Reg was strong enough he might even be able to sit outside in the gardens.

I knew that Reg's presence would bring a lot of attention to the hotel which, on a purely practical level, would be advantageous to them. On the other hand, I was also aware that the seriousness of his condition might deter them from accepting the responsibility of having him as a guest. I was relieved when the manager, Gordon Graham-Hall, agreed and with necessary optimism I booked the room from the end of the following week, an open-ended agreement as I had no idea how long we might stay there . . . or even if we would get there at all.

It was good to have some accommodation sorted. The doctors and nurses, along with members of the administrative staff, various specialists, the occupational therapist and our Macmillan nurse Sandra, all worked together to ensure that Reg could be successfully moved. I can't praise them enough for all they did. The ward sister, Sheila Ginty, was

especially supportive; she helped with many of the arrangements as well as organizing a local GP and district nurses.
She went through everything with me, forgetting nothing,
making sure I was equipped in every way to cope. Sandra
was also excellent. I will never forget her encouragement,
understanding and compassion.

The next week was a frenzy of activity. It began with
a visit from a documentary team. Reg had agreed to give a
final interview. He neither asked for nor received any money
for this. There were simply things he wanted to say and to
share before he died. Above all he wanted to make clear that
the road he had taken was a terrible and painful one, and
if by speaking directly he could deter other people from
making the same mistakes then perhaps something good
could eventually come from it all. He was extremely honest
and open. For a couple of hours the room was full of people,
lights and equipment. Despite his discomfort he tried to talk
for as long as they needed and to answer all their questions.
One moment stands out for me above all others. When asked
if he was bitter about what had happened in his life, Reg
replied, simply, that he no longer had time to be bitter.

It would be wrong to claim that his motive in doing the
interview was entirely altruistic. Reg would never have
claimed it himself. Equally, he was not devoid of good intention. If he wanted to be remembered, he also wanted to make
a difference. He didn't want anyone else to endure what he
had been through. Reg knew what he had lost – and why.
Over half of his life had been taken away. Had it been worth
it? Was reputation and a place in history a fair exchange for
over thirty years in prison? Was respect more important
than love? Was existing in mythology better than existing
in life? For Ron the answer had always been a resounding
Yes. For Reg it had never been quite so clear.

Both he and Ron had always been driven by publicity.
Since childhood the attention of the media had bestowed

some essential meaning on their lives. It was the press that had lifted them out of the East End and on to the front pages of another world. From their early boxing achievements, through street fights, to teenage court appearances, it was the newspapers that provoked an unexpected and gratifying local respect. That respect bred confidence and that confidence, in turn, gradually inspired a very different kind of ambition. Success, at whatever cost, became the imperative. Fame and infamy were just two sides of the same coin. If the twins were entranced, the media were equally so. Throughout the years, especially after their imprisonment, the press continued to simultaneously pursue, encourage, glorify and condemn. Every few months brought a new story. Like resentful but symbiotic partners they fed off each other, both requiring something only the other could provide.

At the end, Reg could have kept his silence. But he was drawn, as he was always drawn, towards some sense of resolution. If he could not openly express all his disappointments, he could at least try to dissuade others from embarking on the same pointless journey. He had walked the path that Ron had designated. It was not his choice but he had accepted it. The responsibility for everything that had happened must be shared between them. In his final public statements Reg tried to find a way to explain.

The evening after the interview was not a quiet one. Reg was restless. Although desperately tired, he couldn't sleep. The day's events ran through his head. He had been forced to face, in the matter of a few hours, many of the major questions about his life. In the ward next door a woman moaned and cried. The sound resounded through the walls, sad and terrible, a pitiful backdrop to our own solemn thoughts. The room was in semi-darkness, lit only by a weak night-light. The evenings grew dark more quickly now and although it wasn't late the sky was almost black. To Reg's side the green numbers blinked on the monitor. It reminded me of the time he had spent in intensive care, of that eternal night when his life had hung in the balance. His victory in the morning had seemed absolute, his survival guaranteed. How impossible that it had come to this. And then, as if our thoughts had mysteriously collided, Reg reached out and took my hand. He said, as he had said once before, 'Thanks for being here, Rob.'

It was late by the time he fell asleep. For a while I watched him. He lay on his back with his head to one side, breathing with steady and peaceful regularity. After half an hour, I slipped quietly out of the room and along the dim and now quiet corridors. I took the lift to the foyer. In recent weeks, because of the constant presence of the press, I had avoided the main door and gone instead to another of the hospital's multiple exits. But it was now 2 a.m. and evasion was unnecessary. There was no one else around. The car park was empty and I went and stood, as I had stood so many times before, by the low wall. Beneath me the second larger car park stretched out. Most of the spaces were vacant. Only the vehicles of the night-staff remained, scattered at irregular intervals. From this height they looked as small as children's toys. The night air was cold but I didn't want to leave. It was here that I had come after Reg's first operation. It was here that I had given thanks for his survival. It was here, night after night, that I had talked on the phone, relaying news, gathering messages, discussing parole and garnering every possible piece of hope. It was here that I had stood alone and prayed. This space, this place, this mundane car park contained so many memories.

Although by the middle of the week everything was in place for the move, one insurmountable problem remained – Reg was still not well enough. He was sedated and taken for another endoscopy. It was established that the artificial tube the surgeons had inserted from his stomach to his intestine remained unblocked. Our biggest fear, that the cancer had spread again and closed it down, was unrealized. Certain muscles in the base of his stomach were simply not working properly. The news, although good, had its downside; there was little they could do, beyond what had already been tried, to force the muscles to work.

The consultant came to see Reg. She offered one last chance. In some cases, she claimed, if the patient ate something solid the muscles would begin to move of their own accord. This would, however, mean removing the thin plastic tube that currently ran through his nose, down his throat and into his stomach, the tube that prevented him from being constantly sick. The decision was his. Reg didn't hesitate; he knew what he wanted. He didn't intend to die in hospital.

The tube was removed the next morning. At midday John Brunton drove from his pub and kindly delivered to Reg the lunch he had requested – a steak and all the trimmings! A part of me was terrified. If things went wrong now, if his stomach rejected the food, then Reg would never leave hospital. He ate his way slowly through the whole steak and thoroughly enjoyed it. It was the first real meal he had consumed in quite a time. He was aware it might also be the last. The next few hours were critical. We waited and waited . . . but there were no ill-effects. The night passed without incident. I knew then, disasters permitting, that we were finally on our way.

Within twenty-four hours the consultant had given Reg permission to leave. It was Friday 22 September. We all knew time was of the essence. By then everything, or almost everything, was in place. Having hoped to leave on the Saturday, it was a bonus to achieve the extra day. Only one problem remained. We had to find a way of getting Reg out of the building without being besieged by the press. The initial plan was for us to leave around midday. John Brunton had arranged for a white Rolls-Royce, which he intended to drive himself, to take us from the hospital to the hotel. He wanted to do something special for Reg and was waiting for our phone call. A hospital manager, the head of security, and the communications manager Mark Langlands, came to talk to me. We had previously gone through various 'escape routes' and made some decisions as to the best exits. All the administrative staff had been extremely understanding throughout Reg's stay and helped to make things more tolerable, especially as regards the media. But now they had an even bigger challenge on their hands; the press were gathering in the foyer and around the hospital – someone had leaked the news that Reg was leaving. There were not, at present, huge numbers but news travels fast. We had to get out as quickly as we could.

Wilf arrived at around 10 a.m. with his friend Alex. They barely had time to get out of the lift and catch their breath before the situation was explained. Our only chance was to leave immediately. Wilf's car was parked outside. We couldn't wait for the Rolls; its presence anyway would only draw attention. We talked to various members of security and staff and started to reorganize. The exit was chosen and a new plan made.

There are many things I could say about the press, not all of them complimentary. I appreciate they have a job to do but sometimes their work seems to slip beyond the parameters of common humanity. In response some would probably retort that Reg was not entirely blameless on that score either and who can argue, except to say that Reg was punished for his sins while the press are constantly rewarded for theirs. It would be hypocritical of me to condemn them out of hand and I don't wish to do so. A small number of journalists and editors gave Reg and myself a fair hearing during the last years of his life and for *their* integrity I will always be grateful. On this particular morning, however, with Reg as ill as he was, their presence was just another mountain to climb. All Reg wanted was to leave hospital quietly. He didn't want to be surrounded by reporters. He didn't want a hundred flashbulbs going off in his face. He was dying and he knew it. His life was almost over.

I helped Reg to get dressed and into the wheelchair. He put on a tracksuit and slipped some trainers on his feet. We both smiled. It was finally happening. While checks were made on his medication, I simultaneously tried to thank the nurses, say goodbye, and pack the rest of our belongings. Pack, in fact, is far too inaccurate a word. I hurled everything into bags; clothes, soap, toothpaste, books, razors, letters and cards found a home in whatever space was available. It was one mad rush. There was little time to think about anything. As we left the room I gave it one final backward glance; we had spent the last five weeks together there and it was full of memories. It was incredible, unbelievable, that we were actually leaving.

We went down in the lift. On the ground floor Wilf and Alex left and went to collect the car. Reg and I, along with staff nurse Sheila Ginty, Mark Langlands and a senior member of hospital security, descended to the basement and from there made our way through the bowels of the hospital. We walked for several minutes until we reached the pre-arranged exit. Wilf, thankfully, was waiting for us. After a quick look round, we helped Reg into the back of the car and then loaded up the luggage. The next few minutes were frantic. Carrier bags, holdalls and cases were forced into every corner. The wheelchair had to be dismantled but our need for haste made simple actions clumsy and we fought and fumbled with the mechanics for what felt like hours. Eventually we squeezed all the component parts into the limited space. Our final thanks and goodbyes were hurried and inadequate. I got into the back with Reg. Wilf started the engine and we pulled away.

We drove unnoticed through the hospital grounds and out through the exit. On reaching the main road there was a common exhalation of breath, a shared relief at what had been avoided. We didn't talk much. Reg was quiet. Occasionally he looked out of the window. As we passed through the Norwich streets I knew this wasn't what he'd ever imagined. His final freedom should have been a time of elation and hope. He should have been looking towards the future. I wondered how many times he had envisaged this day, this moment . . . but never like this. His thoughts were his own. None of us can know exactly what they were.

John Brunton had arranged for help at the Town House. As soon as we arrived Reg was assisted up the stairs and into the room. I think it was at that second, as we passed through the door, that the truth really hit us all. Reg was out of prison and out of hospital. He was finally and absolutely free. As if the knowledge provided a surge of adrenalin, Reg found the strength to move around alone. He walked unaccompanied to the window and looked out over the river. He was pleased with the room and the view. Wilf ordered champagne from the bar. We gathered chairs around the window and all sat down together. It was an incredible moment. Reg was in good spirits, more animated than he had been for many weeks. It was good to hear him laugh again. At one point he got up and made his way to the en suite bathroom. I watched him walk slowly but determinedly across the room. Whilst there he took the opportunity to take a good hard look at himself in the mirror. He wasn't happy with what he saw. A few minutes later he was back, not – as has been claimed – with a tear running down his cheek, but with the perfectly accurate observation that he looked 'bloody terrible'. Self-pity was never in Reg's repertoire.

That first day will always stay with me. After the others had left, Bradley and Donna joined us for an evening meal. We sat and talked. We could have been anywhere, at any time. It was like another beginning. It had, as all beginnings do, an inevitable end, but during these hours we were able to put aside the future. All that mattered was the here and now. Over the following week Reg's condition would worsen but he was able for a few precious days to savour his freedom. He was never going back to prison. That, at least, was over. Our world at the Town House might have been tiny, caught within another four walls, but it was more than enough. There were no bars on the windows, no orders, no demands, and no restrictions. He was free and we were together. The time was our own. These were Reg's real days of liberty and he appreciated them.

It was about 10 p.m. when Bradley and Donna returned to their room. After they had gone, the silence felt immense. It had been a day of constant activity and talk. For a minute I stood by the window and looked out. On the lawn there were benches and tables, all empty now. The air was still and cold. It was almost Autumn. Reg lay in bed, propped up with pillows, sipping a weak Scotch. He said he felt better than he had for weeks. It was as if he was drawing on every last shred of determination and will-power to grant his body a few days' grace from the worst rigours of the cancer. We slept in each other's arms, our first real night together, and woke late the following morning.

The weekend that followed was a good one. Reg could eat and drink a little. On the Saturday the doctor came, shortly followed by the district nurse. They checked Reg's medication and renewed his anti-sickness drugs and morphine. Reg was in bed and when they went to help lift him into a more upright position, he waved them away and heaved himself up with his arms. They could not believe how strong he still was. Before leaving, the doctor left a number in case of emergencies. I put it by the phone. I did not imagine then how soon we'd need to use it.

Outside the sun was shining and we debated whether to go into the garden. In the end Reg decided he'd rather stay put. The press were already ensconced in the bar and around the building; there was slim chance of any privacy if we stepped outside. We heard that one particular newspaper had even hired a boat and were cruising up and down the river, watching the windows. All Reg really wanted was some quiet time. The outside world had become irrelevant. After the chaos of the previous day, we indulged in a slow, relaxing and thoroughly enjoyable afternoon. Bradley and Donna had taken the room next door and they joined us for lunch and again for an evening meal.

There have been many tales not just about Reg and Bradley, but about Bradley and me. It is true, as regards the latter, that we had our differences but I never resented his presence. What I did resent were his actions. In the hospital, when it had become apparent that Bradley *must* have taken the photographs, Reg confronted him. At first he angrily denied everything but faced with the evidence eventually came clean. Why had he done it? Bradley claimed that he believed the publicity would be useful in securing Reg's release. He was unable to explain, however, why he hadn't told him. He also admitted that he'd been paid for the pictures. Reg felt, understandably, hurt and betrayed. He could have asked Bradley to leave – and he certainly thought about it – but with his own life drawing to a close it would have been a terrible way for things to end. Did he forgive him? I think he did. For the last week we tried to put it all behind us.

On the Sunday Trevor Linn and Mark Goldstein, along with his wife Donna, came to visit. It was good to see them. They had developed a unique bond with Reg. They had never let him down and he appreciated it. I was grateful too for everything they had done, for all their hard work, kindness and persistence. Their visit on this occasion was not to do with the law. It was not to do with justice or appeals or any other legal questions. All that was past. They came simply to spend some time with him. Reg, as always,

welcomed and enjoyed their company. Mark told me later
how shocked they had been by his appearance, how much
he had changed even since their last visit. It is to their credit
that they gave no indication of it and for the next couple of
hours proceeded to talk and laugh as they had always done.
When they left, however, it was with the sad and terrible
knowledge that they would never meet again.

Friday, Saturday and Sunday; those were the three
golden days. During them Reg maintained not just his physical strength but also his remarkable spirit. Having fought
and waited for so many years, this was finally *his* time. It
meant everything to him. Although many of his dreams
had been shattered, the most essential remained – he had his
freedom.

It was on Monday that everything began to change. He
woke feeling weak and tired and by midday had not rallied.
Joe Pyle, Johnny Nash and Freddie Foreman had made
arrangements to see him the following morning. Reg said he
couldn't cope with the visit and asked if I could cancel. For
the rest of the day Reg dozed, waking occasionally and then
drifting again into sleep. It was only late in the evening that
he became suddenly and violently ill. Alone I tried to help
whilst simultaneously scrabbling for the doctor's phone
number. It was close to midnight. I held him while I dialled,
hoping and praying there would be an answer. After a few
rings she picked up. I told her what was happening and she
arrived at the Town House within twenty minutes. I had
never been more pleased to see anyone in my life. With com-
petence and compassion she dealt with all his immediate
problems and also took the time, despite the hour, to talk.
Reg asked her some questions and she answered them hon-
estly. He was aware that he had reached another critical stage
– the cancer was spreading quickly. She asked, in return, if
he wanted to be readmitted to hospital. He said no. He
wanted to die in peace with the people he loved beside him.

That night was a turning point. During the week Reg became weaker, unable to eat or even to drink very much. He knew the battle was almost over but still fought to stay alive. He got through the days but enjoyed the evenings most of all, the music and the talk. These were always the hours he was most relaxed. One afternoon, we heard a rumour, relayed on the radio, that Reg had deceived the Home Secretary, the Prison Service and all the specialists at the Norfolk and Norwich Hospital . . . and was not seriously ill at all. He was, it was claimed, living the high-life at the Town House, smoking cigars and swilling champagne. It made Reg laugh. He said, 'Jack Straw must be having a few sleepless nights!'

It was only as the pain increased, and with it his intake of morphine, that Reg began to slip away. By the end of the week his periods of lucidity were rare. It was heartbreaking to watch. He continued to talk but in his own different world. He rarely responded to anything that was said.

On the Saturday night Reg was restless. He was coughing badly. Occasionally he would grasp my hand and murmur a few words. Something would flicker in his eyes, a momentary recognition, there and then lost again. At about 3 a.m., by some incredible effort, he suddenly raised himself up and swung his legs over the side of the bed. He said quite clearly, 'I've got to leave here now.' He tried to stand but his legs weren't strong enough. He sat back down on the bed. It was cold and he was shivering. I wrapped the bedspread round him. He put his head on my shoulder and I held him in my arms, rocking him gently. I think he knew what was happening. I think he knew it was the last night.

I was surprised to be told on the Sunday morning that Joe Pyle, Johnny Nash and Freddie Foreman, despite Reg's wishes, were already on the London to Norwich train. Reg was by now close to the end. He had made the decision not to see them when his mind was clear and their visit in the circumstances felt wrong. This was not the way he wanted to be remembered. There was, however, little I could do. Joe Martin, who had come the previous day, sat with Reg again for a few hours. I was sorry to see him go. He had always been a loyal friend.

The others arrived just after Joe had left. They had been in the bar and came rather noisily through the door, accompanied by Wilf Pine. I stood up and shook their hands; they avoided any eye contact and didn't exchange a single word. It was the first time I'd met any of the three, other than at Chalie's funeral, in the four and a half years I had known Reg. Donna was told to get some drinks. She was (understandably) short with them. If the trio wanted drinks, she said, they could ring room service. They gathered round Reg's bedside instead. Barely conscious, he was unaware of their presence. They bombarded him with questions and remarks to which Reg made no reply. He continued to talk quietly to himself. They seemed vexed by his inability to communicate.

I sat beside Reg. His breathing was laboured. He'd lost a lot of weight and the last of his strength had been ebbing away in recent days. He looked very small and fragile. Despite the morphine he was still in some pain. There was a problem with his right arm and he continued to worry at it, holding and stretching, sometimes grasping it with his other hand. While the chat went on around us, I gently stroked his arm.

As it became clear that Reg could not respond, our visitors turned their attention to me. They embarked on a series of criticisms. The most serious was that I was to blame for what had happened. If I hadn't allowed the first operation Reg would, allegedly, still be fit and well. I could not believe what I was hearing.

I was relieved when the district nurses arrived. They came every day to refill the syringes, to give advice and to adjust Reg's medication if necessary. I asked our visitors if they would be kind enough to wait downstairs. They seemed annoyed by the request but eventually withdrew to the bar. The doctor arrived shortly after. It took over an hour to complete everything they had to do. They treated him as always with kindness and compassion. It was clear he was in distress and they did their best to help. Although they moved him with the utmost care and gentleness, any movement at all caused him pain. As they rolled him carefully on his side he called out my name – for the very last time – and I held him in my arms, stroking his hair and talking softly while the medics completed what they had to do. With the additional pain and the deterioration in his breathing, they decided to increase the morphine and anti-sickness drugs.

After they had left Donna and I sat quietly on the bed. A short while later Bradley joined us. Gradually Reg's coughing subsided. He became less restless and more relaxed. He closed his eyes. He seemed to fall asleep. Although I knew our visitors were waiting to come back up, I didn't ring them. He looked so peaceful I couldn't bear for him to be disturbed.

When they finally returned Reg had completely lost consciousness. I was told they wouldn't stay long but once inside the room they showed no inclination to leave. I thought they had just come to say their goodbyes but, as the time passed, they continued to stand around the bed and stare at him. I sensed more than anything a dogged determination to *be there*. Reg's breathing grew worse. Both Wilf and Donna suggested they should go. I was relieved. I stood up, stood back and waited. None of them moved. There was no response. After a while I sat down beside Reg again. Donna repeated the request. This time she even went and opened the door. Foreman, as if threatened with an undesired eviction, scuttled off to the en-suite bathroom.

It happened quickly. Within a few minutes everything changed. Wilf made a comment; it came back to me in a disconnected form. I felt a kind of dislocation, of incredulity. I looked around and then back at Reg. Donna propelled Joe Pyle and Johnny Nash out of the room. They were just outside the door when Wilf's voice came to me again. I heard him say 'That's it . . .' Reg's breathing stuttered, stopped and then suddenly started again – one last tiny half-breath. And then there was nothing. Silence.

It was the worst moment of my life. I took him in my arms. His skin was warm, his eyes closed as if he were still sleeping. I put my hand on his forehead and stroked his hair. It couldn't be possible. Not this man I had known and loved. It couldn't be over. I was aware, distantly, of Wilf hammering on the bathroom door calling out to Freddie Foreman. When he finally emerged he walked slowly across the room. He paused at the foot of the bed. Then, like some terrible farce, the other two burst in again, fighting and bickering over who had the 'right' to stay. I was holding Reg and crying. It was a nightmare. Donna angrily pushed them all out and locked the door.

What is grief – disbelief, loss, a holding of breath? A fierce angry impossible pain? Hopelessness? Emptiness? There are no good words. There is only a grasping, an absence of understanding. I held him in my arms and cried.

Reg was dead.

EPILOGUE

Reg died a free man on 1 October 2000 just a few weeks short of his sixty-seventh birthday. For a brief period only the door was opened and the future given back to him. He died, as he had always lived, in the midst of controversy. Even in his final hours he was denied the peace he craved.

I returned to Watton dazed and shattered. Later the rage would come, the anger and the bitterness, but for now there was only disbelief. We had spent the last nine weeks together. I felt lost. Was this the truth – I would never see him, never touch him, never hear his voice again? It was impossible. There was no consolation and no comfort. There was no future. To go back in time, that was all I wanted, to relive every moment we had ever shared. Nothing can guide you through that maze of despair. I stumbled through the days and barely slept at night, waking over and over to the same brutal reality.

As I began the difficult but necessary arrangements for the funeral, I was faced with a different kind of nightmare. A newspaper containing an interview with Freddie Foreman was given to me. It purported to tell the story of the last moments of Reg's life. I could barely take in what I was reading. Foreman talked about his visit to the Town House, how he and Reg had chatted for a few hours and how he had finally urged his old friend to 'let go' just seconds before he died. He claimed, astoundingly, 'The last thing he said was he wanted us to be his pall-bearers.' I felt shocked and sickened. I couldn't make any sense of it.

All became clear in a matter of days. I received a phone call and was told that Reg had asked Foreman, Pyle, Nash and Ron's old friend Laurie O'Leary to carry his coffin. It was news to me. This request had allegedly been made not directly but 'through a friend' while Reg was in hospital. Already the story was changing. With too many witnesses, including the doctor and nurses, Foreman's original version of events could not stand up. Knowing Reg's final wishes, and knowing as well that they were lodged securely in his solicitor's safe, I refuted the claim. I asked, 'And what about Bradley?' Despite their differences, Reg had always wanted him to be there at the end. There was an uncomfortable silence followed by a rapid disconnection. A few minutes later I received another call. This time O'Leary had been unceremoniously dropped from the equation. Reg had now asked Foreman, Pyle, Nash and Bradley to be his pall-bearers. If it hadn't been so tragic it might have been funny.

Grief creates its own kind of strength and I refused to be bullied no matter what the consequences. And there certainly were consequences. Rumours began to circulate that I didn't want any gangsters at the funeral and that anyone of the criminal fraternity was unwelcome. It was nonsense. I wanted exactly what Reg had wanted – for everyone who had ever cared about him to be able to attend. Their histories were irrelevant. Reg had a past and a present and it was right that all his friends – current and former – should be there. I asked Wilf Pine to organize half the church and half the cars. In this way, through his contacts with former associates, I hoped to reach all the people who wished to pay their final respects.

For some, it was not enough. It was announced that Foreman was going to 'boycott' the funeral and others, including Tony Lambrianou, quickly followed suit. That any man could refuse to attend the funeral of an old friend because they, or their pals, had not been chosen as pall-bearers seemed a sad reflection not just on their integrity but on any feelings they might have held. It wasn't long, however, before another fact emerged. Foreman had a prior appointment with Scotland Yard. He was due, ironically, to be questioned over the Carlton documentary. His absence from Reg's funeral was far from a matter of principle. It was a necessity.

I should not have been surprised. The world of the old gangsters, as Reg himself had explained, was one of grudges, petty rows and resentments. Like petulant children they bickered among themselves, jostling for status and power. For as long as Reg and Ron were alive they all sought a part in the 'legend', trying to grab a piece of the limelight and a share of the lucrative spoils. To this end they constantly added to the mythology. They iconized the Krays whilst creating larger and more important roles for their own characters. They re-wrote history, made violence glamorous, stupidity admirable and imprisonment heroic. They upheld their reputations and paid their bills off the backs of two men serving life sentences.

Much has been written and will continue to be written about Reg Kray. Most is untrue or grossly distorted, a mixture of exaggeration and fantasy. There were many that perpetuated the myth through the years. It served a useful purpose to present Reg as a symbol, a one-dimensional figure, a personification of the 'glamour' of crime. That image helped to sustain and enhance the reputations of others who moved, or aspired to move, in the same circle. Even after thirty-two years they could not acknowledge or accept the person he had actually become. There was no room in their hearts, minds or ambitions for a different Reg.

He was cast in stone. Reg never attempted to deny who or what he had been. He never turned his back on the past but he no longer lived there; he had moved on and embraced the present. No one is unchanging.

The myth was useful to the authorities as well. While it continued to grow and to flourish, fed by so many books, reports and articles, Reg Kray could still be depicted as a potentially dangerous criminal and a threat to society. The facts were irrelevant. Did Reg deserve the relentless and unforgiving punishment he received? He was certainly guilty of some terrible crimes. His continued imprisonment, however, had little to do with justice or retribution. Many thousands of people convicted of more heinous crimes were released before him. Reg never complained. He had killed and accepted he must pay the price. That his punishment bore no relation to others convicted of similar offences was a truth he had to live with. He knew it was not simply a response to the accusations in the dock. The Krays had jeopardized the old Establishment. They had mixed with lords, MPs and people in 'society' . . . and for *those* sins they could never be forgiven.

What happened in the year following Reg's death was perhaps inevitable. For those who had contributed to the myth there was only one thing left to do – to deconstruct it as quickly and as viciously as possible. Alive they had glorified him; in death they vilified him. The only saleable option was an alternative 'truth', a different kind of lie. Allegation, revelation and insinuation became the new currency. The Kray gravy train was rolling again. It was business as usual.

Reg had anticipated it. There was little he could do but through the terms of his will he did try to prevent two particular people from exploiting his name. Although he had once loved both Bradley Allardyce and Paul Marcus he harboured no illusions. He left them legacies on the condition they did not talk to the media. His bisexuality was common knowledge and he had no reason to be ashamed of it. He did not, however, want me to wake one morning and see the intimate details splashed across a newspaper.

For a while all was quiet. But as it became clear (despite rumours to the contrary) that there were not substantial amounts in Reg's estate, Bradley decided to share some of his experiences. These culminated in a radio interview where he freely admitted his sexual relationship with Reg. His admission came with a speedily added addendum that 'it was against my will and he knew it was against my will'. There is another word for that particular act. It was not one that ever applied to Reg. As if suspecting something of the like might happen, Reg had given me a number of Bradley's letters. He said I might need them one day. Within them the truth is laid out. Bradley's own words betray his later allegations; he talks not just about their sexual relationship but how he himself had encouraged it.

He was not the only one to let Reg down. A few months after his death I logged on to the old Krays' web site and found some of Reg's personal letters up for auction. His old pal Flanagan was trading, like so many others, friendship for cash. His thoughts and feelings were for sale. His Parkhurst weight-lifting certificates were also on offer. Reg had spent six months trying to track them down – everyone, including his surviving relatives, had claimed they knew nothing of their whereabouts.

As arrangements proceeded for the funeral, I was grateful for the support of close friends. Mark Goldstein and Trevor Linn, Marcelle and Stuart Garratt, Donna Allardyce, Donna Cox and of course Wilf were always on the other end of the phone. I must also express thanks to Richard Grayston, who offered once again to organize the security, and to all his men who acted with decorum and dignity on the day. There were, in addition, many people, some of them strangers, who helped Reg during his time at the hospital and at the Town House. It would be impossible to mention them all but special thanks should go to the doctors and nurses, to John Brunton and to John Ledgard, for everything they did.

The date for the funeral was set for October 11. Despite the weather forecast, predicting thunderstorms, gales and torrential rain, the morning dawned bright and sunny. Reg, like Ron and Charlie before him, had defied the elements. A few of us met at Tony and Tracey Mortimer's. They had, kindly, arranged for transport to the East End. The roads were busy and we edged slowly along the Bethnal Green Road until we finally arrived at W. English & Sons. The hearse, with its beautiful black-plumed horses, was already standing outside. It was covered in flowers.

In the church I was glad to see so many familiar faces, including two dear friends called Clell and Janelle Posey, who had travelled all the way from the USA to attend the funeral. Others had also made long journeys. It was a comfort that in these final moments there were people present who truly cared for him. Some of the old associates – as they had threatened – stayed away. It seemed sad that they had chosen to forgo the opportunity to say goodbye. Whatever their feelings it was not the time for recriminations. There were many friends in the congregation, old and new, who said their farewells with genuine love and affection.

It was a long slow drive to Chingford. The cars crawled along the streets. I sat between Donna Allardyce and Donna Cox. We stared silently out of the windows. There wasn't anything left to say. Occasionally a hand crept out and squeezed my own. It was impossible to accept the finality of it all. I would never hear his voice again. I would never hear him laugh. I would never wake and see his face. He would never talk to me again, kiss me, argue with me, or hold me in his arms. There would be no more promises. The time for promises was past.

Reg had at least got the funeral he asked for. There were those who said I wanted him to be buried as someone he wasn't but the people who made this claim had long ago ceased to understand him. At the end Reg was not a 'gangster'. He was no longer thirty-five. He was not an image or a label or a word. He was more than a mere commodity. Having survived over thirty-two years in prison he remained, incredibly, without bitterness or self-pity. Although often portrayed as a caricature he had reason, intelligence and warmth. For all his faults he also had his virtues; his private acts of kindness were always, by their very nature, hidden from the public. He felt fear and doubt and had his share of regrets. He endured the gradual erosion of all his hopes but never gave up on life.

Reg Kray was a man of contradictions and complications, capable of immense love and compassion but also, in his past, of great hate and violence. Part a product of his environment, part victim to his personality, and part inevitably to his twin's, he paid the ultimate price for the terrible choices he made. To say his life was wasted would be a denigration of his incredible spirit and of the joy he brought to me and to others, but what he lost through the years was more than he could ever gain. If there is to be one enduring legacy then Reg would wish it to be this: that no one should ever again take the same long and painful road.

It was early afternoon when we arrived at Chingford. We made our way slowly to the graveside. Only six months before I had stood beside Reg as Charlie was interred. I felt overwhelmed by grief and loneliness. Reg was laid to rest with his twin brother Ron. Nearby lay the graves of his mother and father, his first wife Frances, Charlie and his son

Gary. For the first time in thirty-two years they were
reunited. I dropped a rose on his coffin. As the crowd surged
forward and the ground slowly turned to mud, I remembered the words that Reg had once sent to me. They seemed
to say it all.

'I have spread my dreams under your feet;
Tread softly because you tread on my dreams.'
(W. B. Yeats)

INDEX

A Way Of Life (Reg Kray) 30, 39,
    49, 51, 53, 95, 106–7, 109, 113,
    232
Albany Prison 102–3
Alder Hey Hospital 124
Allardyce, Bradley
    bisexual relationship with Reg
        107–9, 144–5, 153, 156, 157,
        243, 320–1
    chosen as Reg's pall-bearer 300,
        318
    given money by Reg 149
    marries Donna Baker 147–8
    meets Reg for the first time 107
    moved to Elmley Jail 186
    moved to Whitemoor Prison
        108–9, 133
    release from prison 234, 235
    stays with Reg and Roberta at
        the Town House 309–10, 311,
        315
    takes photographs of Reg in
        hospital 311
    visits Reg in Norfolk and
        Norwich Hospital 289, 292–3,
        297
    visits Reg in Norwich Prison
        Hospital 278
    visits Reg in Parkhurst prison
        268

visits Reg in Wayland prison
    245
Allardyce, Donna (née Baker) 149,
    152
    marries Bradley 147–8
    meets Trevor Linn 167
    Reg and Roberta's wedding
        178, 180, 182, 183, 185–6
    stays with Reg and Roberta at
        the Town House 309–10, 311,
        314, 315, 316
    supports Roberta through Reg's
        funeral arrangements 321
    visits Reg in Norfolk and
        Norwich Hospital 289, 297
    visits Reg in Norwich Prison
        Hospital 278
    visits Reg in Parkhurst Prison
        268
    visits Reg in Wayland Prison
        225, 245
Allcock, Michael 91
Allen, Geoff 197
Anciano, Dominic 72, 80
Anglia TV 241, 242–3
Archer, Jeffrey 250
AVP 242

Bailey, David 7, 18
BBC 65, 66

BBC2 257, 270
Beattie, Bernie 23
Becks, Mrs 13
Bejubop (company) 72
Belmarsh Prison 97, 146–7, 173, 175, 271
Bethnal Green police station 271
Betts, Leah 76
Between the Covers (documentary) 257–9
Birmingham Six 69
Blind Beggar pub 21
Bloch, Jonathan 250
Blud, Dr Linda 262, 263
Blundeston Prison, Suffolk 95–7, 98, 120, 128
Bond, James 72
Bone, Fred 51
Boothby, Lord 74
Born Fighter (Reg Kray) 88, 98, 106
Boyce, Christine 24
Boys, R. 117–18
British Telecom 196
Brixton Prison 12–13, 83, 198
Broadmoor 29, 30–1, 32, 42, 45, 48, 54–5, 56, 57, 63, 71–2, 77, 85–6, 99–101, 109, 112, 171
Brown, Sir David 77
Brunton, John 286, 302, 306–7, 309, 322
Burdis, Ray 72, 80–1
Burns, Barbara 183
Burns, Tony 183
Burton, Personal Officer 205–6, 208, 217

Carlton Television 254, 267, 319
Channel 4 241, 242–3
Chelmsford Prison 237
Chingford Cemetery 6, 52, 111, 115, 131, 273, 322, 323

Clark, Charles 16
Clein, Dr 13, 14, 38
Clerk, Carol 88
Coast to Coast (BBC news programme) 66
Cohen, Harry 210–11
Coldingley Prison 62
Coles, Deborah 111–12
Cooper, Dr 26–7, 42, 50, 51, 53, 55, 62–3
Copeland, Mike 14
Copley, John 252–3
Cornell, George 12, 16, 21, 142, 256
Courtney, Dave 257, 258, 259, 270
Cowley, Thomas 13
Cox, Donna 186, 289, 321
Crompton, Carl 149, 150

Daily Mail (newspaper) 212, 215, 220
Daily Mirror (newspaper) 140
Daily Star (newspaper) 99–100
Daltrey, Roger 64, 70, 72, 80, 81
Davis, Sammy, Jnr 65
De Silva, Dr 71
Derbyshire, Beverley 36–7
Dinenage, Fred 64, 72, 74, 98–9, 100
Donoghue, Albert 254
Double R Club, Bow Road 17, 29, 198
Duddy, John 23
Durham Prison 13, 237

Eastern Daily Press (newspaper) 238
Elliott, Martyn 262–3
Elmley Jail 186
Epilogue (tribute video) 4, 130, 131, 132–3

Erlestoke Prison, Wiltshire 173–4
Esquire (magazine) 243–4
European Convention on Human
   Rights 241
Evening Standard (newspaper) 147

Ferguson, Rob 250
Flanagan, Maureen 2, 4, 125, 166,
   321
Fleming, Ian 72
Foreman, Freddie 256
   Charlie's funeral 272–3
   Reg's funeral 318–19
   stars in Carlton documentary
      on the Krays 254–5
   talks to press about Reg's death
      317–18
   visits Charlie when critically ill
      267 8
   visits Reg when critically ill
      298, 312, 313–16
Fraser, Frank 15, 114, 255–6, 292
Front (magazine) 257
Fugitive Films 72, 81
Fun Lovin' Criminals 250

'gangster chic' 158
Garland, Judy 181
Garratt, Marcelle 321
Garratt, Stuart 321
Gartree Prison 68–71, 76, 83, 91,
   128, 202
Gillett, Pete
   alleged bisexual relationship
      with Reg 65–7, 75–6, 89, 243
   gains a part in The Krays film
      80, 81
   makes show biz plans with Reg
      62–3, 64, 65, 66, 76
   meets Reg and gains his sup-
      port 62–3

   relationship with Reg deterio-
      rates 88–90, 92, 94
   released from prison 75–6
   rumours of affair with Kate
      Howard 87, 88, 101
   slips back into life of crime 97,
      107–8, 223–4
Ginty, Sheila 302–3, 308
Gold, Stephen (solicitor) 76–8, 80,
   83, 88–9, 90–1, 94–5, 97,
   101–3, 183
Goldstein, Donna 311
Goldstein, Mark 181, 187, 260,
   289, 295, 299, 300, 311–12,
   321
Gould, Lee 183
Graham-Hall, Gordon 302
Grantham, Roy 25
Gray (prisoner) 103
Grayson, D. E. 206–8
Grayston, Peter 270
Grayston, Richard 270, 321
Great Train Robbers 14
Green, Dr 38, 41, 43
Griffin, Principal Officer 205,
   216–17
Guardian (newspaper) 212, 228
Gudjonsson, Dr 248, 249, 261

Haines, Frank 223
Hames, Carol 112
Hamilton, Dora 35
Hayes, Mr 118
Heatherwood Hospital, Berkshire
   109, 113
Heffer, Simon 212, 215, 220
Henry, Paul *see* Marcus, Paul
Hernu, Piers 257, 258, 259
Highpoint Prison, Suffolk 248
Hill, Billy 73
Hill, Paddy 69

HM Inspectorates of Prisons and
   Probation 242
Home Office 13, 23, 25, 34–5, 54,
   62–3, 84, 102, 189, 204, 208,
   211, 228, 238, 239, 241, 258,
   266, 286, 287, 295, 296
'Homeless Child' (song) 76
Houston, Whitney 114
Howard, Kate (wife of Ron) 71,
   86, 87–8, 99, 100, 101–2, 104,
   224
Hurley, Pete 23

Independent (newspaper) 111–12
Inland Revenue 91
Inquest (pressure group) 111–12
International Record Syndicate
   (IRS) 76
IRA 215
Irving, John 194, 196

Johnson, Harry 'Hate-'Em-All' 97,
   132
Jones, Dilys 113
Jones, John Richard 14

Kane, Lou 196
Keays, Paul 110, 270
Kemp, Gary 78
Kemp, Martin 78
Kiernender, Lee 99–101
King, Principal Officer 214
King, Vicky 119–20
King's Hospital, Camberwell 122
Kingston Prison, Portsmouth 61,
   252
Knox, Billy 289
Kray, Charlie (brother) 35, 37, 39,
   99, 101, 106, 236
   appeals against drugs charges
      234

arrested on drugs charges 146–7
in Belmarsh prison 146–7, 173,
   175
birth date 221
criminal behaviour of 79–80
death 93, 269–70, 274
dislike of Gillett 81
funeral 270–3, 314, 323
illhealth 222, 264–9
and *The Krays* film 82–3, 93–4
in Long Lartin Prison 175,
   211–12, 220–2
manages Double R Club 17
in Parkhurst Prison 264–5
Ron's death and funeral 110,
   111, 114, 115
sentenced to twelve years for
   drug offences 175
son Gary's death 131
son Gary's illness 122–3
trains twins to box 11
on trial for drugs offences 174–5
unable to attend Reg's wedding
   183
visits Ron in hospital 110
works on book 80, 82
Kray, Charlie (father) 11, 13–14,
   323
   attends Violet's funeral 53
   death 56
   grave visited by Reg 115, 273
   ill-health 44, 52
Kray, Gary (nephew) 122–3, 131,
   132, 324
Kray, Reg
   alcohol consumption 158–9,
      216, 217
   Anglia/Channel 4 TV
      documentary 241–3
Between the Covers documentary
   257–9

bisexuality 16, 57–9, 62–7, 75–6, 89, 107–9, 135, 144–5, 151–7, 243, 320–1

blackmail attempts against 151–4, 155–6

boxing 10, 11–12

and Bradley Allardyce 107–9, 133, 144–5, 147–8, 149, 153, 156, 157, 243

Carlton TV documentary 254–5

Charlie Crompton donates windfall to 149–50

Charlie Kray's book 81–2

Charlie's arrest (1996) 146–7

visits Charlie in Belmarsh prison 173

Charlie's trial for drug offences 174–5

visits Charlie in Long Lartin Prison 211–12, 220–2

visits Charlie in Parkhurst Prison 265–8

Charlie's death 269–70

Charlie's funeral 270–3

childhood 10, 11, 28–9

Christmas in Wayland 1997 203–4

Christmas in Wayland 1998 235–6, 237

tries for compassionate parole 288, 289, 290, 295

awarded compassionate parole 295–7, 301–2

craves publicity 10, 72, 199, 303–4

de-categorised to 'B' status 66–7, 83–4, 90–1

death 6, 316, 317

Dinenage book 74–5

enters the dispersal system 33, 68, 84

dreams of the East End 197–8

dreams of Ron 187, 223, 237

early criminal career 10–12

enrolls on 'Lifers' Moving On' course 116

enrolls on Offending Behaviour programme 229–30

Epilogue tribute video 4, 130, 131, 132–3

interviewed by Erlestoke Prison 173–4

exploitation 136–7, 143, 199, 320–1

Family Days at Wayland Prison 224–5

father's death 56

fiftieth birthday 59–60

fights in prison 14, 23

dates Frances 17–18

marries Frances 18

honeymoon in Athens with Frances 18–19

marital difficulties with Frances 19–21, 57, 63

Frances' death 13, 15, 22–3, 36–7, 45, 58, 142, 157, 163, 236

contemplates freedom 77–8, 167–71, 204–14

hopes of freedom quashed 212–13, 214–20, 236

freedom 6, 116, 138

funeral 6, 299–301, 318–19, 321, 322–3

and Gary Kray 123, 131, 132

Georgie Woods' death 252

girlfriends 15–17, 24

gives in 237–8

hero in jail siege 103

illnesses 273, 275, 276–316

suffers diphtheria as child 28

cataracts 195

Otitis Externa 15, 26, 28, 47, 54, 83, 96
experiences stomach pains 140–1, 147, 222–3, 259–61
diagnosed with diverticulitis 259–60
undergoes first major operation 281–2
in intensive care following surgery 282–3
post-surgery pictures taken 290–1
diagnosed with cancer 286–316
undergoes second operation 292–3
condition discovered to be fatal 293–5
last time in the sunshine 301
leaves hospital 306–9
condition becomes very serious 312–16
image 7–8, 137
incarceration 9–10, 12–13
    in Blundeston Prison 95–7, 98, 128
    in Brixton Prison 12–13, 198
    in Gartree Prison 68–71, 76, 83, 91, 128, 202
    in Leicester Prison 22–3, 95
    in Lewes Prison 83–4, 85–6, 90, 95, 106, 128
    in Long Lartin Prison 33–49, 51, 52, 68, 128, 154, 267
    in Maidstone prison 63, 69, 97, 103, 104–9, 115–22, 125, 134–6, 138–9, 144, 147–8, 150, 151–3, 158–9, 164–5, 174, 177–8, 181–4, 187–91
    in Nottingham Prison 90–1, 92, 95, 128
    in Parkhurst Prison 13–15, 22, 23–8, 29–32, 35–6, 45, 46, 48–9, 50–2, 54–62, 63–6, 67, 68, 72, 78, 102–3, 104, 127, 166, 236, 265–9, 270
    in Wandsworth Prison 18, 63
    in Wayland Prison 174, 175, 187, 192–3, 194–8, 200–1, 203–17, 221, 222–3, 224–5, 227, 232–6, 237–41, 244–9, 254–6, 257, 259, 262, 263, 269, 270, 274–8, 286
    in Wormwood Scrubs 63
John Copley's death 252–3
and John Pearson 244
'Lifers' Day' at Wayland 244–8
loneliness following the death of his parents 56–9
makes final documentary 303, 304
thinks of marrying Maureen Flanagan 165–6
media campaign for his release 218–19, 220, 238–9, 290
mental health 25–8, 30–2, 35–51, 53–6, 59–60, 62–3, 69, 83, 85–6, 90, 189
money 148–50
mother's death and funeral 52–4, 58
mother's pain 236–7
moves back to Cedra Court in the East End 19–20
moves on from the gangster life 319–20, 323
moves to the West End 19
mythology surrounding 6–8, 79, 158, 163, 168–71, 198–9, 303–4, 319–20
in Norfolk and Norwich Hospital 280–307

in Norwich Prison Hospital
278–9

choice of pall-bearers 300–1,
318–19

parole reports 116–22, 187–90,
197, 204–10, 261–4
interfered with 227–8

parole review preparation in
Wayland 248–51, 254–5

on his past 9

and Paul Marcus 92, 93, 94,
97–8, 230, 320–1

Pearson book 72–4

real personality 199

and Pete Gillett 62–3, 64, 65–7
75–6, 80, 81, 87, 88–90, 92, 94,
97, 107–8, 224, 243

philosophical nature 171–2,
201

post-mortem removal of Ron's
brain 123–4

proposed incarceration at
Albany Prison 102–3, 104

proposed transfer to Highpoint
Prison 248

psychiatric assessment by
Rampton doctor 45–8

psychiatric medication 25, 28,
31, 39–40, 42, 48, 50, 55, 69,
96, 117, 173–4

psychological examinations at
Wayland 248–9

psychometric testing at
Wayland 209–10, 217, 261,
274–5

public notoriety 120–1, 137–8,
205, 250, 263, 303–4

relationship difficulties 145–6

reputation 142, 159, 198–9

Roberta's first meeting with
1–2, 4–6, 125

pursues Roberta after first
meeting 125–6, 130–1

visited by Roberta for a second
time 131–3

Roberta starts frequent visits to
see 133–5, 138–9

opens up to Roberta 142–4, 146

demands on Roberta increase
150–3, 157–8

proposes to Roberta 159–60,
161–5

marries Roberta 175, 176–87

happy with marriage to
Roberta 196, 200, 225

first wedding anniversary with
Roberta 231–3

testament to Roberta 7

Roberta's fortieth birthday
celebrations 239–41

and Roger Daltrey's film plans
(The Krays) 70, 72, 79, 80–1,
82–3, 93

protective of Ron 141–2

coded letters to Ron 106

reunited with Ron in Parkhurst
23–5, 26–8, 29–31, 46

visits with Ron whilst in Long
Lartin 34, 44

refuses to visit Ron 50

requests to be with Ron after
mother's death 54–5, 56

visits Ron whilst incarcerated at
Broadmoor 71–2, 76–7, 78, 95,
101, 106

visits with Ron whilst in
Parkhurst 63

misses Ron's wedding 87–8

concerned over Ron's marriage
to Kate 101

worried about decline in Ron's
health 109

Ron's death and funeral 110–11,
112, 113–16, 132–3, 172–3, 179,
236, 269
sense of humour 234
sentenced to life 12
sixty-fifth birthday 234–5
sixty-sixth birthday 251
and Steve Tully 59, 62
suicide attempts 39, 40–1, 50
love of talking 132
and the tax man 91
'testing' of 69
Thirtieth anniversary in prison
220
and Tony Lambrianou 256–7
stays at the Town House hotel
302, 309–16
applies for Town Leave 211,
228–9
denied Town Leave 228–9
recruits Trevor Linn 167–8
violent nature 51
wedding photos 184, 186–7,
298–9
missing weight-lifting certificates 321
wives see Kray, Roberta; Shea,
Frances
works on the book A Way Of
Life 106–7, 109
writes Born Fighter 88, 98, 106
writes and publishes Reg Kray's
Book of Slang 59, 64
Kray, Roberta
befriends prisoners' wives at
Maidstone 139–40
and the Between the Covers
documentary 257–8
Bradley and Donna's wedding
148
career history 127–30

celebrates first wedding
anniversary with Reg 231–3
Charlie's funeral 271–3
childhood 126–7
Christmas without Reg 203–4
dislike of publicity 163
father's death 127
first meeting with Reg 1–6, 125
fortieth birthday 239–41
gives media interviews
campaigning for Reg's
release 218–19
gives press conference following Reg's operation 283–4
informed Reg is dying 293–5
informs Reg he has been
awarded compassionate
parole 295–7
makes Anglia TV documentary
241–2
makes plans to move to Maidstone 166
makes plans to move to
Norfolk 192–4
marries Reg 175, 176–87
meets Reg for a second time
131–3
moves to London 127–8
moves to Watton 200
plagued by press 175–6, 178–9,
180–1, 182, 185–6
psychological assessment 210
receives letter from Gillett
223–4
refuses money from Reg 149–50
Reg opens up to 142–4, 146
Reg proposes to 159–60, 161–5
Reg's death 6, 316, 317
Reg's demands on increase
150–3, 157–8
Reg's funeral 6, 318–19, 321–3

Reg's illhealth 140–1, 278–316
Reg's pursuit of following their first meeting 125–6, 130–1
Reg's rejection for parole 214–15, 216, 219–20
Reg's testament to 7
starts frequent visits to Reg 133–5, 138–9
stays with Reg at the Town House hotel 302, 309–16
talks of Reg's love 200
visits Reg at Parkhurst 266–7, 268
visits Reg in Norwich Prison Hospital 278
visits Reg in Wayland Prison 194–7, 200–1, 203–4, 224–5, 245–8
works on own business 129–30, 150–1, 164
Kray, Ron 48–9, 108, 156, 189, 197, 233, 273, 300, 318
boxing 10, 11
in Brixton Prison 12–13, 83, 198
in Broadmoor 30–1, 32, 57, 71–2, 77, 85–6, 99–101, 109, 112, 171
Charlie Kray's book 81–2
childhood 10, 11, 28–9
coded letters to Reg 106
craves publicity 10, 72, 199, 303–4
death 2, 4, 5, 110–16, 132–3, 172–3, 179, 236, 269
Dinenage book 74–5
dislike of Frances 19–20, 21, 57, 162
dislike of Gillett 81, 89–90, 224
divorces Kate Howard 101–2, 104
in Durham Prison 13–14
early criminal career 10–12
Epilogue tribute video 4, 130, 131, 132–3
expresses concern about Reg's mental health 37–8
expresses concern over Reg's prison friends 97
father's death 56
fights in prison 23–5, 99–100
fourth anniversary of his death 251
friendship with Lord Boothby 74
funeral 110–11, 112, 113–15, 270
and Gary Kray 132
health declines 109–10
homosexuality 16, 17
inquest into his death 111–12
and Kate Howard 71, 86, 87–8, 99, 100, 101–2, 166
attacks Lee Kiernender 99–100
love of winning 198
marriage to Kate Howard 86, 87–8, 166
marriage/divorce to Elaine Mildener 86, 87, 166
mental health 13, 29, 57, 85–6, 99–101
mother's death and funeral 52–4
murders Cornell 21, 142, 256
mythology surrounding 8, 79, 142, 158, 169–70, 198–9, 303–4, 319
in Parkhurst Prison 22, 23–5, 26–8, 29–31, 46
Pearson book 72–4
post-mortem removal of his brain 123–4
Reg dreams of 187, 223, 237
Reg is protective of 141–2

Reg laid to rest with 323
Reg refuses to visit 50
Reg requests to be with after
    their mother's death 54–5,
    56
Reg's separation from in prison
    9
reputation 142, 198–9
reunited with Reg in Parkhurst
    23–5, 26–8, 29–31, 46
Roger Daltrey's film plans (*The
    Krays*) 70, 72, 78–9, 80–1,
    82–3, 93
sentenced to life 12
suffers diphtheria as child 28
and Tony Lambrianou 256–7
unconditional love of 157
violent streak 12
visits from Reg whilst in
    Broadmoor 34, 44, 63, 71–2,
    76–7, 78, 95, 101, 106
in Wandsworth prison 17
in Wexham Park Hospital after
    suffering possible heart
    attack 101
wives see Howard, Kate;
    Mildener, Elaine
writes My Story 98–9, 100
Kray, Violet (mother) 35, 37, 38,
    44, 48–9, 50, 87, 267, 323
attempts to reunite the twins in
    prison 13–14
death and funeral 52–4, 56, 58,
    287
favourite song 181
fears for husband's health 52
grave visited by Reg 115, 273
pain at twins' incarceration
    236–7
portrayal in *The Krays* 93
supports Reg in prison 51

twins' childhood 10, 11, 28–9
unconditional love of 22, 157
Krays, The (film) 70, 72, 79, 80–1,
    82–3, 93–4

Lambrianou, Tony 256–7, 319
Langlands, Mark 283, 307, 308
Lansky, Meyer 51
Lavender, Mr 95
Ledgard, John 322
Lee, May (aunt) 22
Lee, Rose (aunt) 22
Lee, Violet (mother) see Kray,
    Violet
Leicester Prison 22–3, 95
Lewes Prison 83–4, 85–6, 90, 92,
    95, 106, 128
Linn, Trevor (solicitor) 218, 221,
    241, 284
attends Reg and Roberta's
    wedding 183
discusses Reg's death arrange-
    ments 299
discusses Reg's parole refusal
    with Roberta 216, 218
expresses alarm at Between the
    Covers documentary 257–8
introduced to Reg 69, 167–8
supports Roberta during
    funeral arrangements 321
visits Reg at the Townhouse 311
works on getting Reg
    'C'-category status 168, 173
works to get Reg
    compassionate parole 289,
    295
works to get Reg parole 197,
    204, 208–9, 227–8, 248
Liverpool School for the Partially
    Hearing 126–7
Liz 223

Long Lartin Prison 33–49, 51, 52, 68, 128, 154, 175, 211–12, 220–2, 222, 267

MacKeith, Dr 113, 248–9
Macmillan nurses 288–9
McVitie, Jack 'The Hat' 12, 22, 53–4, 79–80, 118, 163, 256
Maidstone Hospital 140
Maidstone Prison 1, 2–4, 10, 63, 69, 97, 103, 104–9, 113, 115–22, 125, 134–6, 138–40, 144, 147–8, 150, 151–3, 158–9, 164–5, 174, 177–8, 181–4, 187–91, 200, 203, 205, 223
Mail on Sunday (newspaper) 220
Manning, Patsy 34, 39, 40, 44, 59, 64, 289
Marcus, Paul 92, 93, 94, 97–8, 230, 234, 245, 320–1
Marsh, Paul 109, 110
Martin, Governor 214
Martin, Joe 104, 289, 314
Matthews, Harry 262–3
Mawson, David 112–13
Me and My Brothers (Charlie Kray) 82
Mildener, Elaine 86, 87
Mitchell, Frank 12
Morgan, Huey 250
Mortimer, Tony 187, 225, 289, 300, 322
Mortimer, Tracey 225, 289, 322
Murder, Madness and Marriage (Howard) 100
My Story (Ron Kray) 98–9, 100
Myhill, Adam 225, 289, 300

Nash, Johnny 187, 312, 313–16, 318

News of the World (newspaper) 123, 187, 220, 299
Nias, Dr 208–10, 217
Norfolk and Norwich Hospital 280–307
North London University 127
Norwich Prison 193, 275, 285, 286, 288
Norwich Prison Hospital 278–9
Nottingham Prison 61, 90–1, 92, 95, 97, 128

O'Leary, Laurie 110, 318
Orton, Governor 234–5
Our Story (Dinenage) 14, 64, 75, 80, 81, 88, 91, 99

'Pa' 100
Parkfield (company) 81
Parkhurst Prison 13, 14–15, 22, 23–8, 29–32, 35–6, 42, 45, 46, 48–9, 50–2, 54–66, 67, 68, 72, 78, 102–3, 104, 127, 166, 236, 264–7, 270
Parole Board 204, 208, 210, 211, 212, 214, 215, 217, 220, 227, 228–9, 238–9, 249, 274, 275, 284
Peake, Terry 27
Pearson, John 72–4, 188, 243–4
People (newspaper) 75
Pickering, Dr 45–8
Pine, Ros 266
Pine, Wilf 97
  Charlie's illness and death 266, 267, 269–70
  Reg's death 316
  supports Reg during final illness 281–2, 289, 290, 292–3, 307, 308, 309, 314, 315

supports Roberta during
funeral arrangements 318,
321
Portsmouth News (newspaper) 66
Posey, Clell 322
Posey, Janelle 322
Press Association 140
Prison Reform Trust 139
Profession of Violence, The
(Pearson) 74, 75, 188, 243–4
Pyle, Joe 224, 312, 313–16, 318

Rampton 31, 42, 43, 44–6, 47, 48,
56
Ramsay, Officer 36–7
Raquel's nightclub, Basildon 76
Redgrave, John 177
Reg Kray's Book of Slang 59, 64
Repton Boxing Club, Bethnal
Green 183
Reynolds, Richard 233, 289
Richardson, Eddie 14, 23, 222
Rimini, Ken 273
Roberts, Harry 69
Romero, Dr 112
Rose, Dr 117
Rowe, Raphael 69
Rowlands, Chris 245
Rumball, J. 60–2

St Mary's 266, 267, 268
St Matthew's church 111, 114, 131,
270, 272
Sandra (Macmillan nurse) 289,
302, 303
Scotland Yard 319
Scott, John 272
Shaw, George Bernard 171
Shea, Frances (Reg's first wife) 14,
29, 159, 162, 197, 201, 323
dates Reg 17–18

death 13, 15, 21–2, 36–7, 45, 58,
142, 157, 163, 236
honeymoon in Athens 18–19
marital difficulties 19–21, 57, 63
marries Reg 18
mental instability 19, 20
Reg visits her grave 115, 273
Sidgwick & Jackson 64
Southport 126–7
Squibb, Johnny 289
Squibb, Rose 289
Stallard, Ken 184
Stanley, Judy 94
Stapleton, Paul 93, 135
Stevenson, Melford 12, 46, 76
Stoke Newington 127
Stott, Richard 220
Straffen, John 14
Straw, Jack 220, 227, 228, 239,
241–2, 284, 313
Sugarman, Dr 187–90
Sun (newspaper) 89, 103, 238
Sunday Mirror (newspaper) 97–8
Sunday People (newspaper) 299
Sunday Sport (newspaper) 77
Sutcliffe, Peter (Yorkshire Ripper)
76, 78, 99

Taylor, Bill 107, 109, 193, 232, 233,
247
Tebbit, Lord 220
Tidmarsh, Dr David 53, 71–2
Town House (hotel) 302, 309–16,
317, 322
Tully, Steve 59, 62
Turner, Dr Trevor 208, 210

W. English & Son funeral parlour
113, 124, 270, 271, 322
Wakefield, Doug 27
Wandsworth Prison 17, 18, 63

Wayland Prison 174, 175, 187, 192–8, 200–1, 203–17, 221–5, 227, 232–41, 244–9, 254–7, 259, 262, 263, 265, 269, 270, 274–8, 280, 286
Webb, Dave 183
Weekes, Mr 13–14
West Norwich Hospital 260
West, Pete 110, 118–19, 120
Wetherby, Pete 197
Wexham Park Hospital, Ascot 101

Wheel and Deal (publisher) 64
Whitelaw, J.D.A. 90
Whitemoor Prison 108–9, 133
Whitmarsh, Brenda 289
Whitmarsh, Dave 289
Wilson, Robert 111
Woods, Georgie 245, 252
Woollard, Danny 233
Wormwood Scrubs 63

Yeats, W.B. 324

FREDDIE FOREMAN & TONY LAMBRIANOU

Getting it Straight

PAN BOOKS   £6.99

As never before, Freddie Foreman (who had his own gang in the sixties, which received Jack the Hat McVitie's body at the south end of the Blackwall Tunnel after the Kray murder) and Tony Lambrianou (a noted Kray henchman) in conversation about getting the facts straight, how they went straight – and who they straightened out.

Set against the backdrop of the pub Freddie used to own, and where he was arrested as an accessory to murder, Tony and Freddie's conversations unfold rivetingly, covering not only the goings-on inside during their significant prison terms, but also astonishing fresh information on such notorious incidents as the Krays' murders and the famous Security Express heist, and frank thoughts on the Kray legend and legacy, and crime today.

'Unlike other crook books, this one is a word-for-word transcript straight from the horses' mouths . . . very funny'
Daily Mail

TONY LAMBRIANOU

Inside the Firm

PAN BOOKS   £6.99

Throughout the 1960s, Tony Lambrianou was a key member of the Kray gang. He had a unique close-up view of their reign of terror in an underworld of unashamed evil. Tony Lambrianou knew the whole story, and he served fifteen years for his part in it.

Inside the Firm is the book Tony Lambrianou has written to exorcise the ghosts of his violent career with the Krays and the horrors of his subsequent years in top security prisons. An account more detailed, more impartial and more terrifying than the Krays themselves were ever to reveal. From the murder of Jack 'the Hat' McVitie, and the mystery of the undiscovered body, to the deaths of Ron and Reg, *Inside the Firm* is a brutally honest confession from a gangster determined to turn his back on his criminal past.

REG & RON KRAY

Our Story

PAN BOOKS £5.99

The Kray twins were Britain's most notorious gangsters. For a decade they were the gang lords of the London underworld. Their reign of terror ended on 8 March 1969, when Ronnie and Reg were sentenced to life imprisonment with the recommendation that they serve at least thirty years.

The men whose name was a byword for fear reveal the truth about their violent life and times in *Our Story*. In their own words, they tell the full story of their brutal careers in crime and their years behind bars. Compiled from a series of interviews that took place behind prison walls, *Our Story* is the book that finally explodes the myths that have surrounded the Kray twins.

'An astonishing book . . . you will be astounded by the frankness of the Krays' own chilling story of crime'
Sun

'[This book] reminds the reader that a penal system that does not attempt to rehabilitate the sick in mind is always going to fail the society it aims to protect. The Krays, it would be fair to say, have been left to rot'
Observer

REG KRAY

A Way of Life

PAN BOOKS   £6.99

Over thirty years of blood, sweat and tears

*The story I am about to tell is terrible. For the sake of the young
who I'd like to deter from going to prison, I promised myself
I'd write all the truth in this book, the good experiences
and the bad.*
— *Reg Kray, 1933–2000*

Reg Kray was sentenced in 1968, together with his twin brother
Ron, to serve 'a minimum' of thirty years in jail. Ron passed
away in 1995. After spending over half his life in the prison
system, Reg was finally released in 2000 on compassionate
grounds, before finally losing his battle with cancer in October
of that year.

In *A Way of Life* we come to understand the Reg Kray of
2000, not the one of the 1960s, and how his later life related
to his past. We see the anguish of life inside and Reg's
remarkable influence on many fellow inmates, and how he
handled enforced relationships with characters who ranged
from Lennie McLean to the Great Train Robbers, from John
McVicar to the Yorkshire Ripper, from Frankie Fraser to Ian
Brady – with frank reflections on the penalties of crime.

Concluding with a moving account of Reg's last days by
Roberta Kray, *A Way of Life* is a record for future generations,
putting many misconceptions straight.

OTHER PAN BOOKS
AVAILABLE FROM PAN MACMILLAN

TONY LAMBRIANOU & FREDDIE FOREMAN
GETTING IT STRAIGHT   0 330 49013 3   £6.99

TONY LAMBRIANOU
INSIDE THE FIRM   0 330 49014 1   £6.99

REG & RON KRAY
OUR STORY   0 330 30818 1   £5.99

REG KRAY
A WAY OF LIFE   0 330 48511 3   £6.99

All Pan Macmillan titles can be ordered from our website,
www.panmacmillan.com, or from your local bookshop
and are also available by post from:

Bookpost, PO Box 29, Douglas, Isle of Man IM99 1BQ
Credit cards accepted. For details:
Telephone: 01624 677237
Fax: 01624 670923
E-mail: bookshop@enterprise.net
www.bookpost.co.uk

Free postage and packing in the United Kingdom

Prices shown above were correct at the time of going to press.
Pan Macmillan reserve the right to show new retail prices on covers
which may differ from those previously advertised in the text
or elsewhere.